ph
5.1.07

SOCIAL WORK IN A CORPORATE ERA

Contemporary Social Work Studies

Series Editor:
Robin Lovelock, University of Southampton, UK

Contemporary Social Work Studies (CSWS) is a series disseminating high quality new research and scholarship in the discipline and profession of social work. The series promotes critical engagement with contemporary issues relevant across the social work community and captures the diversity of interests currently evident at national, international and local levels.

CSWS is located in the School of Social Sciences at the University of Southampton, and is a development from the successful series of books published by Ashgate in association with CEDR (the Centre for Evaluative and Developmental Research) from 1991.

Titles include:

Reflecting on Social Work - Discipline and Profession
Edited by Robin Lovelock, Karen Lyons and Jackie Powell

Broadening Horizons: *International Exchanges in Social Work*
Edited by Lena Dominelli and Wanda Thomas Bernard

Beyond Racial Divides: *Ethnicities in Social Work Practice*
Edited by Lena Dominelli, Walter Lorenz and Haluk Soydan

Valuing the Field: Child Welfare in an International Context
Edited by Marilyn Callahan, Sven Hessle and Susan Strega

Social Work in Higher Education: *Demise or Development?*
Karen Lyons

Social Work in a Corporate Era

Practices of Power and Resistance

Edited by

LINDA DAVIES and PETER LEONARD
McGill University, Canada

ASHGATE

Published by
Ashgate Publishing Limited
Gower House
Croft Road
Aldershot
Hants GU11 3HR
England

Ashgate Publishing Company
Suite 420
101 Cherry Street
Burlington, VT 05401-4405
USA

Ashgate website: http://www.ashgate.com

British Library Cataloguing in Publication Data
Social work in a corporate era : practices of power and
    resistance. - (Contemporary social work studies)
    1. Social service
    I. Davies, Linda II. Leonard, Peter, 1930-
    361.3

Library of Congress Cataloging-in-Publication Data
Social work in a corporate era : practices of power and resistance / by Linda Davies and Peter Leonard [editors].
        p. cm. -- (Contemporary social work studies)
    ISBN 0-7546-3883-9
    1. Social service. I. Davies, Linda. II. Leonard, Peter, 1930- III. Series.

    HV40.S61785 2004
    361.3--dc22   2004014023

ISBN 0 7546 3883 9

Printed and bound in Great Britain by MPG Books Ltd, Bodmin, Cornwall

Contents

PART III: NARRATIVE, CRITICAL CONSCIOUSNESS, EMANCIPATION

List of Contributors

Sara Collings is a doctoral student in the School of Social Work, McGill University, Canada.

Linda Davies is Associate Professor in the School of Social Work, McGill University, Canada.

Kamal Fahmi completed his PhD in 2004 from the School of Social Work, McGill University, Canada.

Jan Fook is Professor and Director, Center for Professional Development, La Trobe University, Australia.

Michele Gnanamuttu is a doctoral student in the School of Social Work, McGill University, Canada.

Amanda Grenier is Assistant Professor in the School of Social Work, McGill University, Canada.

Karen Healy is Associate Professor in the School of Social Work and Applied Human Sciences, The University of Queensland, Australia.

Peter Leonard is Professor in the School of Social Work, McGill University, Canada.

Laura Mastronardi is Coordinator of the Certificate Program in Northern Social Work Practice, School of Social Work, McGill University and a doctoral student in McGill's Faculty of Education.

Gabrielle Meagher is senior lecturer in the Discipline of Political Economy at The University of Sydney, Australia.

Anthony Paré is Associate Professor, Department of Integrated Studies in Education, McGill University, Canada.

Nigel Parton is Professor of Child Care and Director of the Centre for Applied Childhood Studies at the University of Huddersfield, England.

Introduction

Linda Davies and Peter Leonard

This book takes a critical stand on the location of social work within the crises and contradictions of this particular juncture in the history of Western countries. At this historical moment, we witness both the increasing exercise of state and corporate power and the growth of new kinds of collective resistance. These forces and counter-forces, and their effects, arise in the context of global problems of economic exploitation, poverty, racism and social exclusion – problems with which social workers are confronted in their own and their clients' experiences, and to which they must respond.

We believe that these structural problems and the crises they create demand a responding dissent at every level, from mass political protest to individual and small-scale resistance. At the level of social work theory and practice, we argue that it is necessary to draw upon the critical tradition embedded in modernity while, simultaneously, confronting the tragic failures of this tradition in the oppressive example of state socialism. A reflective critique of the critical tradition itself should, we maintain, build on elements from a range of 'post-theories' – postmodernism, post-structuralism and post-colonialism. The intellectual and practical problems of rebuilding social work on the theoretical basis of emancipatory narratives, on the one hand, and post-modern deconstructions of those narratives, on the other, are evident throughout this text.

The book is a collective enterprise emerging from discussion and debate among its authors, who wrote and re-wrote our particular chapters as part of an effort to respond to the crises and contradictions that we experienced in social work education, research and practice. The Social Theory Study Group of the School of Social Work, McGill University, has been central to the process of writing the book. This group that consists of the Canadian authors has met over a period of several years. In 2001, a symposium was held at McGill University, which brought the Social Theory Study Group together with academic colleagues from Australia and Britain. At that meeting we decided to collectively publish our contributions. In October 2003, the authors came together again so that we could further reflect on the implications of the positions taken in our individual chapters. The result is a text that is able to draw upon experiences from four countries, three of them clearly complicit in the dynamics of global exploitation.

Before we turn to the individual chapters, we want to first set out our overall perspective on some of the material and ideological forces that are impinging on and reconstructing the practice of social work in advanced or late capitalism. We make a distinction between those forces which appear to be directly antagonistic to a critical social work practice, which we will call *oppositions*, and those forces within critical social work which produce internal debate, quarrels and conflicts, which we will call *tensions*.

Oppositions

A striking feature of the objectives and organization of social services in many Western countries at the present time is the extent to which market relations and the commodification of social care 'packages' has permeated social welfare systems. New technologies are being introduced into the management of services that objectify and make more measurable the relationship between state service providers and those who use these services. Risk management increasingly dominates conceptions of how parents and children living in a milieu of poverty, racism and exclusion are to be defined and responded to. Increasing bureaucratic control, together with reductions in resources, furnish the ideological and material spaces within which social workers are expected to practice as risk assessors and case managers. The role of the social worker as one who engages with the client in a supportive, nurturing encounter appears, at least officially, to be dying.

Regrettably, there are also professional discourses within social work that appear to be eager to adapt to this technocratic managerialism and to the claims to scientific and objective knowledge which accompany it. Within this view, the future of social work is tied to 'mastering' scientific knowledge and new technical skills, those latest and most glamorous forms of expertise that provide the grounds on which, in a world of uncertainty and occupational competition, social work can stake its claim to professional competence. Social work can best defend itself, it is suggested, by claiming to be a science-based profession with an important role in the monitoring and control of problematic populations at risk – the bad, the mad, and the difficult. The classification of 'client problems' becomes a major tool within this scientistic conception of social work. It is a mechanism of objectification and often parallels the reification and stereotyping of 'cultural communities.' Although all social workers and social work educators, including those who practice from a critical position, are daily confronted with their complicity in structures of domination, the perspective that celebrates social work as a socially useful scientific practice proclaims, in effect, its unambiguous and unreflective contribution to the reproduction of the existing capitalist social order.

We might see these manifestations of objectification and the intensive use of panopticon strategies of power as further evidence of Foucault's contention that both modern state organization and the process of professionalization are prime examples of the exercise of disciplinary power. They represent a belief, characteristic of modernity, that the poor and the excluded can only be assisted and supported if such help is accompanied by surveillance and monitoring 'in their own interests'. We might link this Foucauldian analysis to a Marxist view that the liberal welfare state reflects the continuous discursive and material struggle between the interests of the majority subordinate classes and those of the minority dominant class of corporate capital.

The antagonistic relationship between developments in the management of subordinate populations together with the scientization of social work meets increasingly vocal resistance within social work education and practice, a resistance that might signal a significant battle ahead. This often fragmented resistance to managerialism and scientization is mounted, at present, by a diverse crew of critics within social work, exhibiting a variety of bases for their oppositional politics. They include feminists, socialists, anti-racists, defenders of minority cultural rights and opponents of heterosexism and homophobia. Their ideological orientations proclaim their allegiance to a range of social theories and philosophical critiques from, at the one end, Marxism, critical theory, feminism and other emancipatory narratives, and at the other, post-structuralism, post-colonialism and in general the postmodern deconstruction of the very idea of emancipation. The belief in the possibilities of emancipation, it is argued, demands dogmatic, grandiose and inflated claims. However, the diverse oppositional critics have certain things in common as part of their analysis and method: a preference for the narratives of the oppressed over those who oppress them; a demand that the voices of clients and their communities of interest be heard over the buzz of computerized information systems; a recognition of diversity over the classifications of homogenized populations, and over the unceasing form-filling which characterizes the process of individuals being provided with the official identity of client, patient or 'welfare dependent'. Faced with the growth of sophisticated mechanisms of control and the distancing of social service management from the immediate stress and pain of both clients and front-line social workers, we begin to see the possibilities residing in the emergence of a critical re-emphasis on the uniqueness of individual subjects. Such an emphasis becomes, in present circumstances, a radical response to the increasingly objectifying and homogenizing tendencies of social service programmes.

Tensions

This book expands the common ground which might be established among social work critics in the interests of increasing the tolerance between those who maintain allegiance to a narrative of emancipation and those who have already deconstructed such narratives without replacing them with something else. Endless deconstruction tends to follow Zygmunt Bauman's argument that postmodernism 'denies in advance the right of all and any revelation to slip into the place vacated by the deconstructed/discredited rules' (1992, p.xi). A debate about whether it is necessary or even possible to reconstruct a new narrative of emancipation is crucial. The debate is joined between those whose perspective maintains a commitment to the critical, revolutionary side of modernity, among them most

Marxists and many feminists, and those, including other feminists and cultural critics, who are persuaded by a postmodern critique and its scepticism concerning all social theory. This particular, and one might assume fundamental, tension is addressed in this book and attempts are made to develop a dialogue between the various positions represented here.

Whilst the tensions between these critical forces centre on the problematics of emancipatory narratives of practice, they also connect to another source of conflict: the relationship between a social work politics of resistance based primarily on the recognition of difference, and a politics which places emphasis on the interdependence of human subjects and the need for solidarity amongst oppressed populations. Although it might be obvious intellectually that recognition of the importance of both difference and collective solidarity is necessary, in practice this is not so easy to achieve. There is an ethics relevant to both emphases: an ethics of the recognition and celebration of the diversity of human subjects and cultures, and an ethics which acknowledges, contrary to cults of extreme individualism, the interdependence of human subjects. However, the history of many narratives of solidarity are of those which legitimated practices of oppression in the name of the oppressed, most recently practices justified in the name of the redemptive figure of the proletariat as emancipator. This history hurts, as Frederic Jameson (1984) observes, and it must be acknowledged and reflected upon if the ideas of broad-based solidarity are to re-enter strongly into a critical social work discourse, a discourse now heavily influenced by commitments to identity politics and a corresponding postmodern skepticism of any kind of mass 'progressive' politics.

Finally, there is also a tension that arises from the postmodern assault on any kind of certainty. The deconstruction of regimes of Truth as socially and culturally manufactured has effectively put paid to the credibility of dogmatic assertions about both knowledge and values. We have, we hope, learned to be cautious and tentative in the claims we make for our theoretical analyses and our prescriptions for practice. But the authors of this book also believe that such uncertainty must surely have its limits. If we are to engage as moral agents in the struggles for social justice that are integral to critical social work theory and practice, we must depend on strong ethical beliefs, even though such beliefs may no longer be able to claim universal or transcendental moral guarantees. And while we, as social work educators, researchers and practitioners need, perhaps, less intellectual certainty, we might reflect on the fact that most clients of social workers – those living with poverty, racism and social exclusion – are in need of *more* certainty in their material and emotional lives.

Experiences of Contradiction

What are the preoccupations which informed the discussions amongst us which led to this book? We experience being caught within a number of contradictions in our work as both educators and practitioners committed to a critical tradition. On the one hand, these are practices which were established primarily to reproduce the existing social order – to supply appropriate labor for the social services market, to maintain dominant welfare ideologies, to work with the casualties of capitalist economic development and to manage the consequences of social crises. On the other hand, the practices of social work and education carry the potential for resistance against a social order that produces poverty, social injustice and racism. We experience, in other words, a contradiction between the liberatory goals of the critical tradition and the actual oppressive practices that we, as educators and social workers find ourselves engaging in.

How do we attempt to understand this contradiction? Throughout this book, we focus on two recent developments in social work theory and practice, which we agree, have a considerable impact upon us. The first and most overwhelming we might call *managerial scientism*, the advance of a certain kind of rationality in the organization and practice of social work, which claims to be scientific and objective. It is not science as such that we object to, but scientism, a predominantly Western belief that only certain kinds of knowledge count and that other kinds of knowledge are rightly marginalized, especially the stories of those whose voices are rarely heard. We are talking here of the most recent manifestations of Western modernity and in doing so come face-to-face with a critique of that tradition of rationality and objectivity of which we, as 'children of the enlightenment,' are ourselves products. In postmodernism, we draw on a method to deconstruct the foundational assumptions of managerial scientism and the belief that only by becoming 'more scientific' can social work fulfill its mission. Even social work within a critical tradition finds itself reflecting, to a substantial degree, Western economic and cultural hegemony and it forces us to find the spaces where we might resist this hegemony. Yet, postmodernism in some of its versions is so destructive in its practice of deconstruction that some of us approach it with a mixture of fascination and distaste. In this book, we often find ourselves hesitating to embrace either science or post-modern critique, either Western rationality or endless relativist deconstruction. What are we left with, we who see ourselves as part of a critical tradition? The critical social work tradition can be deconstructed as expressing both lofty ideals of social justice together with oppressive practices of racism, cultural arrogance and other expressions of domination. In our discussions together, we spoke of 'dreams of emancipation', a phrase that reminded us that concrete material practices must emerge from these dreams.

Practice and Theory

The history of critical or radical social work has often been one heavy with the theory and rhetoric of progress. Sometimes it has manifested itself in a familiar dogmatic binary: there are 'radical social workers' – feminist, Marxist, structural, anti-oppressive, etc. – who can be usefully contrasted with a social work 'other', those who are 'traditional', or dismissed simply as only oppressive in their practices. We find such dichotomies to be too dogmatic, judgmental and exclusionary to be of much use to us. We believe most social workers struggle to meet their clients' needs as they see them with varying degrees of success and most are aware of the structural barriers their clients face. In the past, it was possible to draw upon metanarrative explanations of total social systems such as capitalism, patriarchy, and colonialism. In the face of postmodern deconstruction, we have learned to be wary of grand and grandiose theory making. As we reflect on practice in this book, we can understand afresh why postmodernism critiques such metanarratives. Theory tends to over-simplify complex social phenomena. The often-experienced separation of theory from practice rests upon the assumptions of hierarchies reflecting, we might argue, the class division between intellectual and practical labor. So, should we who wrote this book have begun in another place? Should we have all started with practice rather than theory? Some chapters are written directly from the perspective of practice and as a group of authors we remain with different strategies regarding the uses of theory.

An over-riding concern for us is how we make explicit the theory that often lies hidden within our daily practices as social workers and educators. It has become evident to us that the role of language is central to both practice and theory, a centrality that has been a focus of much of our writing. To think seriously about the language we use in our work is to confront the need to reflect on deeply internalized ideologies embedded in specific uses of language.

Social Workers as Subjects

One central theme in this text concerns the repositioning of social workers as subjects in the social work labor process. This includes both an emphasis on the subjectivity of workers and an awareness of their capacity to act upon their own intentions both within the organization and in encounters with service users. As subjects with emotions, social workers often experience powerful feelings in their face-to-face practice with clients. In the past, these emotions were conceptualized as transference and counter-transference, with the client fully accounted for in these emotional transactions. Within the rule of managerial scientism, the encounter between social worker and client tends to be objectified in the interests of 'cost-effective' risk assessment measurement and case processing. Both social workers and clients cease to be subjects and become instead the objects of bureaucratic organization.

How can this objectification be resisted? In this book, we argue that reclaiming the terrain of emotional subjectivity is one means of resistance. The opportunity to critically reflect on the emotions aroused for both workers and clients asserts the status of human subject against organizational structures and practices that deny the centrality of such emotion. We are convinced that emotional, reflexive or 'difficult' knowledge must be integrated into critical practice. Recognition of worker subjectivity includes an acknowledgement of their own agency, of their capacity to act. This capacity is dependent on an analysis of the possibilities for taking action within our workplaces. This includes a critical awareness of the language used in constructing both professional and client identities. A necessity facing both practitioners and educators is the struggle to create time and space within our workplaces for a process of critical reflection. We need to establish a climate in which people are enabled to see things differently and imagine steps toward creating change.

In some workplaces, this first requires a struggle for the material pre-conditions necessary to be treated as subjects. The labor force conditions of social workers vary across organizational contexts and location. The process of continuous fragmentation and reorganization of the work process to conform to the dictates of managerial rationality and budgetary control is widely evident. This form of rationality contributes to a deskilling of practitioners and diminishes their sense of agency and accountability in their practice with clients. In the face of this, it is essential, we believe, to reassert the existence of a margin of maneuver for action, however limited. This is a precondition to the development of a critical practice.

The implications of these prescriptions make us as authors reflect on ourselves as educators and practitioners. While not immune to the forces of globalization, academia still represents a privileged space for critical thinking and reflection. From this location the refrain from the practice front – 'it's alright for *you* to talk' haunts us.

The Organization of the Book

The focus of the book emphasizes the necessity and possibilities of resistance to the dominant exercise of power. The book is organized into three parts which explore specific key resources for this resistance – One: *Theory, Reflection, Emotion;* Two: *Cultural Politics, Language, Collectivity*; Three: *Narrative, Critical Consciousness, Emancipation.*

Part One: Theory, Reflection, Emotion

Chapter One, *The Uses of Theory and the Problems of Pessimism*, begins with an examination of some of the political implications for social work of the tensions and oppositions that we have referred to, namely, the challenges which post-theories present for attempts at emancipatory forms of practice. In particular, the problem of growing fatalism and pessimism in the face of globalizing capitalism and its political expression in the liberal 'welfare state'. It is argued that the loss of hope in the possibility of emancipation is a result of the internalization of dominant ideologies that are based upon the assumption that the global capitalist order is here to stay. The development of theory, which attempts to confront the present and conceptualize alternatives, is seen as an antidote to intellectual pessimism.

In Chapter Two, *Critical Reflection and Transformative Possibilities,* the author makes a case that the theory and practice of critical reflection can address some of these dilemmas of fatalism. Critical reflection can provide both a useful way of understanding personal identity and its connection with social context, thereby stimulating transformative effects.

Chapter Three, *Post-Theories for Practice: Challenging the Dogmas,* argues that 'constructive social work' can make a key contribution to the development of critical and reflexive perspectives, and counter the dominance of current managerial practices. Perspectives that draw on or are at least sympathetic towards post-modernism and social constructionism are key for developing theories *for* practice.

Chapter Four, *Subject-to-Subject: Reclaiming the Emotional Terrain for Practice,* contends that the new rationalism evident in technocratic social work practice undermines both the expression of and reflection on the emotional texture of the interaction between social workers and their clients. The authors explore some key concepts in recent feminist psychoanalytic theory that address these often difficult emotions and may allow for more reflexive practice in working with mothers in child welfare contexts.

Part Two: Cultural Politics, Language, Collectivity

Chapter Five, *Whose Side Are You On? Politicized Identities,* investigates the problems created when struggles against racism are linked to a strong identification with particular ethno-racial groups. The Chapter explores how to find ways of fighting racism and other forms of discrimination by valuing individual diversity and multiple social locations. It challenges notions of essential identity, including the mono-racial identity categories that are promoted by both racist and anti-racist ideologies.

Chapter Six, *Texts and Power: Toward a Critical Theory of Language,* maintains that documentary practices play a central role in social work activity. Those practices reflect and construct relations of power, but are treated in social work education and practice as unproblematic. This chapter takes a critical literacy approach to the examination of social work recording. Such an approach exposes the values at play behind the common sense façade of everyday documentary practices.

Chapter Seven, *The Reprofessionalization of Social Work: Collaborative Approaches for Achieving Professional Recognition,* draws on a significant concern amongst critical social workers about the apparently diminishing options for emancipatory work. Specifically, the authors examine the rise of neo-liberal policy regimes and the concomitant dominance of new public management principles in social service organizations. They address the fear that there is no future for critical practice in this new era of social services reform and argue for more collective forms of action.

Part Three: Narrative, Critical Consciousness, Emancipation

Chapter Eight, *Older Women Negotiating Uncertainty in Everyday Life: Contesting Risk Management Systems*, examines the tensions between certainty and uncertainty within the larger stories of managerial and technocratic social work practices, the concerns of critical social work, and the narratives of older women constructed as frail. In social work practice, these strains are evident where imposed ideas clash with diverse experiences and or intentions, such as the new demands for effectiveness and efficiency and meeting client need, and the contradictions between the desire for social justice and increased bureaucratic demands.

Chapter Nine, *Disrupting the Narrative of White Tutelage: Reflections on Post-colonial Social Work Education*, explores the difficulties encountered in bringing an emancipatory orientation to the post-colonial context of social work education and practice with Inuit peoples. The author asks whether we are producing 'new clerks of the empire' who will perform the same state mandated functions previously undertaken by white social workers or whether there is potential for authentic Inuit approaches to social work practice and education.

Chapter Ten, *Social Work Practice and Research as an Emancipatory Process,* explores the potential of Participatory Action Research, drawing upon fieldwork with street children in Cairo. From this base, an argument is mounted that in the current global situation of competing fundamentalisms, a space must be created which focuses on emancipation as a process for both research and social work practice.

A Concluding Reflection emphasizes the importance of using imagination in re-inventing the utopian thinking necessary to conceive of alternatives to the present as a vital part of emancipatory practices.

References

Bauman, Z. (1992), *Intimations of Postmodernity*, Routledge: London.
Jameson, F. (1984), 'Postmodernism or the Cultural Logic of Late Capitalism', *New Left Review*, vol.146, pp. 53-92.

PART I
THEORY, REFLECTION, EMOTION

Chapter 1

The Uses of Theory and the Problems of Pessimism

Peter Leonard

Introduction

Five years after the publication of my book, *Postmodern Welfare* (1997), readers of that text might wonder whether the confidence expressed in the book's subtitle, *reconstructing an emancipatory project,* was justified or whether it was simply a confusing oxymoron. Are the deconstructionists, the relativists, the post-Marxists and many of the cultural theorists right in arguing that the story of emancipation is now at an end? In the global politics of exploitation, racism, starvation and terror, the dreams of social justice and equality for all of humanity, which once produced dread amongst the rulers and hope amongst the oppressed, seem now to have vanished. Such dreams of emancipation appear to be, well *dreams*, appropriately consigned, alongside our own deaths, to that which dare not speak its name. After all, these dreams became, in their most influential form, the nightmare of Soviet oppression of its population, a nightmare from which some projects of emancipation appear not to have recovered. When I visited Britain in 2000, some of my old friends who once shared with me a commitment to a project of socialist social work education were surprised that, though I used post-structural analysis, I also drew on Marxist theory in order to try to understand the relationship between cross-cultural practice and moral agency. For them, my Marxism seemed to be an endearing reminder of a dead past.

Perhaps I should, indeed, at this early point, apologize to the reader for my indulgence in writing about Marxism in a text on social work. And for the lack of good taste, perhaps, in often naming Marxism directly rather than over-using various euphemisms such as *critical* theory to signify an understanding of the world which is based largely on historical materialism.

Certainty and Uncertainty

In place of talk of emancipation, we who engage in the practice of teaching and learning experience, as many others do, the confusion and paradox of living in a dialectic of certainty/uncertainty. The certainty which resides among the leaders of the dominant culture of the West is a product of the end of the Cold War and the belief that capitalism is not only triumphant but also unstoppable. The end of history has arrived, Francis Fukuyama argues, because the world has produced at this point in history a social formation which is the final destination of humanity: global market capitalism. When, in 1992, Fukuyama published *The End of History and the Last Man,* his argument was met with a wide range of responses from acclaim to condemnation. He maintained that the end of the Cold War signalled the working out of the logic of History which had come to its concluding stage with the triumph of capitalist liberal democracy evidenced in the free market economy. Superficial as its treatment of both philosophy and history might be, it was a book which resonated with a widespread belief in the continuing leading role of the West, and the United States in particular, as the civilizing, freedom-loving and wealth-producing dynamic center of the world.

On the other hand, substantial critique was mounted against Fukuyama's thesis from the Left and can be summed up, at this point, by Eric Hobsbawm's sharp comment that 'we are constantly confronted by Western ideologists – Mr. Fukuyama, the Doctor Pangloss of the 1990s comes to mind – for which the rich world's superiority simply expresses its discovery of the best of all possible designs for arranging human affairs, as demonstrated by its historic triumph' (Hobsbawm, 2000, p.166). American triumphalism might be too much to take for many critics, but for those committed to US-led global capitalist expansion, such narratives of overwhelming success provide moral legitimization for the basic experiences of that greed and fear upon which the capitalist social order rests and which so profoundly affects the idea and practice of welfare.

Fukuyama's work is only one example, if a particularly startling and extreme one, of a whole trend of twentieth century theoretical speculation proclaiming the end of phenomena such as history. There are many variants of 'endism' and if they are to function as providing post facto justification of capitalism and supporting self-confident certainty in the virtues of the free market, they have to argue that there can be no alternative to capitalism and that the attempt to pursue the emancipation projects of the nineteenth and twentieth centuries, especially any form of socialism, are doomed to failure. We are urged to embrace the brave new world of unfettered capitalism because this is as good as it gets.

Pessimism

So here we have a ruling ideology in the West which takes the form of a suffocating belief that capitalism is ethically and politically superior to any other conceivable social and economic system.

It is here to stay because it has outlived and triumphed over the particular form of socialism which once flourished in the Soviet Union and other authoritarian state socialist countries. This triumphalism is matched by an overwhelming sense of defeat by many on the Left, and a pessimism which I find shared by many students of social work, especially those at the end of their professional education.

Faced with the aftermath of the Cold War, the Left has either retreated to the 'Third Way' and come to terms with the structures and ideologies of capitalism, or it remains both defiant and pessimistic at the same time. Eric Hobsbawm's book, *The New Century* (2000), illustrates this contradiction. Hobsbawm is a brilliant and immensely influential Marxist historian who, when asked why he stayed in the British Communist Party after the Soviet Union's invasion of Hungary in 1956, explains how conflicted he was, how much he hated the thought of being identified as an 'Anti-Communist', and goes on to explain his own thinking about the relationship between a political cause and the actual practices to which it may give rise:

> If you think that communism is something greater than the history of a backward country in which it happened that communists got to power, then that history is not reason enough to abandon the chosen cause (Hobsbawn, 2000, p.160).

Hobsbawm goes on, however, to mix defiance with pessimism when, in a chilling evaluation of his own history, he says:

> I know very well that the cause that I embraced has proved not to work. Perhaps I shouldn't have chosen it. But ...if people don't have any ideal of a better world, then they have lost something (Hobsbawn, 2000, p.160).

Later, Hobsbawm speaks of the need to have moderate expectations of the world and ends his book by saying that 'at the end of the century, I cannot look to the future with great optimism' (Hobsbawm 2000, p.167). Hobsbawm's pessimistic judgement is, I suggest, widely shared on the Left and perhaps by many of us who have tried to develop a critical social work theory and practice. It has reinforced a pervasive fatalism and a feeling of exhaustion amongst those who might have been expected to continue to support the idea of emancipation. The complex global social system in which we now live is often experienced by us and our students as so overwhelming that we are reduced to feelings of powerlessness. Freire argued, we should remember, that a major obstacle to conscientization in education was 'peasant fatalism' (1970).

Whistling in the Dark

How has the strand of pessimism I have identified on the Left influenced my own work? If I look back at about thirty years of participation in the critical, emancipatory tradition in social work theory and practice, self reflection emerges as one way of moving to counteract pessimism. All of my most significant writing and teaching have been fuelled by a Marxist analysis and, for most of that time, by membership in a Left political party. Have I been optimistic? On the surface, yes. But underneath, in the spaces between the lines of the written text, I can now detect a certain mood in the face of political defeats. My writing was a response, a theoretical practice, in the presence of shifts in the balance of class forces which were profoundly affecting the 'welfare state' and those who worked in it as well as those who used its services. A mood of desperation emerges in some of my writing through an overt focus on feelings of hopelessness about the condition of the poor, subordinated populations with whom social workers practice. My overt focus was on 'crisis', perhaps because thinking and writing about the suffering of actual clients was simply too difficult. The term 'crisis' was the signifier which, for me, represented a depressing reality of major reversals in the struggle for new radical approaches to social work and social policy.

If I take three books written in the last 25 years, it is possible to mark a continuing theme in my justifications for writing predominantly about theory and, in particular, about Marxist theory. In *Social Work Practice under Capitalism,* which I wrote jointly with Paul Corrigan and which was published in 1978, I wrote an editor's introduction to a proposed series of books called *Critical Texts in Social Work and the Welfare State,* of which this book was the first of what would later run to ten volumes. The justification for the planned series was the experience of crisis: that the welfare state in Britain was in a serious condition. This condition was not dependent on the existence of a government with a controlling neo Liberal orthodoxy: Margaret Thatcher was not to gain power until a year after this book was published. In the meantime, however, a Labour government, battered by the international oil crisis and the destructive demands of the International Monetary Fund, was required to preside over the dismantling of its own social democratic welfare state. I wrote:

> Although the precise nature of this crisis is subject to much debate its effects are recognized everywhere, but especially among those working within the apparatus of the welfare state at central and local level, and those most dependent on certain welfare services – the poor, the deprived and the most exploited, including women, the black population and the unemployed (Corrigan and Leonard, 1978, p. vii).

A major threat to the very existence of the welfare state had profound effects on Left critics. Previously, we had an antagonistic relationship to the social democratic ideology which ruled the welfare state and towards the remote, bureaucratic and controlling nature of its services. We had attacked the welfare state: now we found that we were forced to defend it. Even the social democratic welfare state was certainly better than no welfare state. This did not mean that we stopped being critical or engaging in theoretical work. Theory, I argued, enabled us to contextualize attacks on the living standards of a population which included the most vulnerable sections of the working class. But, I pointed out, if we looked further back to the 1960s and early 1970s, we would be able to see, through a Marxist analysis, how naive was the assumption that it was possible to develop humane, universalist and non-stigmatizing social services within the structures of capitalism. This was intended as a challenge to the social democratic orthodoxy of social work education of the day – that if we could get rid of conservative influences in the Labour Party we could return to the old Keynesian welfare state.

So my argument for critical theory rested, as it always does, on a negation of the existing social order, on strengthening resistance at the level of ideology, a resistance which emerges most strongly, perhaps, when political defeats are experienced and pessimism is likely to be growing. More generally, we could see critical theory as primarily *reactive* to wider social and economic shifts and dependent on the prior existence of that dominant system which it opposed. Thus Marxism developed as a reaction to capitalism, and feminism as a reaction to patriarchy; without capitalism, there would have been no Marxism, and without patriarchy, no feminism. As the characteristics of these dynamic social systems change over time a discursive space is created for new social theory which can attempt to explain political defeats and so, at least at the ideological level, counteract the pessimism which frequently appears at these historical junctures.

At the level of the educational process and the dissemination of ideas *Social Work Practice under Capitalism* had its impact in advancing Marxist theory in a form which could be directly used by social workers. At Warwick University we abandoned a revised systems approach which we saw as, despite its potentials, without the critical edge we needed. Teaching and learning about social work was reconstructed to challenge directly dominant ideas about what constituted social work and emphasis was placed on the potentials of Marxist analysis for understanding the material conditions and class relations which constituted the arena in which social work was carried out.

Six years later, in 1984, I published *Personality and Ideology*. Now neo-liberal orthodoxy was everywhere, the 'Thatcher Years' already seemed endless and we were faced with new questions. These questions were not dissimilar to those which were raised by some Marxists in the 1930s and 1940s. Why, they asked, did large sections of the working class support the Right, the figures of authority? The Critical Theory School, first in Germany and then evacuated to the United States, included in its projects the exploration of the critical potential which lay in psychoanalysis. Erich Fromm and others attempted to understand why so many people supported ideas and practices which, from a Marxist perspective, were against their own 'objective' material interests. The answer lay in the intra psychic mechanisms by which dominant ideology was internalized by the individual subject.

My overall intention in this book was to undertake some preliminary groundwork in establishing a materialist theory of the individual subject based on Marxist and feminist analysis. Once again, its justification was indicated in the early sentences of the book's introduction: acknowledgement of the continuing victories of the Right and the defeats of the Left.

Although the political resurgence of the Right characterizes the present period
within many capitalist countries, and often sows despondency and discord amongst
those who oppose it, it is a resurgence which also brings a contradiction: it makes
clearer issues which were previously confused and it compels those of us who
consider ourselves part of the Left to re-evaluate the ways in which we understand
our society and ourselves...[We are led] to explore more fully the nature of human
consciousness, how it is constructed within specific historical conditions, how it is
manipulated in the interests of particular class, gender and ethnic groups, and how
such manipulation might be more effectively resisted (Leonard, 1984, p.1).

Later in the same introductory chapter, I argued that orthodox Leftist thinking
had given priority to the overwhelming effects of the structural forces of class,
gender and racism, the central role of material production and social reproduction,
the controlling operations of the modern state, and the place of the mass media in
the manufacture of 'moral panics'. I suggested that this was an over-determinist
picture which rendered us, together with our even more oppressed clients, only as
victims of a monolithic social order. Such a view is invariably a pessimistic one,
one in which exclusive emphasis on the analysis of wider structural forces may
lead to paralysis when it comes to our own practice. Such an emphasis, I argued,
must be counteracted by understanding more profoundly the dialectic between
determining social forces and the ever-present power of collective and individual
human agency. I had intended this book to be an alternative text for the teaching, in
mainstream social work programmes, of courses variously called Human Growth
and Behaviour, Human Development and Social Environment, and Social
Influences on Behaviour. These courses, as their titles suggested, drew largely
upon what might be called the 'bourgeois' disciplines of sociology, psychology
and psychoanalysis. My approach was an attempt to understand individual identity
as a product of class and gender relations, an understanding within which socialist
feminist social workers would engage in their central counter-ideological role:
contributing to the development of a critical consciousness of how the dynamics of
class and gender relations are internalized and both hold us captive and, at the
same time, encourage rebellious struggles against that which oppresses us.
Subsequently, this Marxist – feminist analysis took a new turn with my attempt to
critique postmodernism as well as to come to terms with it in my teaching of the
social construction of the individual subject.

Postmodern Welfare, published in 1997, continued to reflect the previous
themes of crisis and defeat, but by this stage the defeats were seen as more
catastrophic and the crises more profound. The foundational beliefs in the
possibility of emancipation and social progress are being contested and socialism, I
admitted, was now perceived as having failed as both theory and practice:

In the contemporary political discourse taking place amongst those who assume a
critical oppositional stance to the now triumphal world capitalist order – feminists,
socialists, anti-racists, defenders of minority cultural rights and others – a critical
question is being posed. Is the emancipatory potential of the project of modernity,

which expressed its resistance to domination in the universal terms of justice, reason and progress, now at an end (Leonard, 1997, p. xi)?

Perhaps the combination of the defeat of the very idea of socialism coupled with postmodern deconstruction of all narratives of emancipation provided every justification for feelings of pessimism. Once again, for me, a way forward presents itself, namely theoretical practice which confronts postmodern ideas and attempts to reconstruct the idea of welfare in new terms which take account of the profound critiques of Western cultures produced by postmodern theorizing. But I see now that part of an effective resistance to pessimism lies in a renewed attempt to theorize the whole of the global social system as a dynamic mechanism of exploitation. Here, the Marxist theoretical project of attempting to understand whole social systems becomes relevant again despite the postmodern belief that the grand narratives of social theory are no longer possible or legitimate.

Is Social Theory Possible?

The very idea that it is possible to talk about, let alone begin to grasp, the complex whole of the planetary system of which we are a part, is seen by many as folly. In arguing that effort should be made to try to grasp the whole, Terry Eagleton (1997) maintains that because the Left can no longer think of a political strategy with which to confront capitalism, then it is tempted to stop thinking about it at all, to think only in fragments. In his attack on postmodernism and the impulse to deconstruct concepts of social totality as illusions, Eagleton suggests ironically that 'it does not matter if there is no political agent at hand to transform the whole because there is in fact no whole to be transformed' (Eagleton, p19). So, the attempt to analyse, for the purposes of education and practice, some of the features of the complex whole is likely to be greeted with cries of derision from those who have abjured broad-based social theory in the interests of the marginal and the local. Eagleton admits that trying to grasp a complex totality is difficult, involving as it does a matching complexity of analysis, but argues that this is intellectual work which urgently needs to be undertaken. In the spirit of responding to Eagleton's challenge, I will make some comments, in what follows, on the dynamic of exploitation and accumulation which underpins the project of capitalism at both national and global levels. It is a dynamic which is crucial to the beginning of an understanding of the whole system of which we are part. Relations of exploitation and accumulation underpin class struggles within countries and conflicts between countries, especially those between developed Western capitalism and increasingly impoverished developing countries.

In *The Communist Manifesto,* Marx and Engels argue that the potentially world-wide transformations produced by the development of the capitalist mode of production involve, in their famous phrase, the 'uninterrupted disturbance of all social conditions', crises which are experienced as 'everlasting uncertainty and agitation' (1848/1968). A class analysis of exploitation and accumulation is, I believe, crucial to an understanding of much of the present uncertainty and crisis and the complex interactions that exist between material exploitation, cultural domination and the continuing legacies and re-inventions of colonialism. These are, after all, the interactions which relentlessly work their way through to the experiences of oppression and subordination which characterize the material, social and emotional injuries – the so-called 'risk factors' – which vulnerable populations suffer.

Reconstructing a Class Analysis

I must confess, first of all, that at one time, where class analysis fitted into an understanding of other social divisions and sites of conflict was for me, quite simple: class analysis was central and all other analyses, of gender, racism or sexuality, could be subsumed under the sign of class struggle. Now, of course, the situation is different: in place of those halcyon days of absolute certainty and relative simplicity my identity as a Marxist is problematic.

In Canada, where I now teach, speaking of Marxism in discussions of social policy, of identity, or of practice, is certainly to occupy a site of necessary trouble. For many students, Marxism is the same as Stalinism, or something which went out with the Beatles. And in presenting a Marxist perspective, I have to try to deconstruct Marxism as I go along and once you deconstruct 'the redemptive figure of the proletariat as emancipator,' the idea of the class struggle of the oppressed looks, perhaps, unconvincing. The notion of class, which is conventional in North American education, is as a static description of categories of income and education. This is why poverty can be spoken of quite widely, but a dynamic idea of class exploitation is difficult to grasp and work with because static conceptions of class are so deeply internalized.

For me, one value of a class analysis is that it provides a particular focus of understanding of the context of different kinds of critical practice, but especially those of social work, research and education. Class relations can be seen as embedded in capitalist cultures and their exploitative dynamic hidden in dominant social and economic discourses. In the face of such powerful discourses and their 'common sense' taken-for granted ideological underpinnings, practitioners and educators find difficulty in extracting themselves from dominant understandings and gaining a critical distance from them.

In the context of exploitative economic and cultural globalization – the growing power of multinational corporations, the new uses of technology, the manufacture of desire for commodities, the reorganization of work – there is in many places a weakening of the resistance of organized labour and a retreat from the workplace as the traditional site of class struggle. Under these conditions resistance spreads, as we know, to a large number of sites of identity politics, the politics of gender, ethnicity, culture, sexuality and other locations of domination/subordination.

However, these various identities include class identities, because being class subjects always intersects with and is mediated by these other subject positions: all are subordinated to the social regulation of their labour. This is a process whereby peoples' ability to undertake work is converted into a labour process of value to capital and from which capital extracts its profit. This dynamic of exploitation and extraction constitutes the material relationship to capital of the overwhelming majority of the population. It is one element in being a class subject. The point here is that labour power is disciplined to the purposes of capital accumulation. David Harvey writes that:

> [this discipline] entails, in the first instance, some mix of repression, habituation, co-optation and co-operation, [a process] that has to be renewed with the addition of each new generation of workers to the labour force (1990, p.123).

So capital engages in a continuous struggle to create the appropriate identities of workers as well as consumers as the targets of the manufacture of desire, identities necessary to the maintenance and reproduction of capitalism. Social welfare has, of course, a major role here in the construction of such subjects. The economic system within which welfare functions is dependent on a modernizing process of continuous growth, innovation and the exploitation of labour and of nature. The imperative of the system is to continuously increase this rate of exploitation. The massive casualties of this process in developed countries – the pain produced by capitalist 'progress' – are allocated to social workers and their interventions designed to ameliorate or control the symptoms.

If we look at the old Keynesian welfare state and compare it to the contemporary economies of Late Capitalism, we can decipher the discourses which serve to justify the transformation of the welfare state by reference to economic and technological necessity. In the rhetoric of economic determinism (and the discursive push towards a certain fatalism) we hear that cuts in services are needed because competition in the global market requires it. But Michael Rustin argues that we should see the economic and political changes that have taken place with the rise of neo conservatism:

> ...as specific willed resolutions of conflicts at the level of social relations, and not as the automatic outcomes of [the] technological imperatives [of mass production or its information based successor]. The key to understanding these [changes] are the relations between the strategies of capital and labour, and the material conditions in which they are conducted. These are, after all, relations of power (1989, p.63).

So, we can examine the extent to which the destruction of the welfare state is a process whereby capital has turned the tables on organized labour and interventionist Keynesian governments in order to remove threats to capital accumulation and authority : to increase the rate of exploitation and thus ensure increasing levels of profits and growing corporate power. And with these changes in social welfare, capital is given access to new potential markets: welfare is re-commodified where possible and market principles replace universal service provision.

The Welfare Recipient as a Class Subject

From the abstraction of the global economy and the dynamic of class exploitation we can turn now to a more concrete example of how class subjects are constructed. The subject position of what might be called the *welfare dependent*, dependent, that is, on state resources, is of course problematic for the subject – it invariably involves many kinds of deprivations and abuses, material, social and psychological. The welfare dependent is the object of state monitoring, surveillance and control. But welfare dependency is also a problem for capital. The welfare recipient is dependent on the state and not on the labour market, directly. Being outside the process of exchanging labour for wages – the fundamental dynamic of capitalist appropriation – weakens (it is feared) the subject's allegiance to the *moral necessity,* and not just the material necessity, of paid work, and allows the subject to escape from the social discipline involved in daily paid labour. For most workers in capitalist societies, paid work is, in other words, experienced as a moral obligation, although this dependency on the labour market is re-defined by capital as independence. Through identification with the dominant discourse on work, the subject tends to believe that the ethical imperative to engage in paid labour is autonomously and freely chosen, a belief which we might call a primary *ideological effect.*

One way of managing people's dependence on state welfare payments and legitimating increases in poverty as the price to be paid for increases in the rate of exploitation is to develop an appropriate subordinate social category to which subjects can be consigned, subjects who comprise the segment of the population most likely to be the clients of social workers. This category, variously called the underclass or the culture of poverty, classifies and contextualizes subjects described as welfare dependents, the chronic poor, or often 'bad mothers'.

These categories may be seen as a discursive weapon of class struggle; like the nineteenth century categories of the Residium, the pauper, and the deserving/undeserving, they serve the same or similar purposes. These purposes include directing attention away from the structural forces which determine the distribution of economic and social advantages, avoiding the contemplation of how the State reproduces these distributive mechanisms (by supporting capital's exploitative dynamic), and pathologizing those most injured by shifts in the balance of class forces.

Does this account read as an overly determinist one? Is it likely to reinforce feelings of despair and pessimism in the face of the massive power of international capital? Not, I suggest, if we continue to see class struggle as a two-way process. Although there can be no doubt that the balance of political forces has tilted dramatically in favour of capital, struggles against capital now take place outside the workplace, as well as inside it. Class subjects of many different kinds of social identity are not only victims, they also resist individually and collectively. These subjects are not simply inscribed as inert bodies by the culture of late capitalism, but practice a certain insurgency and recalcitrance in the face of the exercise of power, as Foucault, in his later work, admits.

Difference, Solidarity and Class

In classical Marxism, the solidarity of the whole working class, under the leadership of a revolutionary party, was assumed to be central to class struggle. It was an assumption emerging from a belief in the 'science' of historical materialism, a science which rejected any form of extreme determinism. Marx writes that 'Men (sic) make history, but not under the circumstances of their own choosing' thereby identifying the dialectic between human agency and determining historical forces.

But with the postmodern deconstruction of modern Western ideas of history, science and the narrative of progress, we must now recognize the existence of diverse forms and sites of struggle, diverse histories and cultures. We need to relinquish a linear conception of history as a story of progress and acknowledge the tragic processes at work now and in the past, without succumbing to despair.

So what happens to the ideas of solidarity? Any commitment to solidarity may be seen as dangerous to a politics concerned with the expression of the multiple voices of the excluded Other, who might, once again, be subjected to control justified 'in the interests of emancipation'. Notions of solidarity may not be trusted because in its name it may appropriate difference, smother it in a comradely embrace in the service of a 'higher good'. Some Marxists are deeply critical of the unending deconstruction involved in much of identity politics, seeing it as destroying the possibilities of broad Left alliances against capitalist exploitation, the emergence of 'anti-capitalist' demonstrations notwithstanding. These are perfectly understandable anxieties on both sides and I share many of them, but it seems clear to me that difference must be recognized before we can speak of solidarity.

It is possible to see the convergences between a class analysis of economic exploitation and other related forms of oppression, though the necessary theoretical work is slow to develop. It is clear now that an analysis of class cannot proceed without an accompanying analysis of gender, racism and sexuality, social divisions which involve both economic and cultural domination and exclusion. The family, and other institutions, reproduce gender and sexual identities for the production of gendered heterosexual persons requires the social regulation of the family in the interests of capital's need for the continuous supply of productive and reproductive labour. The capitalist economy is deeply sedimented in patriarchal, heterosexist bourgeois culture and the apparent separation between this culture and the material relations of class is a product of capital itself, another example of a primary ideological effect.

Conclusion

In this discussion I have tried to argue for the uses of theory which might, even in a post-theory period, confront a pervasive sense of pessimism in the face of the massive powers of international capital and its invasion into almost every cultural space on the planet. We can believe in the possibilities of resistance and the struggle against exploitation and cultural domination, however, only if we are able to bring difference and solidarity into a close, symbiotic relationship to each other. We must respect and support difference whenever we can, but we must also acknowledge the interdependence of human subjects.

It is the idea of the interdependence of and between humans and nature that might be a basis for re-establishing solidarity in the interests of difference and the necessities of collective political struggle in the field of welfare and beyond. One element in the kind of solidarity which we might see as necessary could be based on identifying the preconditions for the expression and satisfaction of diverse culturally produced needs, identities and social practices. The expression of diverse needs demands, we might argue, a level of material existence which allows subjects to participate in cultural discourses on needs and well-being, thereby acting as moral agents. Alongside and within a politics of difference lies a common concern with levels of material existence: the global market economy, which is, after all, a class project, benefits a small minority through exploiting the majority. Perhaps this growing perception is one basis of solidarity. If we understand that the exploitative process can be and is contested and struggled against, perhaps this perception and the practice which might emerge from it will also act as an antidote to pessimism.

The shifts in theoretical focus demanded of postmodern critique have enabled some social workers in Western countries to give more recognition and respect to the Other and explore the possibilities of more dialogical and democratic relationships between social workers and service users. These moves are of considerable importance politically, providing a supportive theoretical framework for anti-oppressive practice with marginalized and excluded people. But too great an emphasis on difference, on the cultural relativity of conceptions of needs and their connection to claims for services, can lead to the fragmentation of struggle. We must be aware of the dangers involved in the emergence of forms of small scale collectivism and individualism which ignore the common bonds which may unite exploited populations. At this point in the history of critical social work, it is necessary to grasp hold of both the difference between and the similarity amongst people. This understanding of the dialectic between difference and solidarity is a necessary part of resistance to the deadly pursuit of an organizational practice which both objectifies and homogenizes the growing population of clients who involuntarily join the ranks of the most excluded and subordinated communities. These communities provide the material base upon which new strategies of resistance might be mounted and in which social work could play a crucial part.

References

Butler, J. (1991), 'Imitation and Gender Subordination' in D.Fuss (ed.) *Inside/Out: Lesbian Theories, Gay Theories*, Routledge, New York.

Corrigan, P. and Leonard, P. (1978), *Social Work Practice Under Capitalism: A Marxist Approach*, Macmillan, London.

Eagleton, T. (1997), 'Where Do Postmodernists Come From?' in E.M. Wood (ed.) *In Defence of History: Marxism and the Postmodern Agenda*, Monthly Review Press, New York.

Friere, P. (1970), *Pedagogy of the Oppressed*, Penguin Books, London.

Fukuyama, F. (1992), *The End of History and the Last Man*, Penguin Books, London.

Harvey, D. (1990), *The Condition of Postmodernity: An Enquiry into the Origins of Cultural Change*, Blackwell, Oxford.

Hobsbawm, E. (2000), *The New Century*, Little, Brown and Co., London.

Leonard, P. (1984), *Personality and Ideology: Towards a Materialist Understanding of the Individual*, Macmillan, London.

Leonard, P. (1997), *Postmodern Welfare: Reconstructing an Emancipatory Project*, Sage, London.

Marx, K. and Engels, F. (1848/1968), 'Communist Manifesto' in *Marx and Engels Selected Works*, Lawrence and Wishart, London.

Rustin, M. (1989), 'The Politics of Post-Fordism: Or, the Trouble with New Times', *New Left Review*, Vol. 175, pp. 54-78.

Chapter 2

Critical Reflection and Transformative Possibilities

Jan Fook

Introduction

Is it possible that new ways of knowing can enable emancipation, and can challenge structures and relations of domination?

In the face of current global economic trends, it is easy to feel that possibilities for challenge and change of dominant structures are less attainable. Earlier in this volume Peter Leonard argues that these trends have resulted in a decline in the belief in collective agency and the vision of structural welfare, and that these beliefs are associated with a determinism which results in fatalism. Yet at the same time, the postmodern thinking which is often associated with globalization might potentially unsettle some of our assumed ways of thinking about ourselves in relation to the social structure. It is possible that this unseating of taken-for-granted ways of understanding ourselves in our social worlds might in fact provide a means and a site for challenging and resisting different forms of domination. In this chapter, I aim to explore this issue by examining an approach to unsettling these assumptions. This is the phenomenon of critical reflection. I argue that critical reflection, as a process which is partially based on, and integrates, elements of deconstructive thinking, can provide a means of reconstructing, and thus changing, the ways in which individuals perceive and relate to their social worlds. In this sense, critical reflection holds emancipatory possibilities.

I begin the chapter with a brief description of critical reflection, and then move to a section which develops the idea of critical reflection from a number of different theoretical traditions. After outlining a process for critical reflection which derives from this theoretical background, I then spend some time discussing the emancipatory elements of critical reflection, based on material from existing literature, as well as results of evaluations from my own critical reflection programs. Lastly, I pose some further possibilities for the use of critical reflection in contributing to a transformative social work practice.

What is Critical Reflection?

Critical reflection is most simply understood as an approach to analyzing practice or experience, based on the identification of the assumptions embedded in that practice or experience. Having said that, it is acknowledged that there is wide divergence about what this actually means in practice (Ixer, 1999). Part of the difficulty in being able to pin down the idea of critical reflection with any certainty possibly arises because critical reflection itself seems to derive from a number of different intellectual traditions (which I will describe in more detail in the following section). For instance, it is often used interchangeably with the idea of 'reflective practice', a term which emerges principally from the work of Donald Schon (1983). However, many writers carefully distinguish between reflection, and critical reflection. The latter is also variously defined. Mezirow (1991), writing in the adult education field, distinguishes critical reflection as unearthing deeper assumptions or 'presuppositions' (p.12). Brookfield (1995, p.8) suggests that what makes reflection critical is the focus on power. 'Critical' can also be extended from this to encompass an awareness of how assumptions about the connection between oneself and social context/structure can function in powerful ways, so that awareness of these assumptions can provide a platform for transformative action (e.g. Kondrat, 1999; Fook, 2002). These latter understandings of the term come from a clear critical theory tradition, and this is the perspective that I adopt in this chapter and in my own work more generally.

In order to understand the idea of critical reflection and the processes involved, it is helpful to explore the main traditions of thinking from which it arises. I have identified four main ones which are involved: reflective practice; reflexivity; postmodernism and deconstruction; and critical social theory. In the following section, I will detail each of these and their contribution to the idea of critical reflection.

The Theoretical Background of Critical Reflection

Reflective Practice

The idea of reflective practice is often credited to Argyris and Schon (1976) and later to Donald Schon (1983 and 1987). These works are often used as a basis for subsequent writings in the professional learning traditions, particularly nursing (e.g. Taylor, 2000, Rolfe, 2001). However, in the adult education literature, the much earlier influence of Dewey is noted (Mezirow, 1991). For instance, Mezirow (1991, p.5) notes that for Dewey 'reflection referred to (Dewey, 1933, p.9) 'assessing the grounds (justification) of one's beliefs', the process of rationally examining the assumptions by which we have been justifying our convictions'.

For Schon (1983 and 1987), it was important to acknowledge that professional knowledge involves both 'technical rationality' (rules) and professional artistry (reflection in action), and that very often the 'theory' or rules espoused by practitioners, is quite different from the 'theory' or assumptions embedded in the actual practices of professionals. Reflective practice therefore involves the ability to be aware of the 'theory' or assumptions involved in professional practice, in order to close the gap between what is espoused and what is enacted, in an effort to improve both.

From this has been developed a reflective approach (Fook, 1996), which encompasses the recognition of the intuitive, the artistic and the creative in professional practice. The role of the emotions is also often emphasized (Fook, 1999a).

Put in these terms, critical reflection would involve a focus on assumptions about power, and the corresponding assumptions about links between the individual person and their surrounding social structure. Often a focus on the intuitive and artistic also unearths the role of emotions in supporting particular assumptions. What is difficult, however, in using a simple reflective practice approach, is that often a detailed framework for analyzing the links between the personal and social is not well developed, so it is all too easy to limit focus to personal issues without making a broader connection.

Reflexivity

The idea of reflexivity is perhaps more associated with social science research traditions (Marcus, 1994), and was widely written about in anthropology (for example, Rosaldo, 1993). Lately it has been more developed for use directly in the health and human service professions (e.g. Taylor and White, 2000). Reflexivity, or a 'turning back on itself' (Steier, 1991), again has been variously defined. For example, White (2002, p.102) notes how understandings of reflexivity can range from simple ideas of 'being reflective' through to more complex social science research ideas based on notions of deconstruction. White's own version of reflexivity, of being able to look both inwards and outwards to recognize the connections with social and cultural understandings, is similar to my own, which is also based on an understanding of reflexivity in research practice. In this sense, reflexivity involves the ability to recognize that all aspects of ourselves and our contexts influence the way we research (or create knowledge) (Fook, 1999b). I am using the idea of research in an inclusive sense here, to refer to all the different ways in which we create knowledge – some occur on a more formal and systematic basis, yet others are used daily, and often in unarticulated ways to make sense of immediate surroundings.

If we take this as our base, then it is easy to detail some ways in which we (as researchers and creators of knowledge) might generate knowledge, and this might have some part in influencing the type of knowledge which is produced. For example, knowledge is embodied and social in nature – it is mediated by physical and social lenses. In the same way, knowledge is also mediated by our own subjectivity – our particular being, experience, and social position will influence what and how we interpret. Thirdly, there is a reactivity element – the knowledge we obtain is at least partly determined by the kinds of tools and process we use to create it. And lastly, knowledge is also interactional – it is shaped by historical and structural contexts.

From the reflexivity tradition, critical reflection might be seen as a way of researching personal practice or experience in order to develop our understandings of ourselves as knowers – this helps us make the connections between ourselves as individuals and our broader social, cultural and structural environment.

Postmodernism and Deconstructionism

I have identified these traditions separately from those of reflexivity, although it is clear that they overlap. However, I think it is important to note how the influence of postmodern thinking brings with it particular ways of thinking which to some degree transcend, yet complement, those associated with reflexivity. In this section I also include poststructural thinking as well, and will focus on what I believe to be the common threads which are useful to our understanding of critical reflection. I have developed these ideas in more detail elsewhere (Fook, 1999a). By postmodernism, I am referring simply to the questioning of 'modernist' (or linear and unified) thinking. This postmodern thinking alerts us to the role of dominant discourses in creating what is perceived as legitimate knowledge (and therefore power). Poststructuralists also alert us to the role of language in forming our knowledge, particularly to the role of the construction of binary opposites, and how we make difference, by often attributing inferiority to the second part of a binary category. However, language (and dominant discourse) also has a role in silencing multiple and marginal perspectives, since it is often only the major (unified) voice which is recognized.

Overall then, postmodern and poststructural thinking allows a recognition that knowledge can be socially constructed, often in linear and unified ways, to support a dominant power base, and that we often unwittingly participate in preserving these power relations through the very language which we use to speak about our world. Postmodern thinking opens up the possibilities for contradiction, change and conflict in thinking, thus recognizing that many different experiences can be legitimate.

From this point of view, critical reflection can be aided by deconstructing our thinking in order to expose how we participate in constructing power, and by allowing us to explore conflicts and contradictions which previously we may have silenced. It is particularly useful, I think, in helping to explore difficulties in practice which are brought about because of perceived (binary) dilemmas or tensions. What is still deficient, I believe, about this position, is that details of how to reconstruct power, and how to determine which forms of power actually preserve or challenge domination, are still not clear. A better understanding of how different forms of power can be used and function, and the contradictions involved in this, is needed.

Critical Social Theory

In developing the idea of what is 'critical', the common themes of critical social theory are useful. I have paraphrased and summarized these (Fook, 2002) from Agger (1998), as follows. Critical social theory involves a recognition that domination is both personally experienced and structurally created. In this sense, individuals can participate in their own domination, through holding self-defeating beliefs about their own power and possibilities for change. Social change, in this sense, must therefore be both personally and collectively achieved. This involves a recognition that knowledge often has an empirical reality, but the way that knowledge is used and interpreted may be constructed (socially and personally). Therefore, in bringing about social and personal change, communication and dialogue is important so that shared understandings can be created.

What is important about the contribution of critical social theory for the idea of critical reflection is that it provides a broader framework for understanding what critical reflection can and should help achieve. By helping make connections between the personal and structural, and emphasizing the importance of communication, critical social theory points to how a critical reflection process might help us forge bridges between our own experience and that of others to bring about desired social changes.

In the adult education literature, these aims of critical reflection often translate into specific changes in perspectives. For example, Mezirow (1991, p.14) points out that more inclusive, discriminating, permeable and integrative perspectives are the superior perspectives that adults choose to better understand the meaning of their experience. For him, 'precipitating and fostering critically self-reflective learning means a deliberate effort to foster resistance to …technicist assumptions, to thoughtlessness, to conformity, to impermeable meaning perspectives, to fear of change, to ethnocentric and class bias, and to egocentric values' (1991, p.360).

The Critical Reflection Process

In some ways, what I have outlined above are also different discourses, or ways of talking about, critical reflection. For instance, if we are coming from a reflective practice tradition, we might speak about 'reflecting on' our practice. Alternatively, speaking from the other traditions respectively, we might talk about, 'researching' our practice reflexively, 'deconstructing' our practice, or, from a critical standpoint, 'challenging and changing' our practice. It is helpful to be aware that there may be different ways of talking about a similar process, in which each tradition is integrated with the other in providing different ways to understand and unearth the assumptions involved in practical experience.

Let me illustrate with the following examples of questions, derived from each of the different traditions, which might assist in critically reflecting on our practice. For example, in the reflective practice tradition, critical reflection questions might include: what do my thinking/actions imply about my ideals/the basic social structures I believe in/my beliefs about power?

Using a stance of reflexivity, one might ask, how did I influence the situation through: my actions/my preconceptions/my presence/other people's perceptions of me? How have I constructed myself and the situation in relation to me? How have I constructed myself in relation to power? What have I unearthed about my social beliefs?

From a postmodern/deconstructive perspective, critical reflection might be aided by asking: what language have I used? Are there any binary opposites evident? What perspectives are missing? What are my constructions of power? How do my constructions relate to the dominant discourses? How have I constructed myself in relation to other people, or power?

Taking a critical stance would place the emphasis on how the critical reflection process can bring about change. Questions might take the form of: how might my practice, and my theory of my practice, change as a result of my reflections? How can I change or use my power differently? What different outcomes might I seek, and different processes might I use to challenge different forms of power?

The above list illustrates that although each perspective might provide different ways of asking critical reflective questions, each overlaps in some way. I have found that the above kinds of questions can be used successfully in an integrated way through a process of critical reflection. There is no prescribed way to undertake critical reflection, and, indeed the field is characterized by myriad different process, techniques and exercises which can be used to further critical reflection. This has invited criticism from some quarters (Ixer, 1999) but I believe that this is, in fact, one of the strengths of critical reflection, as it is highly adaptable to situation, place, learner and educator.

However, I do believe that if the critical reflection process is to be used to bring about some kind of change, then it is important to structure the process to bring this about. In my own work, I tend to prescribe two stages to the critical reflection process. The first focuses on exposing and examining the hidden assumptions, and the second on turning these reflections into new ways of understanding practice, our power, and how we might challenge and change our environment in some way. In some ways, the process might be likened to a process of conscientization or consciousness-raising (Hart, 1991) but an included emphasis on how some political options (Heaney and Horton, 1991) arises out of the process. Elsewhere I have likened the process to a first stage of deconstruction and a second stage of reconstruction (Fook, 2002). Other writers also refer to the staging of the critical reflection process (Brookfield, 1991) suggesting that it is a process which is about ongoing development. As mentioned earlier, there are clear commonalities with the conscientization process (Alfrero, 1972) in which there is a shift from first a more fatalistic stage of consciousness in which the person feels dominated by 'facts', through a second stage of awareness of more freedom in understanding the 'facts' from outside, to a final stage of understanding the causal links between 'facts' and social circumstances. With critical reflection there is a fourth stage which links this new critical awareness with possibilities for action.

The process essentially involves a small group of participants who assist each other to critically reflect on their practice in a confidential setting facilitated by someone versed in the approach. A group climate and culture of trust, openness, and non-judgementalism (neither positive nor negative) is essential to the effectiveness of the approach. I ask people to present a concrete 'critical incident' from their own practice as the raw material for critical reflection. The critical incident technique is widely used, and in varying ways (Brookfield, 1995; Davies and Kinloch, 2000). In the critical reflection process that I use, I ask that it be kept deliberately concrete, as someone's 'story' or 'narrative' about an event in which they were involved, and which was significant to them in some way. I find that this focus is helpful on at least four counts: 1/ it allows us to focus on concrete actions as further possibilities; 2/ it allows us to bypass (to some extent) getting caught up in the accepted language or abstracted ways of theorizing practice; 3/ it emphasizes that this is their own construction; and lastly, it has more immediacy for them.

Participants present their critical incidents in two stages according the process outlined above. The first stage focuses on deconstructing the story of the incident. The whole group asks critical reflective questions based on the four theoretical traditions outlined above. Each participant then reflects further on the thinking which has been unearthed in this first stage, and presents their revised 'theory of practice' again (after a period of time, normally at least a week), with a view to devising specific practice strategies from it. The group assists this process by asking a series of reconstructive questions.

How Can Critical Reflection be Transformative?

In order to be transformative, the process of critical reflection needs to be able to counteract feelings of fatalism. What exactly is fatalism and how can it be counteracted through critical reflection? Heaney and Horton (1991, p.86), in speaking of the fatalism often felt by welfare dependants, refer to it as 'an adjustment of the mind to the inevitability of poverty and disenfranchisement'. Fatalism might refer more broadly to feelings of disempowerment, of lack of agency or ability to act upon and effect change. In some senses, this might be associated with an inability to see any connection between an individual person's actions and any broader social concerns, to the point where they do not see any possibilities for action and therefore do not even want to try to think of them. Alternatively, there might be a pervading sense of pessimism, so that there is a belief that even if one could think of changes and could take action to bring them about, it is assumed they would not be successful, or that they will inevitably lead to a negative outcome.

In some of my work with critical reflection, I encounter many constructions which might be associated with feelings of fatalism. For instance, sometimes, along with assumptions that any attempt at changes will not be successful, there might be accompanying beliefs about the 'powerful' people at whom change is targeted, e.g. that they will not listen, that they will find some other way to win, or that they will sabotage the action. Often incidents are constructed in terms which emphasize the powerlessness of the individual person telling the story, and exaggerate the powerfulness of the other person targeted for change. In some cases a form of fatalism is that thinking which consistently constructs actions as not powerful or not powerful enough. For example, I see people who have taken some quite powerful action, but labeled it as unsuccessful because it did not bring about enough 'structural' change, as they saw it. Elsewhere (Fook, 2002, p.110-111), I document this tendency in social workers – change is not seen as good enough unless it is 'structural' and 'total'.

How can such thinking be counteracted by critical reflection? Is it possible that critical reflection can assist people to see how they might become empowered, more effective, or even realize the possibility of their own agency? Whilst there are no definitive answers to these questions, there are several reasons for which I think it is possible that critical reflection can assist in changing personal beliefs about power and their engagement with it, so that new possibilities are opened up for action.

Firstly, the critical reflection process values and validates the personal, and by starting with that, helps to validate the person and their own sense of themselves. Whilst this is not an expressly critical component in an established structural sense, there is growing recognition of the importance of the personal in what is termed 'life politics' (Ferguson, 2001). Thus, critical reflection can be experienced as very liberating, especially by people who assume that their point of view is not important or somehow less valuable. I see this often in the case of human service workers, who are often used to subordinating their own practice wisdom in favor of academic research or theorizing. The novelty of presenting, sharing, and learning from their own practice experience is seen as very validating, and they report increased confidence in their own judgment and creative abilities. Whilst this is a well-known phenomenon in therapeutic circles, it is perhaps less well-recognized in more structural forms of social work which are easily interpreted as focusing only on the social structure, to the point where the personal may be devalued or denied (Fook, 2002).

In addition, people often experience critical reflection as a process which assists them to reaffirm their positive sense of themselves in the face of negative social experiences or social environment. In a recent group I ran with school teachers, participants spoke of being enabled to identify how their social environment (other teachers, school principals, parents of students or the school culture) often negatively affected the value they placed on themselves and their work. They felt they could now distance themselves from needing affirmation from those quarters, and felt empowered by being able to revalue the self-worth or identity which came from their own experience or values.

Secondly, the 'personal' often incorporates an emotional element. Indeed, people often present critical incidents which were significant simply because they were traumatic, emotionally and professionally. Additionally, there are strong emotions often attached to long-held and little-questioned assumptions. Critical reflection can perform a therapeutic function by debriefing, providing support, and clearing emotional blocks. Of course, as therapists, we know that the handling of emotions can be very powerful in inducing change. Whilst this is not a specific goal of critical reflection, and of course needs to be handled sensitively, there is a role for critical reflection in providing collegiate support for the emotional aspects of our work, and in helping colleagues to harness emotional energies for better future practice (Mezirow, 1991, p.17; Askeland, unpub.). I believe one of the strengths of critical reflection is the recognition of the whole person, the physical, social, emotional and cultural being, and how all these aspects are reflected in daily practice. Recognizing these elements, and focusing on how they come together in concrete practice, not only helps removes some blocks which before might have been denied, but also assists people to use all aspects of themselves more productively. There is a better sense of personal integration and integrity. Participants in critical reflection groups often speak about feeling better able to be themselves, and of becoming aware of different strategies they might use at the same time.

Thirdly, by starting with the concrete personal experience, critical reflection is able to make real the connections between the personal and the social. When people are able to get a very specific idea of how a piece of their thinking or action might have influenced a specific thought or action of another person, they are given a clear site to act, and a process for acting. This model can then be applied to many different situations. For example, if a person is reflecting on how they cannot change the organization, it is useful to ask a reflective question about what they are assuming when they talk about 'organization'? What aspects are they talking about? How do they encounter these? Whose attitudes and behavior are they talking about? Which specific behaviors would they like to see changed? What do they mean by change? What would indicate enough change? These questions effectively place the person at the center of their thinking about the organization, and help them to understand how their experience of the organization is mediated by their own thinking about it.

The critical reflection process can be likened to a process of 'laying all the cards on the table'. In this sense, it is about creating a positive climate for change, by emphasizing the potential that change might create, and by framing change in positive terms. What is also important about this is that the person feels free to lay all the 'cards' and to look at them from different perspectives. If such a climate is created, a person can learn to make their own judgments of their own 'cards', simply by seeing them juxtaposed afresh. In this sense, they learn to self evaluate, which is an important process in the achieving of change, and may be more successful in bringing about change than imposing external judgments. It also acts as a form of empowerment, as the responsibility for evaluation is placed squarely back in the hands of the individual.

In a related sense, the critical reflection process also legitimates the person as a creator of their own practice knowledge, and of themselves as social beings. Developing the person as a creator of knowledge has empowering benefits in that it is an aspect of reconstructing the identity of that person as having a role and recognition in contributing to the pool of useful theory. In helping to develop the identity of the person as a social being, the value of that person's contribution is acknowledged as coming from, and influencing, a wider sphere than one's individual experience. It involves the recognition that simply because I am a person in a social context, who cannot be separated from that context (and) who is partially constructed and defined by it, I have wider influence.

This realization extends nicely to the reflexive aspect of critical reflection. This can function to reconstruct the person into many different situations as a responsible actor – one who is able to have influence (indeed who is not able to not have influence because they are inextricably part of their embodied and social context). One of the positive aspects of this is that the influence is of many different kinds – formal, informal, structural, personal, embodied, communicative, positional, subtle, direct, discursive, and so on. This potentially posits many different ways in which influence can be used, and is therefore a potentially more inclusive way of seeing the possibilities of change.

Many of these above changes involve a process of reconstructing the identities of participants as powerful, and, in line with a reflexive awareness, of reconstructing power in inclusive ways. Critical reflection involves an exploration of all assumptions regarding power, and a reconstruction of those ideas which have limited the person to seeing themselves as powerless, or as powerless in relation to other people or structures. This may also involve a deconstruction and reconstruction of beliefs about other types of power inherent in other people or social structures, and about a reconstruction of their own power in relation to this. Because power may be seen to be expressed in many different ways, rather than being the exclusive domain of structurally powerful people, the choices of ways in which to be powerful are increased. This appears to be particularly enabling for people who have not formerly seen themselves as having structural power, for they are able to revalue other aspects of their power. This type of thinking can be loosely equated with a Foucauldian view of power as expressed or enacted, rather than belonging inherently to a person or position (Healy, 2000, p.43).

The reconstruction of powerful identities is based in part on exposing the oppositional thinking involved in assuming that power is structural, and that, by and large, there are two dichotomous groups, the powerful and the powerless. Critical reflection is useful however in deconstructing many binary opposites and in helping to reconstruct binary dilemmas as more complex. Often people freeze into inaction because they have constructed their situation as involving unresolvable tensions. A common one is the conflict between social work values and bureaucratic/management/economic imperatives. Critical reflection exposes these binary constructions, and asks if there are many more varied and more complex ways of seeing situations. What usually happens is that participants recognize that there are many more 'gray' ways of seeing what might have formerly been a 'black and white' situation. This opens up more room for debate, for new strategies. Taylor calls this 'framing the debate in non-dichotomous terms' (1996). In some of the groups I have run, this has involved participants moving on from blaming their supervisors and managers for much of what is wrong with their jobs, to being able to see more and different ways of working with them.

Developing the skill of divergence and a stance of collegiality is related to the above. Mezirow (1991, p.369), sees the skill of divergence as related to 'opening ourselves up to the ideas of others, especially when these provide a new angle of vision'. I have found that learning this skill involves an ability to accept the existence and legitimacy of different points of view (especially those of other people regarded as protagonists in the person's critical incident), even if these might be vastly different, even contradictory, from our own. Often people's abilities to be open to contradictory or divergent viewpoints is enhanced if it is accepted that this does not necessarily mean they have to relinquish their own, but that they can accept that contradictory perspectives can sit side by side, and that all can be 'true' from their respective positions.

The willingness to be more collegiate with fellow workers, regardless of position, is developed in a similar way. Participants in critical reflection workshops often note how the process has made them more aware of their colleagues' situations, has made them more understanding, and able to see more and different options for working with them. They seem to be able to develop more of a shared sense of ideals within an organization, and hence more of an ability to tackle, at least some projects, in a shared way. This contributes to their feelings of empowerment within the organization, and sometimes within their particular job roles. Critical reflection workshops often end spontaneously with plans for shared action, for instance, changing supervision arrangements.

Lastly, an important way in which critical reflection can be transformative is in the ability to develop skills in practicing in uncertainty. Elsewhere I and my colleagues (Fook, Ryan and Hawkins, 2000), have outlined how professional expertise in the current climate involves skills in working with uncertainty, in being able to practice flexibly and with openness, and to be able to modify and create relevant practice theory in an ongoing way. With its inbuilt legitimation of personal experience and practice theory development, critical reflection provides an ideal framework for developing these skills.

Further Possibilities of Critical Reflection

In the foregoing section, I discussed primarily the transformative effects I have observed and experienced in critical reflection programs I have conducted. In this section, I wish to discuss some broader possibilities for the uses of critical reflection which might be posited from my experience.

Firstly, the possibilities for more inclusive approaches have been mooted. Post modern thinking, which allows for more and different ways of knowing, and which underpins critical reflection, also provides a basis for transforming social relations along more inclusive lines. For example, we can use a postmodern analysis to understand the ways in which the fixed identity categories and notions of difference of modernist ways of thinking can work both for or against the political interests of groups defined as 'different'.

For example, an essentialist view of Australian Aboriginal culture has been criticized as one largely constructed by anthropologists and as being too all-pervasive, not recognizing the efforts of many Aborigines to either accommodate or contravene harsh state policies (Finlayson and Anderson, 1996). Noting that Aborigines are increasingly taking responsibility for defining Aboriginality, Lewin (1991) also makes the point that to not recognize that Aboriginality is not homogenous has political consequences, in that an essentialist and structuralist view helps to legitimate government control, and to perpetuate a victim-blaming stance.

Critical reflection therefore possibly has a role in identity politics, that is, the possibility of resisting domination through the recognition of difference, and the creation of new identity categories as a result (Best and Kellner, 1991, p.205). Identity construction plays in important role in the empowerment of previously marginal or disadvantaged groups.

Young notes the politicizing effects of a process of control in the construction of identity:

Assumptions of the universality of the perspective and experience of the privileged are dislodged when the oppressed themselves expose those assumptions by expressing positive images of their experience. By creating their own cultural images they shake up received stereotypes about them (1990, p.155).

I would argue that the methods of critical reflection, used as a tool to research and identify (reconstruct) identities, could function as one of these major empowering methods. The major principle it involves is the idea that critical reflection is a type of narrativity or story telling, in which people can tell (and then possibly deconstruct and reconstruct) specific instances in their own lives or experience. This process of recognition and reflection not only validates experience but opens it up for change by the narrator for her or himself. This latter point is crucial in the politics of critical reflection as an inclusive research method. Many traditional approaches to research and professional practice have placed the power for knowledge making and change within the hands of researchers who have not normally been the people who are the targets of research or change (Smith, 1999). Critical reflection, perhaps unlike many traditional research methods, can only succeed with the full participation and use of participants, and does not necessarily need the participation of an 'outsider' to organize the research process.

There are therefore uses for critical reflection in many different ways and on many different levels. For instance, the process might be used therapeutically to assist in reconstructing damaged personal identities (Sands, 1996, pp.180-183). Alternatively the process might be used with many different types of groups, both service users and workers, to examine marginalized aspects of their identities.

For example, in my own teaching and research experience, I am aware of the use of critical reflection methods being used by indigenous groups in both New

Zealand and New Guinea as a way of researching their own experience. In New Zealand, for instance, I am aware that some Maori social work educators are finding that reflective methods can be used to articulate, develop and write about the Maori approach to social work. In my own teaching, I have found the use of critical reflective methods the best one in working with Aboriginal students to incorporate their own experience into their models of social work practice. For me, this has been the only approach that is effective, since Aboriginal students tend to find what we teach about social work and people to arise from a fundamentally opposed way of seeing the world. In order for any learning to be meaningful, we must engage in a process of developing their own version of social work from their own sets of experiences, taking from bits and pieces of my own perspective along the way. In a way, we engage in a process of reconstructing their identities as Aboriginal social workers, developing a picture of Aboriginal Social Work along the way. Of course, I always participate in the same way all class members do, so I find myself happily involved in reconstructing myself and my own version of social work too. In this sense, I find the whole experience to be as participatory as possible – I learn in the same way all members of the group learn.

Conclusion

In this chapter I have argued that a process of critical reflection, using an amalgam of ideas including reflective practice, reflexivity, postmodernism, deconstruction and critical theory, can have transformative effects. I have illustrated aspects of this argument both from my own experience of conducting critical reflection programs, but also through reference to broader literature. The critical reflection process, as I have outlined it, appears to function similarly to a consciousness-raising process, with an added imperative to develop concrete strategies for action. By engaging with the whole person, and enabling them to make connections with their social and structural environment through the prism of their own concrete experience, the critical reflection process enables individuals to take action in relation to their own social environments. In this way, it is able to counteract aspects of fatalistic thinking, and to open up transformative possibilities. By linking these functions with possibilities for identity reconstruction, the inclusive potential of critical reflection is also realized.

In closing, I do not wish to suggest that critical reflection is the only, or the best method, for enabling transformative practice. In addition, there needs to be continued development of the approach and process for successful use in different contexts and with different groups. However, I believe it is this very flexibility which may mean that it can be effective in different settings and in different ways to enable vastly divergent people, amongst service user and worker groups, to become empowered to take social action within their own environments.

References

Agger, B. (1998), *Critical Social Theories*, Westview, Boulder.

Alfrero, L.A. (1972), 'Conscientization', *New Themes in Social Work Education*, International Association of Schools of Social Work, New York.

Argyris, C. and Schon, D. (1976), *Theory in Practice: Increasing Professional Effectiveness*, Jossey-Bass, San Francisco.

Askeland, G.A. (unpub.) 'Focus on the Facilitator'.

Best, S. and Kellner, D. (1991), *Postmodern Theory: Critical Interrogations*, Guilford Press, New York.

Brookfield, S. (1991), 'Using Critical Incidents to Explore Learner's Assumptions' in J. Mezirow (ed.), *Fostering Critical Reflection in Adulthood*, Jossey-Bass, San Francisco.

Brookfield, S. (1995), Becoming a Critically Reflective Teacher, Jossey-Bass, San Francisco. nloch, H. (2000), 'Critical incident analysis: facilitating reflection and transfer of learning'

Davies, H. and Ki, in V.E. Cree and C. Macauley (eds.), *Transfer of Learning in Professional and Vocational Education*, Routledge, London, pp. 137-147.

Dewey, J. (1933), *How We Think*, Regnery, Chicago.

Ferguson, H. (2001), 'Social Work, Individualisation and Life Politics', *British Journal of Social Work*, Vol. 31, pp. 31-45.

Finlayson, J. and Anderson, I. (1996), 'The Aboriginal Self', in A. Kellehear (ed.), *Social Self: Global Culture*, Oxford University Press, Melbourne.

Fook, J. (1999a), 'Critical reflectivity in education and practice', in B. Pease and J. Fook (eds.), *Transforming Social Work Practice: Postmodern Critical Perspectives*, Allen and Unwin, Sydney, pp. 195-208.

Fook, J. (1999b), 'Reflexivity as method', in J. Daly, A. Kellehear and E. Willis (eds.), *Annual Review of Health Social Sciences*, La Trobe University, Bundoora, vol. 9, pp. 11-20.

Fook, J. (2001), *Linking Theory, Practice and Research*, Critical Social Work, Vol. 2, No. 1, www.criticalsocialwork.com/csw_2001_1.html.

Fook, J. (2002), *Social Work: Critical Theory and Practice*, Sage, London.

Fook, J. (ed.) (1996), *The Reflective Researcher*, Allen and Unwin, Sydney.

Fook, J., Ryan, M. and Hawkins, L. (2000), *Professional Expertise: Practice, Theory and Education for Working in Uncertainty*, Whiting and Birch, London.

Hart, M. U. (1991), 'Liberation through Consciousness-Raising', in J. Mezirow (ed.), *Fostering Critical Reflection in Adulthood*, Jossey-Bass, San Francisco.

Healy, K. (2000), *Social Work Practices*, Sage, London.

Heaney, T.W. and Horton, A.I. (1991), 'Reflective Engagement for Social Change' in J. Mezirow (ed.), *Fostering Critical Reflection in Adulthood*, Jossey-Bass, San Francisco.

Ixer, G. (1999), 'No such thing as reflection', *British Journal of Social Work*, Vol. 29, pp. 513-527.

Kondrat, M.E. (1999), 'Who is the "self" in self-aware? Professional Self-awareness from a critical theory perspective', *Social Service Review*, Vol. 73(4), pp. 451-477.

Lewin, F. (1991), 'Theoretical and Political Implications of the Dynamic Approach to Aboriginality', *Australian Journal of Anthropology*, Vol. 2(2), pp. 171-178.

Marcus, G.E. (1994), 'What comes (just) after "Post"? The case of ethnography', in N.K. Denzin and Y.S. Lincoln (eds.), *Handbook of Qualitative Research*, Sage, London.

Mezirow, J. (1991), 'How Critical Reflection Triggers Learning' in J. Mezirow (ed.), *Fostering Critical Reflection in Adulthood*, Jossey-Bass, San Francisco.

Rolfe, G. (2000), *Research, Truth and Authority*, Macmillan, London.

Rosaldo, R. (1993), *Culture and Truth*, Beacon Press, London.

Sands, R. (1996), 'The Elusiveness of Identity in Social Work Practice with Women', *Clinical Social Work Journal*, Vol. 24(2), pp. 167-186.

Schon, D. (1983), *The Reflective Practitioner*, Temple Smith, London.

Schon, D. (1987), *Educating the Reflective Practitioner*, Jossey-Bass, San Francisco.

Smith, L.T. (1999), *Decolonising Methodologies*, University of Otago Press, Otago.

Steier, F. (ed.) (1991), *Research and Reflexivity*, Sage, London.

Taylor, B. (2000), *Reflective Practice*, Open University Press, Buckingham.

Taylor, C. and White, S. (2000), *Practising Reflexivity in Health and Welfare*, Open University Press, Buckingham.

Taylor, I. (1996), 'Reflective Learning, Social Work Education and Practice in the 21st century', in I. Taylor and N. Gould (eds.), *Reflective Learning for Social Work*, Arena, Aldershot.

White, S. (2001), 'Auto-Ethnography as Reflexive Inquiry', in I. Shaw and N. Gould (eds.), *Qualitative Research in Social Work*, Sage, London.

Young, I. (1990), *Justice and the Politics of Difference*, University of Princeton Press, Princeton.

Chapter 3

Post-Theories for Practice: Challenging the Dogmas

Nigel Parton

Introduction

In this chapter I will be arguing that the contexts in which social work is operating are becoming increasingly complex, fluid and uncertain, and that many of the issues and problems which it is expected to address can be seen as having no easy or unambiguous solutions. As a result, the perspectives critically discussed in this volume and which draw on or are at least sympathetic towards postmodern, constructionist and reflexive perspectives, can be seen as providing crucial insights for developing critical theories for practice. More specifically, they can be seen to develop from social work's traditional strengths and understanding of social processes and where the ability to negotiate, advocate and mediate with creativity are crucial to working with the most marginalized and socially excluded members of society but where the work is becoming increasingly contested and riven with ambiguity. These perspectives provide a potentially productive set of frameworks which practitioners can draw upon in their day-to-day work. However, I will also argue that the requirements made of practitioners by central government in Britain see social workers as little more than organizational functionaries. Here, the requirements made of practitioners are increasingly modernist and rationalist, and it is assumed that the nature of practice simply requires the application of taken-for-granted and codified knowledge often in the form of a very circumscribed and limited notion of 'evidence-based practice' (EBP). The focus for my analysis will be local authority social work in England and Wales. While it is recognized that this is a very specific exemplar and that there will be important differences in other jurisdictions and in other contexts, it is also argued that developments in England and Wales are not unique. Even so, I do recognize that the position of social work in England and Wales over the last thirty years has been somewhat unique in its close association with the central and local state via the establishment and development of local authority social services departments.

My central focus is to try to understand how it is that in an increasingly post-modern world, the responses of official agencies and central government have been so apparently modern and rationalist in nature. At one level, this seems something of a conundrum; at another level, however, I will argue that such developments are quite explicable but at the same time have only limited chances of delivering on what it is claimed are their overriding intentions.

In England and Wales, under the auspices of the New Labor government, we have witnessed a major reassessment of the nature, focus and organization of social work and social care services in recent years. Much of this has taken place under the rationale of 'modernizing' public services (see, for example, DH, 1998). In many respects, the modernization agenda can be seen as an attempt to move beyond the inflexibility, inefficiency and aloofness of large welfare organizations and professional social workers who have played key roles in the delivery of services. The changes introduced are said to make a serious attempt to improve collaboration, inclusiveness and transparency. The visions for the future are articulated in the language of reciprocity and responsibility, justice and fairness, partnership and participation, and crucially recognize that a variety of voluntary and informal services, as well as the state, provide vital contributions to the care and support of individuals and thus strengthen the communities in which they live. However, the way the changes have been introduced has very much been of a top-down nature (Jordan with Jordan, 2000). More particularly, the process of 'modernization' can be seen as furthering the growing instrumentalization and managerialization of social work and social care by its intense focus on performance and efficiency targets, together with the growing emphasis on centralized and formulaic regimes of inspection, audit and scrutiny (Newman, 2001). Thus while many of the more liberatory and radical elements of social work theory and practice can be seen, at one level, to have received official endorsement and to have entered the mainstream, at another level, they can be seen to have been transformed into a variety of mechanisms for the increased regulation of both social workers themselves and the people with whom they work (Langan, 2002). As Stepney has argued, there seems little doubt that practitioners experience these initiatives as increasing managerial control. Moreover, 'the emphasis on technical recording, systematic information gathering, performance indicators, all tend to reinforce mechanistic practice rather than creativity and innovation' (Stepney, 2000, p.12). Social work has become little more than labor in the service of economy, efficiency and effectiveness.

The chapter has four substantive sections. I begin by outlining the way the nature of social work developed from the late nineteenth century onwards through to the late twentieth century. I then discuss in some detail the situation in which social work now finds itself in England and Wales at the beginning of the twenty-first century, and how this seems to be increasingly characterized by more intense systems of surveillance and rationalization. I then briefly discuss the nature of evidence-based practice (EBP), but conclude by trying to demonstrate that such a narrow and circumscribed version of EBP is neither appropriate nor helpful. However, it may be on this terrain that more creative and reflexive versions of what constitutes evidence might find it productive to engage and thus develop the space for developing perspectives and practices that are not only critical and reflexive but also constructive.

The Emergence of Social Work: Between Private and Public

I have argued previously (Parton, 1991; 1994; 1998) that the emergence of modern social work is associated with the transformations that took place from the mid nineteenth century onwards in response to a number of interrelated anxieties about the family and the community more generally. It developed as a hybrid in the space, 'the social' (Donzelot, 1980), between the private sphere of the household and the public sphere of society.

The emergence of the 'social' was seen as the most appropriate way for the state to maintain its legitimacy while protecting individual children. For liberalism, 'the unresolved problem is how child rearing can be made into a matter of public concern and its qualities monitored without destroying the ideal of the family as a counterweight to state power, a domain of voluntary, self-regulating actions' (Dingwall, Eekelaar and Murray, 1983, pp.214-215). Social work occupied the space between the respectable and dangerous classes, and between those with access to political and speaking rights and those who are excluded (Philp, 1979; Stenson, 1993). Social work fulfilled an essentially mediating role between those who are actually or potentially excluded and the mainstream of society.

Turning to the post-war welfare state, we can see that it was based on a particular model of the economy and the family. Not only did it assume full male employment, it also assumed a traditional role for the patriarchal nuclear family. The family was also assumed to be white. The notion of the 'family wage' was central, linking the labor market to the distribution of social roles and dependency by age and gender within the family. Within the family, women were to trade housework, childbirth and child rearing and physical and emotional caring in return for economic support as a 'labor of love' (Finch and Groves, 1983). In practice, therefore, much welfare work was expected to be undertaken within the family either using the family wage to buy goods and services or by women caring for children and other dependents. The provision of state welfare was intended to support the patriarchal nuclear family, which was seen as central, positive and beneficent.

Clearly, therefore, social work would be subjected to a whole series of tensions and difficulties if any of the underlying assumptions supporting this notion of 'the social' were to be seriously questioned, or if there were to be significant changes in the key institutions which provided the framework for 'social' work, whether this be the labor market, the patriarchal white nuclear family, or the other more universal social services, particularly health, education, and social security. Beyond this, further stresses would be created if the political consensus that underpinned the post-war welfare changes was itself put under serious strain. Both the institutions of the family and the labor market changed considerably in the subsequent thirty years.

However, it was not simply that there were changes in some of the major social institutions. The political climate itself began to change significantly. For just at the point at which modern social work emerged in the early 1970s to play a significant part in the welfarist project, 'welfarism' itself was experiencing considerable strains and ultimately crises. At one level, the criticisms leveled at social work from the mid 1970s onwards can be understood as a specific case of the neo-liberal and New Right approaches to government which dominated from the election of Margaret Thatcher in 1979, in terms of: an antagonism towards public expenditure on state welfare; an increasing emphasis on self-help and family support; the centrality of individual responsibility, choice and freedom; and an extension of the commodification of social relations. However, to see the challenges to social work as arising only from the New Right would be simplistic, for increasingly it was felt that social work was failing to meet the aspirations expected of it and vocal criticism was also evident from a variety of other quarters, including the political left, feminists, anti-racists, as well as from a variety of user groups and other professional and community interests (Clarke, 1993). Social work, particularly that practiced in social service departments, was seen as costly, ineffective, distant and oppressive, leaving the user powerless and without a voice. Thus, not only were certain key social institutions changing – particularly the family, the community and the economy – but it was increasingly subject to political criticism for its inefficiency and insensitivity as well as having new demands made upon it, particularly from new user groups. As a result, its already fragile authority and status was seen as having little solid foundation and it was subjected to skepticism about its claims to knowledge.

Risk and uncertainty can increasingly be seen to characterize contemporary times (Beck, 1992; Adam et al., 2000), such that more and more social conflicts are seen as having no easy and unambiguous solutions, and which are distinguished by a fundamental ambivalence that might be grasped by calculations of probability but certainly not removed by them. So long as traditions and customs were widely sustained, experts were invariably seen as people who could be turned to or who could make key decisions and, in the public eye at least, science was imbued with a major sense of monolithic and generic authority. In effect, science and experts were invested with the authority of a final sovereign court of appeal. But increasingly shorn of formulaic truth, all claims to knowledge have become corrigible and subject to skepticism. Increasingly, it seems, we are now living in a world of multiple authorities and wide-ranging knowledge. In many respects, the history of state social work in England and Wales over the last thirty years can be seen as a fascinating case study of these major and more wide-ranging social changes. It is as if the modern, certain, positivistic forms of knowledge and practice, and the social conditions within which they were located, have now become subject to increasing critique and doubt. The growing awareness of the constructedness of social reality makes the political issue of justification, therefore, highly problematic. It is in this context that concerns often associated with debates about postmodernity move center stage. For the notion of postmodernity recognizes that persons now inhabit a world that has become increasingly disorientated, disturbed, and subject to doubt. The pursuit of order and control, the promotion of calculability, the belief in progress, science and rationality and other features intrinsic to modernity are increasingly being seen as undermined by a simultaneous range of negative conditions and experiences and the persistence of chance and the threat of indeterminacy (Wagner, 1994). Postmodernity can be characterized as the fragmentation of modernity into forms of institutional pluralism, marked by variety, difference, contingency, relativism and ambivalence – all of which modernity sought to overcome (Smart, 1999). A constant and growing questioning of modern solutions has been diagnosed as symptomatic of the postmodern condition. Even those who are highly critical of claims that society is moving towards the postmodern recognize that the average person is experiencing a considerable loss of confidence in science and experts providing solutions to economic, social, and human problems (Tayler-Gooby, 1994). Increasingly, it is accepted that, whether one characterizes the contemporary as postmodern or not, the notion of contingency of all social phenomena is evident and needs to inform conceptions of both community and selfhood and what we do and how we do it, whether this applies to social research, professional practice or day-to-day life.

Contemporary Mainstream Social Work

It is perhaps ironic that in this increasingly uncertain and fluid situation, the primary response for reforming social work has been to introduce a plethora of changes that are clearly modernist and rationalist in both conception and implementation. However, it is my argument that it is precisely because of the need to try and increase control in the context of this growing and wide-ranging uncertainty that such approaches have been adopted. Essentially, the last twenty-five years have seen the growth of managerialism and audit in mainstream social work in England and Wales. Since the late 1970s significant changes in the organization, practice and culture of all public services have occurred. Beginning with the election of Margaret Thatcher in 1979, the primary impetus for such change was initially driven by the attempts to rein in public expenditure and introduce some of the disciplines of the private sector via the quasi-market, the purchaser-provider split and the growth of a contract culture. However, the changes have moved far beyond simple attempts to exert tighter fiscal control. Not only have we witnessed the emergence of neo-liberal ideologies of micro-government, political discourses concerned with accountability and performance, and attempts to improve economy, efficiency and effectiveness, but we have seen the growing emphasis on the need to make the actions of professionals and the services they provide far more 'transparent' and 'accountable' (Power, 1997). What has occurred is a significant shift towards giving managers the right to manage, instituting systems of regulation to achieve value for money and thereby producing accountability to the tax payer and the paymaster on the one hand and the customer and the user on the other (Clarke, Gerwirtz and McLaughlin, 2000).

While these changes were originally introduced under the auspices of the Conservative administration, since 1997 the changes invoked by the New Labor government have been even more rapid and intensive. In particular, the promulgation of a whole range of new performance targets, inspection regimes and continual attempts to maximize 'best value' and ongoing effectiveness regimes has had the effect of both rationalizing on the one hand and centralizing on the other. As Stephen Webb has suggested, there is currently: 'a double discursive alliance of scientism and managerialism in social work which gears up to systematic information processing operations to produce regulated action. We thus have the assimilation of a form of "scientific management" in social work' (Webb, 2001, p.74). What seems to have happened is that in the current context for the state, there is a paradox of the simultaneous demand for certainty together with the denial of its possibility; professionals cannot provide certainty and consistency and are, in any case, not trusted to do so. The net result seems to be that the various changes introduced act to side-step this paradox and to substitute confidence in systems for trust in individual professionals (Smith, 2001). Thus, whilst the wider environment seems to becoming more uncertain, fluid and contingent, the micro world of the practitioner is being subject to a whole variety of processes of standardization and regularization.

Under New Labor, these changes go under the broad banner of 'Modernizing Social Services' (DH, 1998), which is the White Paper providing the framework for the subsequent changes. It is primarily concerned with regulating local authority departments through a series of supervisory and monitoring bodies, with setting new standards and targets with which to measure performance, and for agencies to enforce these, and with establishing a new system for placing social care workers under the guidance of new regulatory bodies.

Managers continue to play a key role but are now not simply concerned with managerial control, but are seen as being in the vanguard of taking forward these new visions. In contrast to the Conservative changes, this version of managerialism is presented as empowering and emphasizing partnership (Glendinning, Powell and Rummery, 2002). It purports to speak for service users so that any resistance to managerialism by social workers is easily attacked as being elitist. Rather than managerialism being seen as simply concerned with the power of managers to enhance cost effectiveness and efficiency, New Labor sees its managers as operating towards a much higher order. As Newman (2001) has argued, the key aspects of modernizing managements' higher purposes have been presented as the updating of services to match the expectations of modern consumers, empowering citizens and communities and social inclusion. However, the public sector is enjoined to deliver these new services within the discourses of quality management, customer service and user involvement – all of which require not simply continual improvement but also the need to break traditional models of both service provision and professional self-interest. Public social services are to become more like the private sector with an emphasis on entrepreneurialism and modern commercial practices.

In this context, it may seem odd that the changes have introduced such apparent emphasis on the need for rationality and bureaucratic procedures. Superficially, it seems that the changes are not only extremely modernist but Fordist as well. I would suggest this is only partly correct. In many respects, the repositioning of the central state and the local state can be seen as having many of the characteristics of

McDonaldization (Ritzer, 1998; 2000) and franchising. As John Harris (2003) has suggested, this New Labor vision of how modernization translates into local authority businesses has emanated from strong central government control of the agenda to be implemented. Like the corporate headquarters of a modern business, New Labor has defined social work's objectives at national level, set outcomes to be achieved locally, and monitored the results in considerable detail. The emphasis on local leadership, entrepreneurialism and a strong performance culture with regard to standards and quality has been pinned to the achievement of targets set by central government. Harris argues this is close to a public sector model of franchising, for franchise holders, although legally independent, must conform to detailed standards of operation designed and enforced by the parent company, in this case central government. In this franchising arrangement there is limited operational autonomy and the threat of having the franchise taken away, if performance is not up to scratch, is considerable. The introduction of league tables and stars for good and bad performance all point to this. It now appears that those local authorities which perform well – gaining maximum stars – will be given much greater freedom from central government strictures. It is in this context that notions of quality take on a particular significance, as illustrated by the Quality Strategy for Social Care (DH, 2000): 'Delivering high quality social care services is essentially a local responsibility. The Quality Strategy will set a national framework to help raise local standards, but this will only be achieved through local policy and implementation' (DH, 2000, para 18). Elements of the design of the quality system were set out in the Quality Strategy and included national service frameworks, national standards, service models and local performance measures, against which progress within an agreed timescale would be considered. While the process can be seen as increasing rationalization and centralization, is also clear that the responsibility for delivery is with local service providers.

Evidence-Based Practice (EBP)

The other key element I wish to draw attention to in this new era for social work practice in England and Wales is the increasing emphasis on the importance of evidence-based practice (EBP). An important element in the rationale of the quality movement in social work and social care has been the argument that practitioners adopt a more rigorous application of critical appraisal skills to their practice. They should draw upon clear guidelines and protocols developed from research findings. EBP is the doctrine that professional practice should be based upon sound research evidence about the effectiveness of any assessment or intervention. At a superficial level, it is very difficult to argue against something that seems so commonsensical. Two key assumptions underlie the strategy. The first defines 'sound evidence', which may be relied upon to contribute to the classification of an intervention as effective or ineffective, as evidence derived from studies conducted in a certain way are held to be 'scientific'. The approach is based on that developed within medicine and is typified in the influential 'hierarchy of evidence' which is seen as definitive of what constitutes sound scientific research, and where the strongest evidence is seen to emanate from at least one systematic review of multiple, well-designed, randomized trials. The principle that underpins the hierarchy is that of validity, that is the elimination from research findings of bias arising from any difference between those treated by the intervention being researched and patients not so treated.

The second key element underpinning EBP is based on the notion that the most useful, though not necessarily exclusive, method for disseminating sound research evidence is via appropriate guidelines. It is recognized that practitioners cannot be expected to read every research study relevant to their practice and that such guidelines are meant to be accessible and authoritative. The logic of the guidelines is essentially algorithmic, in that it guides its users to courses of action, dependent upon stated prior conditions. In general, such guidelines do not claim to determine professional action completely, and degrees of discretion are still allowed.

Clearly, however, the emergence of EBP is closely associated with some of the changes discussed above. Its growth and official legitimation has taken place in a context where there are considerable concerns about risk, uncertainty about traditional science and professional expertise, and growing concerns about effectiveness and the impact on users. It seems to provide coherent and practical input into overcoming some of these problems and, at the same time, reinforces a number of the elements around the increased emphasis on accountability, transparency and monitoring. The hierarchical preference for RCT (randomized control trial) is interesting. As such, it consists primarily of the inference of cause-effect relationships from past statistical relationships between interventions and outcomes. It is, therefore, less concerned with causative processes than with establishing what interventions are likely to be effective, irrespective of why. In this sense the model is a probabilistic (that is, one where the cause-effect relationships are inherently uncertain), and empiricist (that is, one where knowledge can only justifiably derive from past experience). Further, as Liz Trinder (2000) has demonstrated, the development of evidence-based practice in relation to social work is at a very rudimentary stage of development. In many respects, the knowledge base and professional standing of social work is very different to that of medicine where the approach has originated. Similarly, the nature of the work does not lend itself nearly so easily to such an approach. Even so, the language of EBP has become increasingly powerful and in this respect can be seen as a key contributor to the growing dominance of the rationalistic and managerialist approaches I have been looking at in this chapter. In some respects it has the effect of legitimating and providing a rhetorical backcloth for such developments. As I will argue by way of conclusion, I am not, in principle, against the notion of EBP. It is certain versions that cause the problems. The bigger issue is more how such an approach has been used as part of the more general drifts I have been analyzing. In some respects, EBP might provide quite an interesting vehicle for some quite new and critical departures. My concern is that it has been used in a quite specific way that has the impact of reinforcing the political instrumentalism and the aspirations for growing central control that are being implemented by the modernization agenda. The latter is primarily premised on attempts to provide certainty in an increasingly uncertain world. It is in this sense that recent developments can be seen as superficially consistent with modern approaches in an increasingly fluid and postmodern world.

While skeptical of the current emphasis on evidence-based practice, it is the particular versions that are currently being promulgated and used within the rationalist and managerialist approaches that give cause for concern. It is my view that the notion of 'evidence-based practice' should take on a support role, rather than be promoted to the front line in the development of a certain instrumental form of practice knowledge, as seems to be the case currently. Reasons for its current hegemony in social work practice and education seem to have more to do with the political agendas of New Labor and its modernization programme than the needs of practitioners and service users. I am concerned that it is often conceived in a very narrow form and in a top-down nature. The approach adopted is excessively utilitarian and instrumental in intention.

There are two approaches that tend to dominate debates about EBP. The naïve rational approach that research leads practice (knowledge-driven model) and which places the researcher in a very powerful position; and the problem-solving approach where research follows policy, and where practice issues shape research agendas. Here the researcher is much more at the behest of the policy maker. However, both models assume a linear relationship between research and practice; the difference is in the posited direction of the influence. Clearly, the relationship between research and practice is much more uncertain and contradictory than such approaches recognize. Increasingly, it has been recognized that the relationships between research and decision makers – whether these be politicians, policy-makers or practitioners – is much more subtle and complex than the EBP approach often assumes. Research is better understood as just one of the factors which might play a role in decision-making, so that the relationship is much more nebulous and interactive in nature.

Many years ago, Weiss (1979) outlined at least six models for the way in which research might be conceptualized as impacting on decision-making. Recent commentators have argued that it is much better to talk in terms of 'evidence-informed' practice, rather than 'evidence-based' practice and see the most appropriate approach as being characterized as an 'enlightenment model' (see, for example, Young et al., 2002; Packwood, 2002). Here research is seen as standing a little distant from immediate practice concerns; the relationship is much more indirect. The focus is less likely to be the decision-problem itself, but the context within which the decision might be taken, providing a frame for thinking about it. Research aims to illuminate the landscape for decision-makers and actors more generally. The role of research becomes one of primarily clarifying issues and informing debate, and less one of problem-solving. Research thus takes on the role of aiding the democratic process, rather than being part of a narrowly focused decision-making process and recognizes that evidence is likely to be contested and subject to debate.

Clearly, however, such debate is likely to be more reasoned when research is part of the equation than if research was not available in the first place. Research on process as well as outcomes is equally, if not more, relevant in these circumstances. We should not dismiss the emancipatory potential of research. Clearly research can throw important insights into the nature of society, how it is changing, as well as the important social structural factors which impact on everyone's day-to-day life. When we talk about 'evidence-based' practice this does not have to be simply that based on the clinical trial or the random controlled test. In some respects, the accumulation of evidence and different types of research could well provide a vital vehicle for critically commentating upon and resisting some of the centralizing and dehumanizing elements of contemporary policy and practice, which is reducing practitioners to organizational functionaries and community members to 'service users'. As ever, the key issue is invariably related to power and knowledge and crucially who asks the questions and with what import. Not only can research encourage enlightenment and emancipation, it can act to empower the most powerless. It can help to provide information and insights which otherwise would not become available. Not only does this challenge some of the assumptions of those currently holding power but some of the more traditional and long-standing seats of power, as well, including those occupied by professionals. Simply because research can have negative and unintended consequences does not mean that it cannot have positive impacts as well. What I am suggesting is that in the process of trying to deconstruct evidence-based practice we can also act to try and distance it from some of the managerialist and rationalist practices and discourses it has currently become implicated in.

Conclusions

It is in this changing social and professional context that I have attempted to develop the notion of constructive social work (Parton and O'Byrne, 2000; Parton, 2003). It has been developed as an explicit counterweight to some of the developments in official policy and practice that I have outlined in this chapter. As I have argued, the predominant response to the growing risk, uncertainty and fluidity of current times in social work since the 1970s has been to construct ever more sophisticated systems of accountability for practitioners and users, and thereby attempted to rationalize and scientize increasing areas of social work activity with the introduction of complex procedures and systems of audit, together with a narrow emphasis on 'evidence-based practice' – where it is assumed the world can be subjected to prediction and calculative control. A major concern has been two-fold. Not only do these developments misconstrue the nature of recent changes, and thus have considerable risk of a range of unintended consequences, they are in great danger of failing to build on the range of skills which have traditionally lain at the core of social work, particularly those related to process and where the ability to negotiate and mediate with creativity has been of central relevance. As a result, any allegiance to notions of emancipation and 'emancipatory politics' is being lost. The central emphasis of constructive social work that we have developed is upon process, plurality of both knowledge and voice, and the relational quality of knowledge and language. It is consistent with the core values and traditions of social work, and proceeds on an assumption that users, no matter what their circumstances, have significant resources within and around them in order to bring about positive change. This argues that social work is as much, if not more, an art than a science, and proceeds on the basis that practice should be understood as much as a practical-moral activity as a rational-technical one. It is affirmative and reflexive and focuses on dialogue, listening to and talking with the Other. An ability to work with ambiguity and uncertainty, both in terms of process and outcomes, is seen as key. The principle of indeterminacy suggests the fluid, recursive and non-determined way that social situations unfold. The general thrust is that social life is replete with possibilities and that the linguistic social bond proposed is more open to alteration and expansion than is often assumed but does not underestimate that those on the receiving end of social work are usually the most constrained and marginalized of those in our society. Even so, it recognizes that the traditional core of social work attempts to care as well as control, to liberate as well as regulate. Such principles are as relevant to frontline practitioners as they are to the people with whom they work. More particularly, and theoretically, it draws on certain versions of social constructionism and the feminist ethics of care (Meagher and Parton, 2003).

Such an approach is thoroughly consistent with contemporary debates around the nature of theory and practice in contemporary social theory. The individual of modernity is seen as reflective while that of the late modern or postmodern as reflexive. To reflect is to somehow subsume the object under the subject of knowledge. It presumes a dualism, a scientific attitude in which the subject is in one realm, the object of knowledge in another. Drawing on the work of Kant (1952), Scott Lash differentiates between what he calls determinate judgment and reflexive judgment; and it is reflexive judgment that is seen to lie at the core of the contemporary fluid, risk culture of the postmodern. However, determinate judgment is seen as the sort of judgment that aims for objective validity – it is the model of physics and mathematics. Its conditions of possibility are the categories of logic. In contrast, reflexive judgments do not operate from given rules of logic but operate on the basis of finding the rule. Unlike the propositional truths that are determinate judgments, reflexive judgments are seen as estimations that are based on 'feelings' of pleasure and displeasure but also on feelings of shock, overwhelmedness, fear, loathing, as well as joy. They have less to do with the predictive statements, validity claims and rational arguments associated with determinate judgments. Determinate judgments involve some assumption of events under the logical categories of the understanding; whereas reflexive judgments – which are estimations based on theory – take place not just through understanding but through the imagination and, more immediately, through sensation. Determinate judgment is perceived as drawing on various technico-scientific processes in an attempt to map and then control external and objectively recognized dangers; whereas reflexive judgment is described as involving more imaginative and inter-subjective approaches to uncertain or contested areas of knowledge – with interpretation and negotiation replacing calculation and prediction.

Whereas determinate judgment is seen as linear, reflexive judgment is seen as non-linear and this is seen as thoroughly consistent with the parallel non-linear changes in the role of the state, the family, ethnic groupings, and changes in social class and the labor market more generally. The roles that reproduce linear agents and systems under the auspices of modernity are seen to have been progressively erased. However, the result is not the disappearance of the subject, or of a general irrationality. The subject relating to contemporary fragmented institutions has moved from a position of reflection to one of reflexivity. Yet because this subject is so constantly in motion and is so involved in the world, it makes little sense to talk about subject position in any kind of knowing or fixed sense. Knowledge is increasingly uncertain even though we are more knowledgeable than ever. The key issue is that the type of knowledge at stake changes. It is itself precarious as distinct from certain, and what that knowledge is about is also uncertain – probabilistic, at best; more like, according to Lash (2003), 'possibilistic'. Whereas determinate judgment depends on prescription and on determinate rules, increasingly the subject must now be the rule-finder.

It is thus much more appropriate to see that what is required is the encouragement of this reflexive judgment as opposed to the determinate judgment, but of course this is precisely not what is happening. Yet in reflexive judgment it is the practitioner who must invariably find the rule when working with the service user. It is not simply that with reflexive judgment we are concerned only with uncertainty and risk, but it also provides the possibility for creativity and innovation. The increasing complexity and non-linear nature of the world means that the world is less predictable, therefore less regularized. This is not to say that the practitioner is likely to be in control in these situations. It is to suggest, however, that there is far more room for maneuver than may at first appear. As Lash (2000, p.52) suggests, 'reflexive judgment is always a question of uncertainty, of risk, but it also leaves the door open to much innovation'. In the process, the individual practitioner is forced into a much more independent stance, with this notion of proactive 'rule finding' displacing the dependence on the rules and norms of bureaucratic procedures and guidance. Issues around the non-linear, complex nature of contemporary decision-making and the culture in which professional practice takes place is not recognized in the modernizing agenda of New Labor and other advanced liberal regimes.

It is in this context that we have attempted to develop this notion of constructive social work as providing a positive framework while not simply critiquing the contemporary dominant dogmas associated with socio-technical emphasis and narrow emphasis on 'evidence-based practice'. We also provide a positive contribution for creatively taking forward our notions of theory and practice in and of social work. Notions of critical reflexivity lie at its core. What the work of Lash and others suggests, however, is that issues around the emotions and aesthetics are key and that the way our feelings interrelate and inform our judgments should not be underestimated. However, rather than see these as being impediments simply to be eradicated or overcome – as is the case with the rational-technical approach – they are seen as lying at the core of what needs to be recognized and worked with. It is in this context that we can begin to see some interesting connections emerging both theoretically and practically between approaches which are sympathetic towards social constructionist and postmodern perspectives and those which are rediscovering the insights of psycho-dynamic work and object-relations theory (see, for example, Froggett, 2002 and the chapter by Davies et al. in this volume).

References

Adam, B., Beck U. and van Loon, J. (eds.) (2000), *The Risk Society and Beyond: Critical Issues for Social Theory*, Sage, London.

Beck, U. (1992), *Risk Society: Towards a New Modernity*, Sage, London.

Clarke, J. (ed.) (1993), *A Crisis in Care? Challenges to Social Work*, Sage, London.

Clarke, J., Gewirtz, S. and McLaughlin, E. (eds.) (2000), *New Managerialism, New Welfare?*, Sage, London.

Department of Health (1998), *Modernizing Social Services: Promoting Independence, Improving Protection, Raising Standards*, Cm. 4169, The Stationery Office, London.

Department of Health (2000), *A Quality Strategy for Social Care*, The Stationery Office, London.

Dingwall, R. and Eekelaar, J. (1988), 'Families and the state: An historical perspective on the public regulation of private conduct', *Law and Society*, Vol. 10(4), pp. 341-361.

Dingwall, R., Eekelaar, J. and Murray, T. (1983), *The Protection of Children: State Intervention and Family Life*. Basil Blackwell, Oxford.

Donzelot, J. (1980), *The Policing of Families: Welfare Versus the State*, Hutchinson, London.

Finch, J. and Groves, D. (1983), *A Labor of Love: Women, Work and Caring*, RKP, London.

Froggett, L. (2002), *Love, Hate and Welfare*, Policy Press, Bristol.

Glendinning, C., Powell, M. and Rummery, K. (eds.) (2002), *Partnerships, New Labor and the Governance of Welfare*, Policy Press, Bristol.

Harris, J. (2003), *The Social Work Business*, Routledge, London.

Hirst, P. (1981), 'The genesis of the social', *Politics and Power*, Vol. 3, pp. 67-82.

Jordan, B. with Jordan, C. (2000), *Social Work and the Third Way: Tough Love as Social Policy*, Sage, London.

Kant, I. (1952), *The Critique of Judgment*, Oxford University Press, Oxford.

Langan, M. (2002), 'The Legacy of Radical Social Work', in R. Adams, L. Dominelli and M. Payne (eds.), *Social Work: Themes, Issues and Critical Debates*, (Second Edition), Palgrave, Basingstoke.

Lash, S. (2000), 'Risk Culture', in B. Adam, U. Beck, and J. van Loon (eds.), *The Risk Society and Beyond: Critical Issues for Social Theory*, Sage, London.

Lash, S. (2003), 'Reflexivity as Non-Linearity', *Theory, Culture and Society*, Vol. 20(2), pp. 49-57.

Meagher, G. and Parton, N. (2003), 'Modernizing social work and the ethics of care', *Social Work and Society*, Vol. 1(2), pp. 35-40.

Newman, J. (2001), *Modernizing Governance: New Labor, Policy and Society*, Sage, London.

Packwood, A. (2002), 'Evidence-based policy: Rhetoric and reality', *Social Policy and Society*, Vol. 1(3), pp. 267-272.

Parton, M. (1994), 'Problematics of government, (post)modernity and social work', *British Journal of Social Work*, Vol. 24(1), pp. 9-32.

Parton, N. (1991), *Governing the Family: Child Care, Child Protection and the State*, Macmillan/Palgrave, Basingstoke.

Parton, N. (1998), 'Risk, advanced liberalism and child welfare: The need to rediscover uncertainty and ambiguity', *British Journal of Social Work*, Vol. 28(1), pp. 5-27.

Parton, N. (2003), 'Rethinking professional practice: The contributions of social constructionism and the feminist 'ethics of care', *British Journal of Social Work*, Vol. 33(1), pp. 1-16.

Parton, N. and O'Byrne, P. (2000), *Constructive Social Work: Towards a New Practice*, Palgrave, Basingstoke.

Philp, M. (1979), 'Notes on the form of knowledge in social work', *Sociological Review*, Vol. 27(1), pp. 83-111.

Power, M. (1997), *The Audit Society: Rituals of Verification*, Oxford University Press, Oxford.

Ritzer, G. (1998), *The McDonaldization Thesis*, Sage, London.

Ritzer, G. (2000), *The McDonaldization of Society*, (New Century Edition), Pine Forge Press, Thousand Oaks, CA.

Smart, B. (1999), *Facing Modernity: Ambivalence, Reflexivity and Morality*, Sage, London.

Smith, C. (2001), 'Trust and confidence: Possibilities for social work in high modernity', *British Journal of Social Work*, Vol. 31(2), pp. 287-305.

Stenson, K. (1993), 'Social work discourse and the social work interview', *Economy and Society*, Vol. 22(1), pp. 42-76.

Stepney, P. (2000), 'Implications for social workers', in P. Stepney and D. Ford (eds.), *Social Work Models, Methods and Theories*, Russell House, Lyme Regis.

Taylor-Gooby, P. (1994), 'Postmodernism and social policy: A great leap backwards?' *Journal of Social Policy*, Vol. 23(3), pp. 385-404.

Trinder, L. (2000), 'Evidence-based practice in social work and probation', in L. Trinder and S. Reynolds (eds.), *Evidence-Based Practice: A Critical Appraisal*, Blackwell Science, Oxford.

Wagner, P. (1994), *A Sociology of Modernity: Liberty and Discipline*, Routledge, London.

Webb, S. (2001), 'Some considerations on the validity of evidence-based practice in social work', *British Journal of Social Work*, Vol. 31(1), pp. 57-79.

Weiss, C.H. (1979), 'The many meanings of research utilization', *Public Administration Review*, Vol. 39, pp. 426-431.

Young, K., Ashby, D., Bozaz, A. and Grayson, L. (2002), 'Social science and the evidence-based policy movement', *Social Policy and Society*, Vol. 1(3), pp. 215-224.

Chapter 4

Subject-to-Subject: Reclaiming the Emotional Terrain for Practice

Linda Davies and Sara Collings

Introduction

Contemporary child welfare policy and theory have become increasingly influenced by discourses of accountability, risk, and surveillance. The deaths of children on child welfare caseloads have sparked intense scrutiny of child welfare practices. Governments and child welfare agencies have responded by standardizing procedures, intensifying documentation practices, and adopting seemingly objective and scientific frameworks that aim to guide workers in the detection and management of risk. Within these approaches, 'child abuse' is officially understood as a phenomenon open to discovery, and, more and more, orthodox social work theory in child welfare is guided by the positivistic ethos of risk management as it strives for the appearance of a rational and rigorous discipline. These shifts in theory and practice have led to increased pressure on workers who are expected to carry large caseloads, document extensively, and bear the burden of liability for managing 'risk'. Child welfare workers are left with very little time for direct engagement with clients, or for the contemplation necessary for thorough assessment.

Despite the veneer of rational certainty that is reflected in dominant child welfare policy, there remains what might be understood as a hidden 'truth' of actual child welfare practice: daily child welfare is often messy, difficult to chart and irrational. It is, by its very nature, an intensely human endeavor that involves emotion, uncertainty and moral ambiguity. Child welfare workers' emotions play a role, consciously and unconsciously, in every element of practice with clients, including child welfare decision-making. This is so whether or not the emotional terrain is officially acknowledged as integral to the child welfare investigation and intervention. In this chapter, we wish to consider emotions in child welfare work and to suggest that reflection on this area of practice might offer a source of knowledge and creativity for front-line workers. We will engage in a renewed examination of the 'art' of child welfare practice and of emotions as a 'way of knowing' for both social workers and their clients.

To begin, we will identify those current trends in practice that undermine expressing and reflecting on the feelings aroused in the course of child welfare work. We then explore the potential of some feminist psychoanalytic ideas for understanding this area of practice and assessing how these ideas may be applied in child welfare settings. Specifically, we examine psychoanalytic ideas about maternal ambivalence and the concepts of transference and counter-transference in relation to work with mothers who are involved with child welfare agencies. Psychoanalytic theory once dominated social work practice and was later criticized for its patriarchal underpinnings. Recent feminist reconstructions of psychoanalytic ideas, however, can make an important contribution to critical analyses of gender, race and class and might even be understood as a form of resistance to dominant rational/technical approaches to practice.

Social Work as Rational

The notion of the 'therapeutic relationship' was once considered to be the cornerstone of good casework practice. Developing relationships with mothers who were clients of child welfare agencies required that social workers focus on developing trust with their clients while paying attention to their own feelings and reactions within the casework relationship. Although social work theory has been influenced by scientific discourses almost from its inception (Moffat 2001, Swift, 1995), these discourses were mitigated by counter-discourses of art and intuition. As Florence Hollis claimed in 1970:

> casework is both art and science. Intuitive insights and spontaneity are combined with continuous effort to develop and systematize knowledge and understanding of objective truths about man (*sic*) and his social expressions, relationships, and organizations (1970, p.38).

Conversely, in recent years, child welfare social work appears to have embraced rational and technical approaches to practice with very little appeal to the intuitive and relationship-based forms of practice formerly referred to as the 'art' of social work. Instead, much of child welfare practice has centered on the science of detection with a focus on searching out and responding to specific observable behaviors. Seemingly objective methods of assessment are continuously researched and updated to guide workers to look for and document those behaviors associated with high risk. Where social workers once wrote and assessed according to the more detailed and individualized style of the narrative report, more prescriptive and behavior-based recording tools have become central to child welfare assessment. This style of assessment can lead social workers to consider their clients' acts as though they were disembodied from the clients themselves. The context of clients' lives and their individual subjectivity remain unexplored and instead clients are described according to visible or surface behaviors: 'Social workers now ask what clients do rather than why they do it – a switch from causation to counting, from explanation to audit' (Howe, 1996, p.88).

Similarly, it might be suggested that the social worker herself is symbolically extracted from the child welfare encounter. Child welfare supervision increasingly focuses on ensuring that child welfare workers have followed correct procedures and made safe decisions with little if any attention placed upon the social worker's subjective self in relation to her client. The child welfare worker learns to write official documents in an 'objective' style. She refers to herself using the generic - 'the worker' – and presents 'the facts' in a professional and detached manner, suggesting that any other qualified onlooker would have perceived the events in an identical manner. In some ways, and certainly within her official and institutional capacity as a child welfare worker, the social worker is distanced from her subjective and emotional relationships with her clients.

What is the effect of this attempt to erase emotional contradiction and complexity from child welfare practice? Some have suggested that the proceduralism underlying the prescribed routines and responses to child welfare situations provokes a tendency to provide standard assessments of each child welfare situation (McMahon, 1998). It might be suggested that falling into routines can serve dual purposes for child welfare workers and for child welfare organizations. In one sense, a habitual form of practice can allow workers and agencies to find shelter from the anxieties associated with their work (Davies, 1990, Foster, 2001). In the face of intense workload, the child welfare worker can become sheltered from the emotional reactions that devolve from their encounters with clients by retreating into the safety of routine procedures. In turn, workers can similarly become more distanced from their organizations as supervision and support is replaced by performance review.

Conversely, the stringent and emotionally detached nature of standardized child welfare practice may heighten anxiety for workers who struggle silently with both the emotional impact of their relationships with mothers and the bureaucratic organizational tasks required for risk management procedures. Parton charges: 'there is a hole in the center of the enterprise' (Parton, 1994, p. 101), claiming that social work has lost the discourses of practices that supported the ability to listen and talk with people. Current frameworks for practice discourage thorough analyses of client's situations, or what Howe describes as 'depth explanations' (1996), and they provide little room for creativity and uncertainty.

While dominant theories of social work may be neglecting the potential of relationship-based practice, the work nevertheless remains emotionally stressful and highly charged. Today's child welfare workers find themselves in a field that faces ongoing problems with burnout and increased violence directed at workers from clients (Regehr et al., 2000). Although a concern over worker stress and burnout is reflected in many professional journals, most seem to emphasize helping workers to minimize the emotional impact of the job through individual self-care and through strategies to avoid 'taking it home'. Workers' emotions are not acknowledged as a normal effect of practice that could be productively explored as a source of creative insight. As we will discuss below, this is one of the strengths of psychoanalytic approaches. Instead, the subjective experience of practice is all but ignored within most child welfare organizations. The emphasis on rationality filters through to our expectations of clients who are required to present themselves as emotionally controlled and acquiescent in order to be deemed 'good clients' (McMahon, 1998; Forsberg, 1999).

The rational ethos of official child welfare discourse is perhaps particularly incongruous in a field so concerned with notions of mothering (Davies, Collings and Krane, 2002). Ideas and feelings about mothering can be contentious and often seem to rise more from the pit of the stomach than from the intellect. In child welfare settings, social workers directly encounter mothers whose parenting may deviate sharply from the idealized norm of the 'good mother' who is depicted as loving, sacrificial and devoted to her children. The maternal performance of these clients is often severely undermined by poverty, unemployment, lack of childcare and racism. When the normative category of the 'good mother' is disturbed, child welfare workers can be confronted with a range of uncomfortable emotions. This occurs despite the theoretical framework or ideological position that a worker may espouse. For example, a social worker who holds a well thought out feminist critique of women's oppression may nonetheless still experience disconcerting feelings of rage towards a mother who stays with an abusive partner and thus endangers her children.

Closer attention to the non-rational emotional aspects of practice is thus essential for engaging in therapeutic relationships in child welfare. This requires a theoretical lens that can guide an examination of the complex relationships that develop between workers and mothers and attend to the suppressed emotions and motivations that are not necessarily clearly apparent to social workers. At present, there are a few writers who are beginning to respond to this void (Lawrence, 1992; Featherstone, 1997; Foster, 2001). Here we will consider a selection of feminist psychoanalytic theorists whose work offers insight into worker/client inter-subjectivity.

Psychoanalytic Theory and Feminism

Psychoanalytic theory has clearly been controversial for feminists. It has been criticized for its lack of attention to the social context in which women's emotional development occurs and for its practitioner's long-standing history of mother-blame. Nevertheless, some feminist clinicians have returned to psychoanalytic ideas and contributed to its continued development and change (Lawrence and Maguire 1999). As Einhorn puts it: 'psychoanalysis describes how we internalize the external world and then reproduce and develop it through our personal relationships' (Lawrence and Maguire, 1999, p.vii). These theorists suggest that women's personal change cannot come about purely through cognitive therapeutic approaches but must delve more deeply into how unconscious feelings and fantasies influence our motivations and behavior (Featherstone, 1997; Lawrence and Maguire, 1999).

Feminist psychoanalytic theory has begun to explore the psychic consequences of oppression and how differences in race, culture, and class can have an impact on the therapeutic relationship. The social location of the client and the therapist affects the therapeutic relationship and the processes of transference and counter-transference (Lawrence and Maguire, 1999). In addition, where traditional psychoanalytic literature emphasized the needs and developmental progress of the child within the mother-child relationship, this feminist psychoanalytic literature has also considered the mother's needs and development within the social context in which women raise their children (Lawrence, 1992, p.33). When applied to child welfare assessment and treatment, these theories imply that those working with mothers need to incorporate a consideration of both their material and psychological deprivation, and to challenge the expectation that women should be 'copers' despite their material circumstances. Thus, feminist psychoanalytic theorists advocate for a full analysis of women's subjectivity, connecting the emotional functioning of women to their structural/material contexts.

These developments in feminist psychoanalytic thinking provide a rich theoretical resource for child welfare practice. There is, by now, a wide spectrum of such psychoanalytic literature available.[1] Here we address three basic psychoanalytic concepts that might be especially applicable to an analysis of child welfare practice: ambivalence, transference, and counter-transference. We will offer a brief examination of these ideas and consider how they might be applied to a child welfare setting. The selective use of these psychoanalytic concepts may help social workers move towards a subject-to-subject relationship with their clients, rather than the object-to-object relationship that characterizes contemporary child protection practice.

Transference and Counter-Transference

Psychoanalytic theory is noted for recognizing the significance of practitioners' and clients' emotional reactions, and for developing conceptual tools for processing them. For example, many proponents of psychoanalysis claim that clients relive unresolved hurts within their relationships with therapists. The well-established concept of transference 'the process by which the client transfers feelings applicable to a previous relationship into the present one' reflects this notion. The analogous concept of counter-transference considers the emotions that clients provoked in social workers and suggests that these emerge 'either in response to the transference, or as a result of the (usually unresolved) personal issues which the practitioner brings to the relationship' (Erooga 1994: 207-8 cited in Featherstone, 1997). The emotional triggers leading to such reactions can be fundamental to the process of examining and enriching therapeutic relationships between clients and social workers. Tapping the therapeutic potential of transference, however, requires reflection, support and time. Child welfare workers need to be able to recognize the existence of transference or counter-transference, and they also need to be guided as they explore possible interpretations – with either their client or their supervisor.

Feminist psychoanalytic theorists propose that the notion of transference should be understood in relation to specific socio-cultural factors, claiming that the unconscious feelings that can emerge through the individual therapeutic relationship are socially mediated. Unequal status associated with differences of gender, race and class will have psychic consequences. The therapist struggles to disentangle these complex issues, while sorting out what belongs to past experiences (her own or her client's) and what is part of the dynamic of the present therapeutic relationship. For example, a social worker's feelings of anger towards a mother who is a child welfare client might arise partly from the worker's past relationship with her own mother, or from her insecurities about her own mothering performance.

Unfortunately, in most child protection organizations there is less space for social workers to talk about or process the uncomfortable feelings that are aroused in the course of their practice. This can have negative repercussions for workers and clients. Rather than process these feelings, agency cultures of risk, surveillance, and blame may offer an avenue for avoiding self-reflection so that workers might play out counter-transference as they apply blanket approaches in their work with mothers.

Ignoring counter-transference in the mother/worker relationship may have negative consequences for mothers and their children. Social workers who are unequipped theoretically to examine mother-child relationships and the feelings arising from these relationships may, in fact, worsen their clients' emotional difficulties. This is suggested in Marilyn Lawrence's work, where she points out that when women clients under scrutiny by child welfare are forced to hide their own needs (and thus suppress the 'child-in-themselves'), they may be even less likely to be able to offer their children nurture and care. For example, Lawrence (1992) suggests that in some child protection cases, the social worker continually exhorts the mother to care for her child's needs and points out her responsibilities as a mother – thereby exacerbating the mother's guilt and paralysis. If the mother's emotional state is not addressed, the demands of the needy child she is responsible for may overwhelmingly trigger her own childish needs and perhaps lead to abuse. Child welfare workers thus must be able to reflect on the feelings emerging from their own counter-transference when confronted with a non-coping mother.

Social workers, who notoriously resist taking care of their own needs, might experience anxiety in these situations. Lawrence argues that social workers are the good daughters who have repressed the needy, 'messy, envious, upset, childish parts of themselves' (1992, p. 41). The prospect of engaging with a mother who outwardly expresses these repressed needs may be very frightening for some workers. While some mothers have difficulty allowing their children full freedom of emotional expression, it might be similarly argued that some social workers may have difficulty allowing mothers to express negative feelings: 'It is quite possible for social workers and other 'caring' professionals to make the mistake of expecting too much of their clients, much as abusing parents often do of their children' (Lawrence 1992, p.40). On the other hand, Lawrence points out that some feminist social workers, in misplaced sympathy for their women clients, may be inclined to overlook a mother's involvement or culpability in cases of child abuse.

Much of the resistance to both the non-coping and culpable mother can be understood by considering normative constructions of the 'good mother'. Examining transference and counter-transference within worker/mother relationships necessarily involves examining how such cultural prescriptions impede the expression of healthy ambivalence for both mothers and workers (Swigart, 1991; Parker, 1997; Featherstone, 1997).

Maternal Ambivalence

The important concept of ambivalence is well established within psychoanalytic theory and was central in the theoretical frameworks of Klein and Winnicott. It is usually examined from the infant's point of view. The infant's experiences of both love and hate for the mother marks an important developmental stage. However, maternal ambivalence has recently been explored by a number of feminist psychoanalytic theorists. Rozsika Parker describes maternal ambivalence as an emotional position constituting a 'complex and contradictory state of mind, shared variously by all mothers, in which loving and hating feelings for children exist side by side' (1997, p.17). Ambivalence is central to mother-child relationships, according to Parker, and yet it is 'curiously hard to believe in' (p. 17) and very painful to experience.

While these concurrent feelings of love and hate are socially silenced and thus difficult to acknowledge, ambivalence can function as a source of creative insight when it is expressed and managed. Parker (1997) points to the value of healthy ambivalence: 'When manageable, the pain, conflict and confusion of the coexistence of love and hate actually motivate a mother to struggle to understand her own feelings and her child's behavior' (p. 31). The conflict between love and hate can be so intense that it mobilizes the capacity for 'creative aggression'. To resolve the discomfort of ambivalence, a mother may be prompted to reflect productively on her relationship with her child and discover possibilities for change.

When unmanageable, however, ambivalence may arouse intolerable levels of guilt and anxiety and can be a source of extreme distress for a mother, as well as a potential danger for her child. Parker argues that the taboo on the expression of maternal ambivalence is one of the central factors that renders such ambivalence unmanageable for mothers, and can therefore lead to violence and abuse. The guilt and anxiety experienced by mothers is intensified by narrow cultural representations of 'good' and 'bad' mothers. This is particularly so in a culture where dominant constructions of the 'good mother' as an idealized nurturer persist. Any feelings or behavior that fall outside this impossible ideal are thus the source of a lot of fear for mothers. Mothers who are in the grip of these turbulent emotions often feel as though they are unnatural: 'It is the denial of the feelings of fury, boredom or even dislike towards children, all of which are part of motherhood, that makes the burden hard for women to bear, and can so often result in these negative feelings being expressed in secret and perverse ways' (Maynes and Best, 1997, p. 126). The conspiracy of silence around such negative feelings leaves mothers with no place to turn to diffuse or process their feelings of ambivalence and guilt. Instead, women fear social denigration as failed mothers. In this culture, we have difficulty not splitting mothers into categories that either deify her or condemn her.

Workers, in turn, may split mothers into binary classifications of 'good' and 'bad'. In the climate of anxiety around child abuse, there is little space for workers to take risks and thus explore the normal feelings of ambivalence that all mothers experience. Winnicott's supportive construct of the 'good enough' is overshadowed by the requirements placed upon workers and institutions to predict and control the care of children (Winnicott, 1960). This term, 'good enough mother', recognizes diversity in mothering experiences and acknowledges an image of 'mothering that is acceptable, not perfect' (Silva, 1996, p.2). Parker similarly speaks of a process of 'maternal individuation' (borrowing from Jung's concept) where the mother, '...to regain her sense of well-being, needs to abandon impossible maternal ideals which dangerously magnify both self-hate and child-hate' (1997, p.25). This healthy process, however, is jeopardized in the current climate of fear about expressing negative feelings towards motherhood or toward children.

Possibilities for Child Welfare Practice

A move towards reclaiming and revising some psychoanalytic approaches to understanding child welfare relationships involves calling on social workers to develop more therapeutic relationships with their clients, and this in turn requires difficult emotional work. The social worker must both contain the pain expressed by their client, and simultaneously maintain enough emotional distance to view their client's situation clearly. Obviously, this is not easy. Workers often find themselves needing to examine feelings about clients that they are consciously or unconsciously trying to avoid. Foster (2001) argues that helping professionals who are working in agencies where there is a statutory 'duty to care' may need to temporarily 'split off' part of their emotional experience in order to preserve their own mental health and provide reliable services to their clients. Yet doing good therapeutic work requires us simultaneously to reintegrate these splits of emotions so that we can be emotionally 'in touch', 'some or enough of the time' (Foster, 2001, p. 81).

A worker who finds herself experiencing strong feelings of anger or dislike towards a client can easily find recourse in the risk assessment mode of practice where social workers are guided to manage clients' behaviors and classify them according to grades of risk. Foster suggests that risk-management social work practice can become a comfortable style of practice for social workers who are experiencing persecutory anxiety. This form of anxiety is defined as an emotional reaction within a relationship that may cause us to overlook any of the client's positive attributes while projecting any and all negative attributes on to them: 'Winnicott alerted us to the danger in our clinical work of being unable to recognize our hatred of our clients, of their thoughts and their actions, when he wrote, 'however much he loves his patients he cannot avoid hating them and fearing them, and the better he knows this, the less will hate and fear be the motives determining what he does to his patients' (Winnicott 1947, p.195 in Maynes and Best 1997, p.126). As Maynes and Best explain, Winnicott is reminding us that therapeutic relationships are also open to abuse. In relation to this, Foster (2001) points to the precisely mapped out organizational procedures that can support a mechanistic and numbing form of 'going through the motions' (p.86) rather than facing persecutory feelings and building a therapeutic human relationship.

In contrast to this tendency, there is a danger that some workers might develop an idealized picture of their clients. Bolstered by the dominant ideal of the harmonious mother/child relationship (Featherstone, 1999), social workers might hold onto a romantic assessment of some women clients and resist taking measures or coming to any conclusions that might contradict such a fantasy. Foster describes this emotional state as one where we are '...split from experience often by colluding with our clients by focusing on the good aspects of the relationship while overlooking their destructiveness' (2001, p.85).

Looking at each of these emotional states might mean that workers must examine their own experiences with their mothers and face those fears and anxieties that their unconscious had displaced. Foster describes an optimal state for child welfare workers as one 'which enables us to hold on to ambivalent feelings of love and hate and to sustain successful loving and caring relationships with others' (2001, p.81). In order to support this optimal level of functioning, social workers require the space to reflect, process and contain their reactions to their clients.

Strong supervision is necessary to this process. Foster (2001) describes supervision as a method of containment: she suggests that social service organizations require 'reflective spaces' that serve to safely 'contain and modify' individual and organizational anxieties. These spaces are traditionally, although not necessarily, obtained through individual supervision, and allow social workers to explore those feelings that might feel risky and that reflect feelings about their clients that might seem inappropriate.

Foster's remarks about supervision within a 'culture of blame' (p.85) point to the barriers to supportive supervision within child welfare organizations. At the individual level, social workers are the target of child welfare investigations, and so their decisions and behaviors are always potentially open to scrutiny. The prospect of undergoing such an enquiry looms for workers as they sort out their relationships with mothers while they work to ensure the safety of children. At the organizational level, child welfare agencies reflect this fear of scrutiny. The focal point for supervision can therefore tend to be a response to the 'culture of blame' by examining worker's procedural decisions at the expense of considering their therapeutic relationships with clients. Rather than supporting workers in taking emotional risks and assessing mothers' ambivalence (as normal or potentially dangerous), workers are directed to follow the proper prescriptions for practice. This undermines therapeutic possibilities and, sadly, in the current climate, rarely results in respite services or concrete supports to lessen the burden of mothering or the difficulties of working in child protection.

Conclusion

Child welfare's current organizational and emotional climate appears to be stifling therapeutic work with clients and thus a number of critics have called for a radical shift in the field's orientation. In this chapter, we have offered a brief exploration of the potential of some psychoanalytic concepts for child welfare practice, and considered how these insights may contribute to such a shift. This is not to suggest that psychoanalytic approaches are the only way forward (see, for example, Fook, in this volume). We must also recognize the earlier feminist misgivings about psychoanalytic theory and maintain a critical stance towards its application, particularly with marginalized populations. As well, there are, of course, other helpful practice approaches that have the potential to resist the objectification of clients and workers.

We are, however, convinced that reclaiming the emotional terrain for social work practice is necessary. We have suggested that this could be beneficial for clients and would be a welcome change to what has become essentially soul-destroying work. Ultimately, we are advocating for a renewed consideration of the inter-subjectivity between workers and clients. This is not to minimize the difficulties of child protection work and the range of power relationships it entails. As Featherstone (1997) points out, practitioners in child protection do not have the luxury of simply concentrating on a therapeutic relationship with their clients. The legal mandate to protect children requires that they hold mothers accountable for the safety of their children. Nevertheless, as workers engage in child protection assessment, the emotional terrain that characterizes their relationships with clients should not be ignored – indeed, it might be seen as a valuable source of insight for practice.

Note

1   Lawrence and Maguire's 1999 volume cites influences as varied as Freud, Jung, and contemporary British and North American theorists. There is also the overlap with various postmodern theorists including Jane Flax and French postmodern feminists.

References

Davies, L. (1990), 'Limits of Bureaucratic Control: Social Workers in Child Welfare' in L. Davies and E. Shragge (eds.), *Bureaucracy and Community*, Black Rose Books, Montreal, pp. 81-101.

Davies, L., Collings, S. and Krane, J. (2002), 'Mothering and Child Protection Practice', Association for Research on Mothering, 'Mothering and the Academy' Conference, York University.

Featherstone, B. (1997), 'I Wouldn't do Your Job! Women, Social Work, and Child Abuse' in W. Hollway and B. Featherstone (eds.), *Mothering and Ambivalence*, Routledge, New York, pp. 167-192.

Featherstone, B. (1999), 'Taking Mothers Seriously: The Implications for Child Protection', *Child and Family Social Work*, vol. 4, pp. 43-53.

Forsberg, H. (1999), 'Speaking of Emotions in Child Protection Practices' in A. Jokinen, K. Juhila, and Tarja Poso (eds.), *Constructing Social Work Practices*, Ashgate, Burlington, pp. 116-132.

Foster, A. (2001), 'The Duty to Care and the Need to Split', *Journal of Social Work Practice*, vol. 15(1), pp .81-90.

Hollis, F. (1970), 'The Psychosocial Approach to Casework' in R. Roberts and R. Nee (eds.), *Theories of Social Casework*, University of Chicago Press, Chicago.

Howe, D. (1996), 'Surface and Depth in Social Work Practice' in N. Parton (ed.), *Social Theory, Social Change and Social Work*, Routledge, London, pp. 77-97.

Lawrence, M. (1992), 'Women's Psychology and Feminist Social Work Practice' in M. Langan and L. Day (eds.), *Women, Oppression and Social Work: Issues in Anti-Discriminatory Practice*, Routledge, London, pp. 32-47.

Lawrence, M. and Maguire M. (1999), *Psychotherapy with Women: Feminist Perspectives*, Routledge, USA.

Maynes, P. and Best, J. (1997), 'In the Company of Women: Experiences of Working with the Lost Mother', in W. Hollway and B. Featherstone (eds.), *Mothering and Ambivalence*, Routledge, New York, pp. 119-135.

McMahan, A. (1998), 'Boilerplating' in A. McMahan, *Damned If You Do, Damned If You Don't*, Ashgate, Vermont, pp. 57-73.

Moffat, K. (2001), *A Poetics of Social Work: Personal Agency and Social Transformation in Canada, 1920-1939*, University of Toronto Press, Toronto.

Parker, R. (1997), 'The Production and Purposes of Maternal Ambivalence' in W. Hollway and B. Featherstone (eds.), *Mothering and Ambivalence*, Routledge, New York, pp.17-36.

Parton, N. (1994), 'The Nature of Social Work under Conditions of Postmodernity', *Social Work and Social Services Review*, vol. 5, pp. 93-112.

Regehr, C., Leslie, B., Howe, P., and Chau, S. (2000), *Stressors in Child Welfare Practice*, University of Toronto Faculty of Social Work and Toronto Children's Aid Society, Toronto, pp. 1-15.

Silva, E.B. (ed.) (1996), *Good Enough Mothering? Feminist Perspectives on Lone Motherhood*, Routledge, London.

Swift, K. (1995), 'Missing Persons: Women in Child Welfare', *Child Welfare*, vol. LXXIV, pp. 486-502.

Swigart, J. (1991), *The Myth of the Bad Mother*, Avon, New York.

Winnicott, D.W. (1960), 'Ego distortion in terms of true and false self' in D.W. Winnicott, *The Maturational Processes and the Facilitating Environment. Studies in the Theory of Emotional Development*, Hogarth Press, London.

PART II
CULTURAL POLITICS, LANGUAGE, COLLECTIVITY

Chapter 5

Whose Side Are You On? Politicized Identities

Michele Gnanamuttu

Sorry, Our Translator's Out Sick Today[1]

You, a Black
Don't see why you should take Chicano studies, Asian-American studies, or even
Native American studies – or why I do
You, an Indian
Ask me over and over why Blacks hang out more with each other than they do
with tan people
You, a white
Think I have a duty to answer any goddamn personal question that comes into your
head
You, a Black
Get offended when I tell you you're not capable of advising me on how to put
together a powwow
You, an Indian
Look at me like I just told you I'm going to the moon and say, 'Why do you want
to go to Nigeria?'
You, a white
Don't believe me when I say it doesn't work to teach about Native Americans the
same way you teach about African-Americans
YOU
Ask me questions
And won't believe the answers

Did you ever think that
Maybe I get tired of translating?

(Bandy, N. in Camper, 1994, p.8)

Introduction

Whose side are you on? This question reflects the common underlying expectations and consequent judgments made about the identity choices of certain groups of people, particularly those from minority communities. It may be said that all identities, those we claim ourselves and those we give each other, reflect some political stance. If we examine western hegemonic and critical social work[2] perspectives, we see that both have expectations of what is an appropriate identity choice for each group within society. What is considered an *appropriate* identity depends on which side you are on. The way to make public 'where you stand' and 'whose side you're on' is to name yourself according to the language of a particular group. Most people working against various and intersecting forms of oppression choose a particular identity that names their critical understanding of dominant society, such as feminist, anti-oppressive, etc., and their own locations as women, Black, people of color, etc. For some of these people, not identifying *appropriately,* according to the language of the critical perspective, may be understood as not being critical of or, in fact, supporting the dominant western ideology. The identity choices of people with mixed family backgrounds are often judged to reflect their family and political loyalties. In this chapter, I am using *people with mixed family backgrounds* to refer to people whose families are racially and/or ethnically diverse through adoption, fostering, birth, and step families. While the focus of my examination will be on their choices, people from other minority groups living in white, Anglo, Christian dominant societies also experience many of the complexities discussed.

This chapter explores the contradictory personal and political meanings of ethnic and racialized identities. It examines how the choice and implications of a particular identity, for example a minority one, can challenge and reproduce both hegemonic and critical understandings of identity. In the chapter, I discuss how the judgments of these identity choices by others, such as family, friends, teachers, colleagues, social workers, strangers, and wider society also reflect these inconsistent understandings of identity. These dominant and critical understandings are inextricably tied up with (neo) colonial and patriarchal notions of ethnicity, race, sexuality, gender, and class. They create Others in the more obvious ways of racialized and gendered labels, but also through more subtle and often internalized divisions like class and ethnic distinctions in accent and use of language, and the differential status of shades of skin color among people of color. I will be discussing some of these identity paradoxes in the current contexts of Britain and several of its former settled colonies: Canada and Sri Lanka mainly, with some references to Australia and the USA whose minority-majority identity relations are similar to those in Canada and Britain.

The number of ethnically and racially diverse people in North America is growing due to the birth of children from increasing numbers of mixed couples (Fong et al., 1995) and the increase in international and trans-racial adoptions (Bagley, 1993 and Kim, 1978). Similar trends are happening in Britain (Tizard and Pheonix, 2002, and Parker and Song, 2001). Popular discourse about people with mixed family backgrounds portrays them negatively as confused, marginal, and not belonging anywhere (Root, 1992; Tizard and Pheonix, 1993; Ifekwunigwe, 1999, all cited in Mahtani, 2002). Immigrants from minority groups are portrayed similarly as being confused and not belonging, as the title of the recently aired CBC Documentary *Caught between cultures* (Canadian Broadcasting Corporation, 2003) implies. As social workers and educators, particularly those of us claiming a *critical* perspective, we must learn to understand, hear, and ally with them/us in ways that do not further marginalize and reinforce negative and deficient stereotypes. I believe this kind of understanding involves more than just listening to Other's stories and that it begins with opening ourselves to hearing those stories by interrogating our own privileged and/or marginalized positions.

'You Don't Look Like A...,' 'Where Are You From?' and Other Stories from the Front[3]

The following stories are about confronting and negotiating the boundaries of dominant and critical understandings of identity. Like the poem that began the chapter, they are presented to give some insight into the real life complexities and contradictions of identities and to give a context to the analysis that follows this section.

The following three excerpts are from a discussion about identity I had with a woman of Black and white Canadian ancestry, who was adopted by white British Canadian parents. The first excerpt is an example of how other people try to contain her self-identification within *their* own understandings of identity:

No matter how much I immersed myself in the Black community, I obviously cannot be seen as a Black person [because she appears white]. So I get a lot of rejection from the Black community, but I never really put myself forward. People assume I'm white, all the time, completely. If I am at certain events, I am assumed to be one of these white people who are trying to be hip and happening or an activist ...When I go to an event [I've been] refused to get in because it's a Black event, even when it is about my ancestors.

In the excerpt above, she described experiences of having her claim of a partly Black identity denied by people in that community. In refusing her admission to a Black event, they may have been resisting what they perceived as her sense of white entitlement to be included everywhere because they saw no visible proof of her belonging to that community. Another situation when she was rejected because her chosen multiethnic identity and her appearance do not *match*, was when identity politics interfered with a friendship:

... one black friend of mine cut me out of her life for a while. She became a fairly militant Black activist. ...I felt like I couldn't say my opinions or that I'm Black. ...You can't talk about it unless it's part of your identity and because I wasn't considered really Black. ...it was an era where everything was appropriation and colonization. ...Identity politics is what people call it now [late 1990s].

Finally, she explained how her understanding of what has influenced her identity had changed over time, so that she self-identified in a way that felt true to her even though it did not fit with the expectations of other:

> ...Every year it changes how I identify racially, but generally I just say *multiethnic, ½ Black, ½ white biologically, raised in a multiethnic family*, because I feel that way with my [adoptive] brother being [a different mix] and my [adoptive] parents being [British]. I used to identify as just [British] ... people see me as white, so why not just say I'm white. And then it's less upsetting to other Black people. It's very upsetting for Black people when I say I'm... it's less confusing for white people. Then I went through a stage where I said I was ½ Black, ½ white, but at this point I feel like it's not as honest, because I feel like my environmental influences are very strong. So it can't just be a biological thing as an identity. So that's [in italics above] how I identify myself, if I'm forced to and how I identify myself when I'm doing [diversity] workshops. I'll identify myself in those workshops.

As a woman of color with a mixed family background, my own experiences and those reported by others have inspired my interest and informed my critique of the contradictions of identities.

I was born in London, England, and lived in Sri Lanka for a few years before coming to Canada as a young child in the early 1970s. I have Canadian and British citizenship and passports. I grew up with my father and stepmother in a mid-sized town in south-western Ontario, in central Canada. My father was born and raised in what was then the British crown colony of Ceylon, and is now Sri Lanka[4] and immigrated to England as an adult. His family was ethnically Tamil and Methodist, and although he was English speaking, he also knew some Tamil. My stepmother was born and raised in England and her parents were of white Scottish and English ancestry. My parents, my father and (step) mother, immigrated to Canada, from England, in the early 1970s when there was a shortage of practitioners in their health care professions.

My birth mother's family is Roman Catholic and English speaking, although most also speak Sinhalese and/or Tamil. My maternal grandfather's family came to Sri Lanka from what was then India and is now Pakistan. My maternal grandmother's French ancestors came to Sri Lanka in the eighteenth century. I am told that, until my grandmother's generation, they had intermarried with only other white Europeans,[5] of which there were many with the three successive European colonial regimes of Portuguese, Dutch, and British. While being subjects of British colonialism, my Sri Lankan parents' families were also relatively privileged in Sri Lanka, by their westernization. My mother's family would have been part of a subgroup of society who had European ancestry (called Burghers) and were highly represented in the bourgeoisie (Jayawardena, 2000). Although my father's family struggled to make ends meet after his father died young, they would have been a part of a group that:

colonizers had an interest in converting ... not only to Christianity,... but also to a western way of life, thereby creating a local group that spoke, dressed, ate, drank, lived and thought like themselves (Jayawardena, 2000, p. 247).

In Canada

I grew up in a white, mostly middle-class and Christian neighborhood in a town that is still surrounded by farmland. All of my close childhood friends were white and Christian, but not all middle class. Twenty-five years later, a few of them still are among my closest friends. In elementary school, the few friendships I had with children of color, including a Chinese girl, a Black Guyanese girl, and an Indian girl, did not last long because their families moved away within a couple years.

In addition to being socialized into my parents' mostly *western* ways of life, I believe they also wanted us to be *Canadian,* but not to the extent of using Canadian English slang as they wanted us to speak *proper* English, i.e., British English, which was what they knew. The only times I heard Sinhalese or Tamil spoken were in parts of conversations my father had with his Sri Lankan friends. He did not teach or encourage us to learn either language. My family life was the same as most of the white Canadian, Christian, Anglophone, and middle-class people around us. I spoke English with a Canadian accent, had Christian names, celebrated Christmas and attended church, was a Girl Guide, played sports, dated, went to university, worked part time, went to and had parties, and got into trouble for drinking too much too young. Our family vacations often took us camping, skiing, and visiting family in England. Until I was a young adult, I thought most Sri Lankans lived more or less like us.

There were no discussions about prejudice or racism in my family, although occasionally racist comments were made. My critical understanding of racism and prejudice only developed as an adult. As I child I remember knowing that somehow it would be better to be white and occasionally wished I were, but did not understand why and was not that concerned. In my childhood world, being female left me with much more to contend with than being brown. Perhaps if I had been subject to name calling, bullying, or being excluded from groups and activities, I would have seen things differently. I know that there must have been some incidents that I did not realize were racist, but in some ways, I believe I was fortunate to have grown up not expecting to be discriminated against based on my skin color. I can now see how I must have been protected by my (step) mother's white privilege and by my family's class and cultural privilege, which did not make anyone in our circle feel threatened by our few, but significant, differences.

I recognize that there are questions to be asked about the *appropriateness* of *minority* children being brought up in relatively uncritical mainstream *Canadian* ways and, although I will not be discussing them in this chapter, they do arise in the debates about trans-racial /ethnic adoption and foster placements.

Although I did not have many nasty experiences of racism and discrimination, most of the time I was conscious of looking different, especially when I was one of few, if any, people of color at an event. While I sometimes felt uncomfortable, I got used to it and also learned early on that there are benefits and dangers, as a female, of being considered exotic and attractive. It was much later that I understood the interconnections between racism and sexism. Much as been written on the ways racism and sexism intersect to create the prevalent and disturbing notion that women of color, and particularly ethnically and racially mixed women, are exotic Others (Hooks, 1992, Camper, 1994).

In Ontario and Quebec, the provinces where I have lived in Canada, I am often asked 'Where are you from?' If I answer with the name of my hometown or home province, I then get part two of the question, 'No, um, where were you born?' The answer, 'England,' is followed by, 'Okay, well, where are your parents from?' At any point during this interrogation, if I say *Sri Lanka*, the questions end. Those are the words, the place that most people, regardless of their skin color, ethnicity, or politics, are looking for. In asking this question their assumption is that I am not from Canada. Since I was not born in Canada, I *am* from somewhere else, but England is not the answer they are looking for either; they want to know why my skin is brown. I am asked this question in bars, workplaces, homes, when walking down the street, and often by complete strangers. Sometimes the question is asked by a person of color who may think I have the same ancestry as he/she does, but most often it is white men using this question as an opening line.

In Sri Lanka

On a visit to Sri Lanka recently, I did not expect to be asked, 'Where are you from?' so often. My answer was that, 'I live in Canada.' 'Ah, but you look like a Sri Lankan.' 'Well I am, my family is from here.' They look curiously at me and, having taken in my short hair cut, western accent, dress, and passport, and the white woman (my step-mother) with me, tilt their heads to the side and say, 'Ah, I see.'

I reach the limit of being seen as a westerner when I go swimming at a public beach in a bathing suit and am stared at constantly. It seems only *white* western women can do that.

Although some things are vaguely familiar even after twenty six years of not being there, I do not feel *at home* in Sri Lanka and that is a little disappointing. I've heard many people of color, in particular those who do not feel accepted in Canada and Britain talk about finally feeling at home when they returned to the country of their family's ancestry. This is not my experience and I later realize it is because I feel Canada is my home. While I feel connected to Sri Lanka, Canada, and Britain, it is only Sri Lanka whose languages and ways of life I do not know, and where I do not have citizenship or the rights to live, work, or own property. Despite this reality, many people would say I ought to feel more Sri Lankan than Canadian or British.

In Britain

It seems to be my Canadian accent that provokes people to ask, 'Where are you from?' or 'Are you American?' My accent is important enough that 'Canada' or 'I'm Canadian' is the answer most people are content with. This is not to say skin color is not important in the UK, as I experienced and witness more racism and prejudice in my six months spent here recently than ever before. However, I am also surprised and not sure how to interpret the number of people of color and white people who say 'So, you're one of us then' when I explain that I have British citizenship by birth and do not need a visa to work here.

It is people of color who teach me that in Britain with my Sri Lankan ancestry, I am considered part of the *Asian (*and *South Asian*) ethnic community, and that I am *Black* when I want to align myself with other people of color.

In My Shoes

'Where are you from?' If you were me, what would you say?

Location, Language and Critical Social Work

Prejudicial, intolerant, and discriminatory behaviors can result from un*conscious* beliefs and feelings. Comments have been made to me by critical colleagues, most of whom were white, that left me wondering about their critical consciousness. Questions such as, 'You're not really mixed though, are you?' and comments that I am *trying* to claim many ancestries are not uncommon. These kinds of comments have been made by people, often women, whose work I admire and who have been supportive of my work in the area of identity. I was once asked, 'How did you end up with a name like *that* (Yvette Michele)?' by a female, critical social work professor of color. I interpreted this to mean that she thought these western, Christian names were not quite right for me with my brown skin and south Asian family name. She asked this while handing over some flyers that she wanted me to give to people in *my* community who might be interested in a conference on issues for people of color. Later when I thought about her question, I wondered what she assumed *my* community was. Prejudicial and dismissive comments from colleagues of color are more disappointing than from white colleagues, because they are more unexpected.

At a particular social work agency in Canada, I was assigned disproportionate numbers of families of color and, particularly, Sri Lankan families compared to my white colleagues. Presumably this was based on the assumption that I could work better with them because we were all people of color and Sri Lankan. In regard to the latter families, this may well have been true despite the fact that we were different in religion, ethnicity, class, language, and that they had very recently immigrated to Canada, while I had grown up here. Some of these are differences that divide the dominant group from the marginalized in Sri Lanka and have fuelled an eighteen-year civil war. It was also assumed that no special cultural knowledge was needed to work with my white, Christian, English-speaking clients. The irony of this is that I likely do understand more about mainstream Canadian culture than Sri Lankan, but I doubt my managers knew this. Similarly, while working in England in an apparently progressive local authority, I asked why I had been given a particularly complex case since I had little experience. 'They like having Black workers on those cases,' I was told.

The language of identity discourses is inconsistent and debated across social, political, and geographical contexts. There are complexities and contradictions in the commonly used labels, even before taking into account multiple ancestries. In Canada, Sri Lankans are considered *South Asian*, whereas in the UK, *Asian* commonly refers to people from the Indian subcontinent. In North America, Asians are people with east and south East Asian ancestry. To ally myself politically with others who experience racism in Canada, I call myself a person of color or a visible minority, while in the UK, I was Black. In North America, Blacks are people with African ancestry. This means, depending on whether it is taking place in Canada or Britain, different people are welcome at a meeting for *Black* social workers. When I was working in Britain, there was such a meeting and I knew I could attend. On the other hand, several years earlier while working at a Canadian social work agency, there had also been a meeting for *Black* social workers and, understanding that in Canada *Black* does not include Sri Lankans, I did not attend. Such differences reflect the way the language of identity is shaped by the ideology and politics of a community (Lionnet, 1989).

The terms *people of color*, *visible minority*, and *ethnic and cultural communities* are commonly used within critical and dominant discourses. Although I continue to use them, I find these terms problematic and awkward, because they all maintain white, straight, Christian, English (and in Quebec, French) speaking as the norm. The invisibility of what is *normal* reproduces the *Other*-ness of *visible minorities*, people *of color*, and *ethnic* and *cultural* communities who are defined by their difference from the accepted norm. It raises the question, 'In relation to whom are some people *visible, minorities,* or *of color*?' Frankenberg (1997) observes that leaving 'whiteness unexamined is to perpetuate a kind of asymmetry that has marred even many critical analyses of racial formation and cultural practice' (p.1). Left unexamined, the dominant groups also appear to be homogeneous, which is not the case when you consider how many shades of *white* people there are when apparently they do not have any color. I also find it awkward to say woman or person *of color*, because it sounds so passive.

While in the UK, I quite liked referring to myself as *Black,* although I used it only in the political sense of being a person of color. I think it is because the word itself does not mean inferior or sound passive, like visible minority and person of color do. I also liked using the term because it confronted the racism against people of African ancestry that I have found exists within the Asian-South Asian community. Within all social subgroups, there are members who are conscious of their own oppression, while oppressing others.

Identity Choices and Contradictions

In this section, I will discuss three possible identity choices for people with mixed family ancestries. Much of the following discussion is also relevant for people with various ethnic, racial, or cultural minority backgrounds living in white dominant societies. The first identity choice is a dominant, national identity, such as Canadian or Australian. The second is a minority identity like Jamaican or Jewish, or a double-barreled, hyphenated identity, such as Chinese-Canadian or Indo-Canadian. The third option, a mixed identity, is chosen to acknowledge their known diverse family ancestry.

I have already discussed my experience of being asked 'Where are you from?' in different contexts and how it reflects others' perception of difference and, sometimes, a common difference. This is a question people of color are asked regularly in Canada (Palmer, 1997). Since the majority of the population of Canada (and the US and Australia) have arrived here in the last several hundred years, relatively recently compared to the thousands of years Aboriginal peoples have lived on these lands, it is not so surprising that attention is paid to people's ancestry. Thus, it is not so problematic that this question is asked at all, but that it is asked mostly of people of color with the implication that we have *just* arrived. People with non-Canadian accents are also asked this question, regardless of their skin color. However, their accents indicate that they have grown up or lived a substantial part of their lives in another place. So there is some logic in assuming that there is another place that they called home before Canada even if this is home now. However, people of color are assumed to be from elsewhere even when we have Canadian accents.

Although both white people and people of color ask this question, from my experience it seems to be with different intentions. People of color seem to want to point out what we have in common and some even guess that I am from the same place as them, whereas white people seem to be more interested in my difference from them. Although it is disproportionately white people who ask, in both cases the underlying assumption is that people of color are from somewhere else. People who are seen as white[6] and who have the *appropriate* accents, names, and dress are not usually asked this question. It is this absence that reveals the racism at the root of who is *seen* as Canadian and who is not. The assumption underlying this is that Canadians are white (Palmer, 1997). A very good friend who, like me, was born in England, emigrated to Canada at a young age, and grew up in the same small city as I did, does not have strangers ask where she's from. She is white.

Some people from minority groups, including people of color, feel that a dominant Canadian identity best represents their lived realities and some want to be *just* Canadian. For people who were born here or arrived as young children this may be the only place they know as home. For those whose ancestors came here many generations ago, their lived realities may have little, if any, similarity to that of the people living in the countries where their ancestors came from. This is as true for people from minority groups as it is for Canadians of white European ancestry. However, the descendants of the Africans who came to Canada as slaves starting in the early seventeenth century and of the Chinese, Japanese, and Sikhs who started arriving in the last half of the nineteenth century (Henry et al, 1995) are still asked where they are from. It is ironic that white Canadians, who *chose* to acknowledge their ethnic ancestry, may say they are second or third generation Irish or Polish, while people of color are having to prove their connection to Canada by saying they are second or third generation *Canadian.*

Some people with a critical perspective would not support the choice of a dominant *Canadian* identity for a person with mixed ancestry or a person of color. The critique of this identity could be that it is a result of the person wanting to deny their minority identity because they have internalized the dominant message that their minority identity is inferior. Appiah (1997) explains that not identifying with their minority ancestry is judged more harshly for people of color than for ethnic minority whites in the US. I would argue this is also true in Canada and Britain. A person of Irish American descent who fails to acknowledge this descent 'is generally not held to be inauthentic' (Appiah, 1997, p.79). On the other hand, an African American who can pass as white and chooses a white identity is 'thought of by many as being not merely inauthentic, but dishonest' (p.79). However, if they are visibly mixed they are thought to be inauthentic, but not dishonest because their appearance reveals what they try to deny (Appiah, 1997). The political significance of skin color in these countries cannot be minimized; that a white woman can give birth to a Black child, but a Black woman cannot give birth to a white child (Hollinger, 1995) exemplifies the powerful personal and political contradictions of racialized, ethnic, and minority categories.

From another political perspective, a national Canadian identity for a person of color could be seen as resisting being forced into the position of Other in ones own home. It challenges the dominant belief that Canadians (Americans, Australians, and British) are white and that since we are not, we must be from somewhere else. It argues that like whites, people of color can also be fully Canadian.[7] However, as mentioned above, some people choose a dominant identity to disassociate themselves from a minority identity of which they are ashamed. So, we must carefully consider when a person of color or from a minority group, says they are *Canadian,* whether it is a form of resistance to the racist dominant culture or a reflection of some internalized oppression. For example, in answering the question, 'where are you from?' with the name of the south western Ontario town where I grew up, it is with the awareness that I am contesting the prejudgment that since I am not white I must be from a place outside of Canada.

The second choice is to identify according to the minority and/or visible part of ones' background, e.g., Chinese, Jewish, Jamaican-Canadian or Sri Lankan-Canadian. This is a very common choice for people from minority groups. Most people with a critical perspective would agree that '(in) a society in which racial discrimination and disadvantage are an everyday reality for minority ethnic groups, the importance of (a positive) identity based on racial, cultural, religious and linguistic aspects is crucial' (Barn, 1999, p.7). Since people of color will be identified by their appearance and consequently discriminated against, feeling connected to and proud of this identity affords some defense against internalizing the belief that they are inferior. This need for group belonging and strength also applies to people from minority groups who look white or are considered white, because they can also internalize the inferior status dominant society gives to their group.

However, by self-identifying as a minority we also reproduce colonial and essentialist identity categories. Choosing and advocating identities that label people according to how they are different from white, western European, Christian, or Anglophone people reproduces the myth that these people set the norm in Canada (the US, Australia, and Britain), and that only they can be *just* Canadian. This is not by coincidence, as these countries have 'a history of the self naming of white people as white that (was) linked to imperial and colonial expansion...and the making of (white dominant) nation states' (Frankenberg, 1997, p.8). Another critique of hyphenated identities comes from Neil Bissoondath (1994), and although he was not only discussing people of color, he asks why should we be people for whom the countries of our ancestors are always more important than that Canada is our home.

Another consequence of people self- identifying with a particular minority group is that it divides people and groups that may have similar political goals. There are different groups with the same political goals who are not working together and compete against each other, as individual *ethnic* and *cultural* groups, for the same limited resources provided by the government. Another cultural policy that undermines political change is '(multicultural) policy, where ethnicities are celebrated as a backdrop for Canadian identity, often (ensuring) that forms of institutionalized racism are rendered invisible' (Kobayashi, 1993 and Kymlicka, 1995 in Mahtani, 2002, p. 475). When resources are focused on 'celebrating diversity,' we may be distracted from seeing racism and intolerance. Whether by design or as an unintentional outcome, the affects of these policies are to divide community groups who together could more powerfully challenge multiple forms of oppression. Martinez (2000) argues that 'liberation has similar meanings for all people of color engaged in struggle' (p.93).

Minority identities can be particularly problematic for people with mixed family ancestries. Even when promoted for anti-racist and anti-oppressive purposes, these identities can be experienced as inauthentic and oppressive because they force the person to choose one part of their family over another. Thus, the third identity option is to choose a mixed or multiple identity. The negative connotation of terms like mongrel, mulatto, half breed, half-caste, etc. reveal how people with mixed ancestry have been labeled as oddities and unnatural in the not too distant past (Mahtani, 2002). More recently there have been significant moves away from this negativity and toward claiming positive mixed identities (Mahtani & Moreno, 2001; Mahtani, 2002;Parker and Song, 2001; Root, 1997 and 2000). In the US, in particular, there are growing numbers of political and social organizations for people with mixed family backgrounds who choose to identify that way.[8] Choosing mixed and multiple identities acknowledges a person's diversity in ways that challenges the existing dominant labels, including Black, white, and hyphenated identities, that are also advocated by those with critical perspectives. Mahtani (2002) talks about mixed race identities as '(providing) a way to identify outside of the constraining racialized categories of identity' (p.469).

There are important benefits to identifying diversely, but because identity labels have 'implications for access to power, distribution of resources, and for social policy and practice' (Asamoah et al, 1991, p.9), they may also have political implications. They can undermine solidarity based on existing identity categories and the relative power these groups have attained. Civil rights leaders in the US are concerned that the choice of a mixed category will reduce minority group populations enough to detrimentally affect 'civil rights programs, including those related to housing, employment, and education' (Fong et al, 1995, p.727).

There are a few other contradictions in mixed identities that need to be acknowledged, although I will not be discussing them further in this chapter. A critique of mixed *race* discourse, in particular, is that it perpetuates the belief that there are biologically distinct races (Mahtani, 2002). How do we talk about and challenge racism, while also dispelling the myth that there are distinct biological *races*? Another problem is that much of the popular discourse on mixed identity seems preoccupied with those who have some white European ancestry, leaving the voices of *non-white* mixed-race people in the margins (Mahtani and Moreno, 2001). Lastly, 'disparities in class and education also serve to shape the experience of multi-raciality' (Mahtani, 2002, p. 474). This limits the scope of this discourse because most of us who are publicly writing about multiethnic identities and interrogating essentialist identities, including ethnicity, race, culture, gender, and sexuality, are doing so from within the privileged spaces of universities. In examining the choice of a *mixed race* identities, Mahtani (2002) notes that, unlike the middle and upper class women in her study, 'other "mixed race" women who may be economically disadvantaged… may not have access to a university education where many of the women interviewed learned about the identification of "mixed race" identity' (p.474).

Implications for Critical Education and Practice

'I shake people's notions of what race…is. They would rather deny my existence than grapple with how that shakes what they think race or ethnicity is' (Gnanamuttu, 1999, p.16). The three narratives presented at the beginning of this chapter reflect experiences of having one's own understandings of ourselves challenged and minimized by others, because we do not fit with *their* understandings of us. We need to move away from these *either/or* and *neither* understandings of the identities of people with mixed backgrounds and toward the language and conceptualization of *both/and*. Mahtani (2002) talks about moving away from the *out of place* metaphor and looking at where people with diverse backgrounds feel '*in place*' (p. 471). At least conceptually and linguistically, this would open up space for multiple self-identifications that foster personal belonging and political solidarity with multiple groups. Essential identity categories and, particularly, their mutual exclusivity would still be deconstructed, although not completely abandoned. The deconstructed and deliberate use of essential identity categories is reflected in Gayatri Spivak's notion of 'strategic essentialism,' about which she says, when discussing political representation, 'no representation can take place without essentialism' (Harasym, 1990, p.109). Within this conceptualization of identity, I could provisionally self-identify in personally meaningful and politically (representative) strategic ways with various marginal and privileged locations to which I *(essentially)* belong, for example as a Canadian, a Canadian woman of color, a person/woman with mixed ancestry, and a Sri Lankan-Canadian, etc. This is a personally and politically useful way to bridge difference and solidarity. In general, people for whom multiple identities feel the most authentic, including those with mixed ancestry, could self-identify diversely and yet continue to be part of a political group and/or movement.

While we are working out these linguistic and conceptual spaces in our heads (and hearts), we also need to be working for change in our lives and work. In advocating resistance to the identities prescribed and explanations expected by others, Root (2000) has created a Bill of Rights for Racially Mixed People.[9] Although it is specifically referring to mixed *race*, I suggest its premises could be used to challenge fixed and essential constructs of ethnic, cultural, and sexual identities.

In educational and direct social work practices, social policy, political strategies, and research methods we need to be conscious that there are issues particular to people's experiences of having mixed ancestries. For example, at an individual level, we may assume that people from minority groups receive positive messages about their identity from family and community that counteract the negative ones from dominant society. However, people with diverse ancestry may receive contradictory messages about their worth and belonging in the family and community. Root (1997) suggests that therapy with mixed race women may bring particular issues around uniqueness, acceptance and belonging, physical appearance, sexuality, self-esteem and identity. When gathering demographic data for research, social policy, or at an agency level, we need to account for people's individual diversity and self-definition. In research, 'When studying populations that include people with mixed race and ethnicity, an increasingly likely circumstance, researchers will have to question to what extent race or ethnicity in fact has a meaningful explanatory capability' (Fong et al., 1995, p. 727).

Critique, Location, and Risk

As students, educators, and workers '(in) the social work profession we confront history at its deepest and most personal level, that is a vivid part of each person's daily life' (Deer, 1994, p. 71), including our own lives. In this chapter, I have critiqued some aspects of critical social work and some people who claim this perspective, and that feels awkward and risky. As a female post-graduate student of color, I am writing, some would say predictably, about identity, race, ethnicity, and politics and critiquing dominant discourses. However, since my critique is also of critical perspectives that have been part of successful challenges to oppressive beliefs and practices, I worry that this may lead some to wonder 'Whose side is she on?' in these struggles. Despite my belief that the authors in this book share a critical perspective, I must admit I would feel more secure if I were not one of only three people of color and one of three Ph.D. students of the twelve authors of this book. The feeling of risk is increased because I have disclosed quite a lot of myself and my family. Although my own story was used to illustrate the complex, contradictory, shifting, and slippery nature of these debates and although I believe it is important for authors to acknowledge their own location and interest within a discourse, criticism of this work may now feel a little too close to home. (This makes me appreciate why some critical authors represent others and distance themselves from their work.)

Despite being critical of the western, middle class, masculine hegemony that is the norm in western academic institutions (and their critical subgroups) and societies, I am aware that my (relative) career success so far is due, in part, to having been socialized into it. All of these factors led me to worry about perceptions of tokenism, of *letting the side down*, and that people of color will see me as a *coconut/Oreo* (brown/ black on the outside and white on the inside) in its derogatory sense. Most importantly, I do not want to be understood as trying to undermine the fight against racism and ethnic prejudice. These perceived risks led me to consider withdrawing my chapter from this book on several occasions. It is often awkward and uncomfortable for you, the reader, and me, the writer to examine how those of us with critical social work and education perspectives can be oppressive. However, those of us trying to question, teach, work, and live our lives from critical perspectives need to look more critically at our own insecurities, assumptions, privileges, interests, and agendas. Hopefully opening ourselves up to hearing these stories of racism, prejudice, and discrimination will increase our consciousness, and improve our understanding and our ways of fighting oppression.

Acknowledgements

Copyright © 2000 from 'Readings from Diversity and Social Justice' by M. Adams et al. Reproduced by permission of Routledge/Taylor & Francis Books, Inc.

Bandy, N. (1994), 'Sorry, our translator's out sick today' in C. Camper (ed.), *Miscegenation Blues. Voices of Mixed Race Women*. Toronto: Sister Vision Press. Every effort has been made to trace the copyright owners. However, if advised of any inadvertent omissions, the publishers and I would be pleased to incorporate proper acknowledgement in future editions.

Notes

1   The author is a woman of mixed ancestry living in the USA. Terms: In the U.S., Chicano refers to people with Mexican heritage and Asian usually refers people whose ancestors originate from the countries of east and south east Asia. In this poem, Indian refers to Native American.

2   Throughout this chapter, I have use the terms critical social work and critical perspectives to include people who are questioning and working against hetero-sexism, homophobia, racism, ethnic prejudice, ageism, global capitalism, and other oppressive forces from sometimes contradictory and, at other times, collaborating perspectives.

3   *Noun:* that part or side that is forward or most often seen; outward aspect or bearing; people with a common goal; military: the total area in which opposing armies face each other. Collins English Dictionary, 2002, p.477.

4   Demographics of Sri Lanka. There were indigenous peoples on the island when the Sinhalese came from northern India in the 6thC BC claimed the island and were later invaded by the Tamils. European domination began in the 16th century with arrival of the Portuguese. In 1653, the island became a Dutch colony and by 1796 it was a British colony. In February 1948, Ceylon as it was still known, became independent. In 1972 it became the Republic of Sri Lanka and, in 1978, the Democratic Socialist Republic of Sri Lanka. In 2003, of Sri Lanka's population of about 19 million people, 74 per cent are Sinhalese, 18 per cent Tamil, seven per cent Moors, and the remaining, one per cent of the population was made up of Eurasians/Burghers (with Sri Lankan and European ancestry), Malays (ethnically Indonesian and Malaysian), and Veddas (the indigenous peoples). Although most Sinhalese and Tamils are Buddhist and Hindu, respectively, many are Christian; 70 per cent Buddhist, 15 per cent Hindu, eight per cent Christian, and seven per cent Muslim. Sinhalese is the official and a national language and Tamil is also a national language, English is commonly used in government and is spoken competently by about 10 per cent of the population (http://www.nationmaster.com/encyclopedia/Demographics-of-Sri-Lanka).

5   When my mother's siblings were immigrating to Australia thirty years ago, they documented their maternal family ancestry because they, I'm told, had to prove they had at least forty percent white European ancestry.

6   Who is considered white, in North America at least, has changed significantly with time. (See *How Jews became white folks and what that says about race in America* [1998] by Karen Brodkin, and *How the Irish became white* [1996] by Noel Ignatiev.)

7   All of us who live here are already *Canadian* in that we are at the very least benefiting from the continuing colonial exploitation of Aboriginal peoples and their lands, as all Canadians, Americans, and Australians do.

8   The MAVIN Foundation (mavinfoundation.org), Interracial Family Support Network, Association of Multiethnic Americans – AMEA, Harmony, Prism, Project RACE – Reclassify All Children Equally (cited in Parker & Song, 2001 and Mahtani, 2002).

9   Bill of Rights for Racially Mixed People
    I have the right
          not to justify my existence in this world
          not to keep the races separate within me
          not to be responsible for people's discomfort with my physical ambiguity
          not to justify my ethnic legitimacy
    I have the right

To identify myself differently than strangers expect me to identify
To identify myself differently than how my parents identify me
To identify myself differently than my brothers and sisters
To identify myself differently in different situations
I have the right
To create a vocabulary to communicate about being multiracial
To change my identity over my lifetime – and more than once
To have loyalties and identify with more than one group of people
To freely choose whom I befriend and love (Root, 2000).

References

Appiah, A. (1997), ' "But would that still be me?" Notes on gender, "race", ethnicity, as sources of 'identity', in N. Zack (ed.), *Race/Sex: Their Sameness, Difference and Interplay*, Routledge, New York, pp. 75-81.

Asamoah, Y. et al. (1991), 'What we call ourselves: Implications for resources, policy, and practice.' *Journal of Multicultural Social Work*, Vol. 1(1), pp. 6-22.

Bagley, C. (1993), 'Chinese adoptees in Britain: a twenty year follow-up of adjustment and social identity.' *International Social Work*, Vol. 36(2), pp. 143-157.

Bandy, N.A. (1994), 'Sorry, our translator's out sick today', in C. Camper (ed.), *Miscegenation Blues. Voices of Mixed Race Women*, Sister Vision Press, Toronto.

Barn, R. (ed.) (1999), 'Racial and ethnic identity', *Working with Black Children and Adolescents in Need*, British Association of Adoption and Fostering, London, pp. 7-17.

Bissoondath, N. (1994), *Selling Illusions: The Cult of Multiculturalism in Canada*, Penguin, Toronto.

Camper, C. (ed.) (1994), *Miscegenation Blues. Voices of Mixed Race Women*, Sister Vision Press, Toronto.

Canadian Broadcasting Corporation (2003), *Caught Between Cultures*, (Holly Preston, producer), First aired on December 16, 2003 on CBC Newsworld, Canada.

Collins English Dictionary and Thesaurus 21st Century Edition, (second edition) (2000), HarperCollins, Glasgow.

Deer, A. (1994), 'Multiculturalism and Activism: The Role of Social Work Education.' *Journal of Progressive Human Services*, 5(1), pp. 6373.

'Demographics of Sri Lanka' at *http://www.nationmaster.com/encyclopedia/Demographics-of-Sri-Lanka*. Website visited January 19, 2004.

Fong, R. et al. (1995), 'A Multiracial Reality: Issues for Social Work', *Social Work*, Vol. 40(6), pp. 725-727.

Frankenberg, R. (ed.) (1997), 'Introduction: Local Whitenesses, Localizing Whiteness', in R. Frankenberg (ed.), *Displacing Whiteness: Essays in Social and Cultural Criticism*, Duke University, Durham and London.

Gnanamuttu, M. (1999), *Towards an Understanding of Individual Diversity: Multiple Identities*, Unpublished Master's Independent Study Project, McGill University, Montreal.

Harasym, S. (ed.) (1990), 'Practical politics of the open end' in Gayatri Chakravorty Spivak, *The Post-Colonial Critic Interviews, Strategies, Dialogues*, Routledge, New York.

Henry, et al. (1995), *The Colour of Democracy. Racism in Canadian Society*, Harcourt, Brace and Co., Toronto.

Hollinger, D. (1995), *Post-ethnic America: Beyond Multiculturalism*, Basic Books, New York.

Hooks, B. (1992), *Black Looks Race and Representation*, South End Press, Boston.

Jayawardena, K. (2000), *Nobodies to Somebodies The Rise of the Colonial Bourgeoisie in Sri Lanka*, The Social Scientists' Association, Colombo.

Kim, D.S. (1978), 'Issues in transracial and transcultural adoption', *Social Casework*, Vol. 59(8), pp. 477-486.

Lionnet, F. (1989), 'The politics and aesthetics of metissage.', in S. Smith and J. Watson. (eds.), *Woman, Autobiography, Theory: A Reader*, The University of Wisconsin Press, Madison, Wisconsin.

Mahtani, M. (2002), 'What's in a name? Exploring the employment of "mixed race" as an identification.' *Ethnicities*, Vol. 2(4), pp. 469-490.

Mahtani, M. and Moreno, A. (2001), 'Same difference: towards a more unified discourse in 'mixed race' theory,' in D. Parker and M. Song. (eds.), *Rethinking 'Mixed Race'*, Pluto Press, London.

Martinez, E. (2000), 'Seeing more than Black and White', in M. Adams *et al.* (eds.), *Readings for Diversity and Social Justice*, Routledge, New York and London.

Palmer, H. (1997), *'...But Where Are You Really From?' Stories of Identity and Assimilation in Canada*, Sister Vision Press, Toronto.

Parker, D. and Song, M. (eds.) (2001), *Rethinking 'Mixed Race'*, Pluto Press, London.

Root, M. (1997), 'Mixed-race women', in N. Zack (ed.), *Race/Sex: Their Sameness, Difference and Interplay,* Routledge, New York.

Root, M. (2000), 'A Bill of Rights for Racially Mixed People', in M. Adams *et al.* (eds.), *Readings for Diversity and Social Justice,* Routledge, New York and London.

Tizard, B. and Phoenix, A. (2002), *Black, White or Mixed Race? Race and Racism in the Lives of Young People of Mixed Parentage*, revised edition, Routledge, London and New York.

Chapter 6

Texts and Power: Toward a Critical Theory of Language

Anthony Paré

Introduction

> ...ideology is minutely inscribed in the discourse of daily practice (Berlin, 1996, p.78).

In answer to a question about how they learned to write social work documents, new practitioners said the following:

> I learned mostly by ... I wrote it, and I showed it to my supervisor and, I mean, all the information was right but it was under the wrong headings and so I had to end up shifting things around and then I re-did it and it was fine, I guess...

> ...I would give it to [my supervisor] to read and then she would say, 'Well, the language here is a little too strong. You might to change the way you've phrased this. This is good, but I think you should include something else which you have not said...'

> ...I think I've learned how to write the way [my supervisor] wants me to write, because now I go and she says, 'Yep, that's fine...'

What is taught and what is learned in this apprenticeship? What values and beliefs pass down from generation to generation of social workers through this heritage of literate practice? This chapter addresses these and related questions by considering the social regulation of discursive labor – that is, the control of the production of meaning – and the ways in which social workers might resist the imperatives of institutional recording practices and thus control the means of producing the realities that social work texts construct.[1] In what follows, I propose that a hidden ideology of oppression infuses social work recording practices – an ideology that seeps into daily work through the repetition and replication of documentation habits learned uncritically during initial practice.

Social work practitioners and educators wishing to resist that ideology would be helped by increased awareness of language and its effects. Becoming critically literate – sensitive to the ways in which textual practices locate workers and clients in relations of power – is an essential first step towards taking an active and informed part in resisting those practices and escaping what Nietzsche called 'the prison house of language.' In other words, a theory of language can be used to counteract the effects of language.

The chapter begins with a consideration of the nature of language and the link between language and discourse. Next, it examines how ideology works invisibly within discourses to produce common sense. Then, in order to demonstrate the ways in which professional textual practices subtly implicate workers in oppressive relations, the chapter offers samples of social workers talking about recording. The chapter ends with suggestions about how social workers might resist the influence of these practices by becoming more conscious of their effects and by developing counter-practices.

What is Language?

This overview of language-related concepts is not meant as remediation, or as some sort of punishment for having failed to pay attention in secondary school English class. In fact, most English classrooms do not equip us to think about language in any very practical or useful way. So, although we actually know much more about language than we realize, most of us do not have easy access to that knowledge – that is, we cannot examine or articulate it – so we have difficulty reflecting on or revising what we know.

What is language, and how does it work? Answers to those questions consume entire careers and occupy whole floors of library space, so the discussion that follows will be necessarily brief and consequently superficial.

First, it helps to remember that language is a human invention. In a very real sense, it is a technology, a tool, a human-devised means of acting in and on the world.[2] We may be, as Pinker (1994) suggests, genetically programmed for language ('hard-wired,' as they say), and we are certainly marvelously suited for language physiologically: the human tongue and mouth are capable of shaping the noise produced by our vocal chords into an infinite number of sounds. But beyond biology, human society and culture take over, and language can be seen to be a vast, living contract – an agreement among people over time and space about what particular spoken or written symbols will mean and how we will use them to make meaning together.

For most of us, that social contract and its many sub-clauses are invisible; language is just there – a human activity that surrounds us, as natural and ubiquitous as air. Day in and day out, we participate in it with ease, and in all manner of settings language spills from our mouths or finger tips without apparent effort, or even much thought. And yet, language is a complex set of regulated, interrelated systems, and we must know the systems to employ language correctly, appropriately, and effectively.

Two questions about our language knowledge are worth considering here: What is it we know? And, how do we know it? What we know is incredibly complex. People who wish to participate in English, for example, must know the English lexicon – the list of currently acceptable words – or at least a sufficient number of those words to engage in any sort of meaningful exchange, and they need to know how to pronounce them. If they hope to be understood in writing, they must know the rules of English spelling and punctuation. The lexicon alone is not all that useful, however, unless people know how to place words or parts of words into acceptable, meaningful combinations and sequences.[3] To do that requires knowledge of morphemes (prefixes, suffixes), grammar (parts of speech, agreement, tense), and syntax (sentence types and structures). Beyond the sentence, there are rules governing cohesion in multi-sentence passages – rules that allow us to recognize an extended utterance or written paragraph as more than a random assortment of sentences.

Two speakers of English, even in casual conversation, are performing an extraordinary feat. With dizzying speed and fluency, building on each other, they explain, agree, respond, question, elaborate. To an observer, they do this without apparent reference to rules of any sort; instead, they 'shape at the point of utterance,' in the words of James Britton (1980) – that is, they make meaning on the fly, adhering all the while to rules of semantics, grammar, syntax, and cohesion.

It is important to note that authority or control over these rules is also part of a social contract. Words have no direct or intrinsic connection to the objects or actions they represent; they are simply agreed-on sounds or graphic representations of those sounds.[4] Words are symbols or signs that stand-in for something else. Likewise, a particular sentence is considered grammatical because we, or some sub-set of 'we,' decide that it is. So, for example, the sentence 'He ain't here' is deemed unacceptable in certain social groups, and perfectly fine in others. There is nothing intrinsically *wrong* (inaccurate, illogical, incomprehensible, immoral) with the sentence, but custom (and, truth be told, class) determines its propriety. We'll return to this point in the next section, where we consider what happens to language when it comes to life within different communities.

The answer to the second question – how do we know all of this? – is central to the argument of this chapter: we know language procedurally but not declaratively; that is, we can *use* language, but most of us cannot explain in any detail what we know that allows us to use it.[5] This notion of knowledge-in-use, or procedural knowledge, is crucial. The complex linguistic systems we employ – whether they are called English, Arabic, or Urdu – are deeply rule-bound. They are intricate and tightly constrained social agreements that allow us to produce shared meanings. Yet even those of us who were subjected to years of grammar instruction could only explain a fraction of the decision-making process that a speaker or writer employs at any given moment. And yet, people who would not know a gerund from a conjunction use them both constantly, correctly, and effectively, and have done so since a very early age – even before the dubious benefits of grammar lessons.

How we gain this knowledge – that is, the process of language acquisition – is not important for our purposes here. What *is* important to recognize is the vast, largely inexpressible knowledge of language that each of us possesses and employs. And so far we have only considered the linguistic systems that allow us to produce acceptable sentences. There are also rules governing such things as the style, tone, topic, format, timing, and length of a particular utterance. In the next section, we will look at how language rules become instantiated or enacted within particular contexts and communities. To do that, we will consider the relationship between language and discourse.

Language and Discourse

One of the most commonly used words in contemporary intellectual life is *discourse.* Widely and loosely employed, it sometimes seems to be synonymous with language, but at other times seems to refer to something bigger than, but including, language. James Gee (1996) offers this definition:

> A Discourse is a socially accepted association among ways of using language, other symbolic expressions, and 'artifacts', of thinking, feeling, believing, valuing, and acting that can be used to identify oneself as a member of a socially meaningful group or 'social network', or to signal (that one is playing) a socially meaningful 'role' (p.131).

Lemke's (1995) definition is simpler but similar: 'the social activity of making meanings with language and other symbolic systems in some particular kind of situation or setting' (p.6). Common to both definitions, and most relevant to this chapter, is the notion of specificity: Gee points to *a* 'Discourse' within *a* group; Lemke writes of 'particular' settings.

This use of *discourse* reflects a marriage of ideas from language study (e.g., linguistics, literary theory, composition and rhetoric, literacy studies) with ideas from social and critical theory, particularly the work of Foucault (e.g., 1972).[6] It recognizes that social collectives of various sorts develop and design particular ways of using language and other meaning-making practices. In much the same way that dialects and accents develop in distinct language groups because of commonalities of class, race, region, and historical period, specialized discourses evolve within what are sometimes called 'discourse communities.'

There has been considerable debate about the use of the word 'community' to draw boundaries around discourses (e.g., Faigley, 1992). I share discomfort with the rosy view implied by 'community,' a word Raymond Williams (1976) called 'warmly persuasive' (p.66), especially since I wish to draw a more sinister portrait of collective discourse in this chapter. Moreover, it is important to note that each of us is a member of many communities and that a collective such as 'social workers' will consist of many sub-cultures and, consequently, many different discourses. However, the term 'discourse community' does conjure a commonality of location and attitude that is appropriate for the analysis I offer in this chapter.

Such communities might be formally constituted and distinct, such as history professors or dentists, or they might be ill-defined and amorphous, such as sports fans or skiers. But whether clearly distinguished or vaguely defined, discourse communities devise and enforce rules for the production of meaning. Sometimes those rules are codified – for instance, in regulations concerning legal proceedings or the submission of academic articles or the conduct of committees – and sometimes they are widely but tacitly accepted and honored, much like the rules described in the previous section.

In fact, linguistic systems – grammar, syntax, semantics, and so on – only take shape within a discourse, and are regulated or legislated by the discourse community. As Gee (1996) says, 'Language makes no sense outside of Discourses' (p.viii). So, for example, split infinitives, double negatives, slang, profanity, contractions, sentences beginning with 'and' or ending with a preposition, and other such variations in language use are judged acceptable or not within a group that shares a discourse, and adherence to group norms marks one as a member. Once again, it should be noted that explicit knowledge of norms is not essential for adherence; we learn to speak and write like the people with whom we identify, not by instruction, but by a slow process of osmosis.

However, beyond a community's special lexicon and its tolerance for variations in grammar and syntax, there exist other systems of discourse control, more or less prescribed and explicit, that determine who speaks (or writes), as well as when, why, where, how, and to whom. In highly formalized communities, these control systems often take on the trappings of ritual or drama: in courtrooms, the lawyers make opening and closing arguments, evidence is deemed admissible or inadmissible, juries listen in silence, judges rule on objections, witnesses answer questions. For the most part, however, even when tight constraints are operating, these rules for discourse production, like grammar proscriptions, are obeyed without much conscious or critical attention.

Obedience comes at a cost, as Norman Fairclough (1992) notes: 'Discourses do not just reflect or represent social entities and relations, they construct or 'constitute' them' (p.3). That is, communities and their members are shaped by their discourse, even as they shape it. Participation in a discourse locates one in relationships to others and to ideas; it implicates one in the ethos of the discourse. Gee (2001) again: 'Operating within a Discourse, we align ourselves with and get aligned by words, deeds, values, thoughts, beliefs, things, places, and times so as to recognize and get recognized as a person of a certain type' (p.360).

Before considering the ways in which controls on discourse affect social workers and their recording, I would like to explore the relationship between discourse and ideology, and the process by which that relationship disappears into common sense.

Discourse, Ideology, and Common Sense

In this book's introductory chapter, Peter Leonard makes the following observation:

> Class relations can be seen as embedded in capitalist cultures and their exploitative dynamic hidden in dominant social and economic discourses. In the face of such powerful discourses and their 'common sense' taken-for granted ideological underpinnings, practitioners and educators find difficulty in extracting themselves from dominant understandings and gaining a critical distance from them. (p. 23).

One of the chief ways that unexamined 'dominant understandings' are maintained in social work (and other fields) is through texts and textual practices, especially those that are regulated and repeated. Such patterns in documentation are often called 'genres' in studies of discourse.

Traditionally, the term 'genre' has been applied to text types: the genres of literature (poetry, short stories, drama, etc.) or business (quarterly and annual reports, sales letters, business plans, etc.). But following Miller (1984), there has been a growing realization that repeated institutional texts lie at the center of a larger pattern of repetition that includes parallel activities (e.g., meetings, various related texts), methods of collecting and analyzing information, standard distribution routes, predictable reader responses, pre-determined consequences or follow-ups, and so on. As Fairclough (1992) puts it, '[a] genre implies not only a particular text type, but also particular processes of producing, distributing and consuming texts' (p.126). In addition, genre studies have indicated the extent to which regular textual practices and the documents they produce elicit particular attitudes and values (e.g., Freedman and Medway, 1994; Dias, Freedman, Medway, and Paré, 1999; Coe, Lingard, and Teslenko, 2002).

Repeated documents and the procedures for producing them – as well as the attitudes and values that are evoked by them – take on an air of normalcy; they become simply 'the way things are done.' For one thing, many such practices pre-date individual workers, so they appear immutable; for another, their automatic enactment at particular moments in institutional activity makes them seem inevitable. Here again, at a much higher level of operation, are the rules we follow in the production of language and discourse. Embedded within the rules governing a genre are regulations about lexicon, grammar, syntax, style, tone, arrangement, and a whole host of other discourse features. We come to know these practices as newcomers to the community through our participation in their enactment. They become second nature, as it were.

In fact, Fairclough (1995) argues that repeated texts and textual practices are a key force in what he calls the 'naturalization of ideology':

> A particular set of discourse conventions (e.g., for conducting medical consultations, or media interviews, or for writing crime reports in newspapers) implicitly embodies certain ideologies – particular knowledge and beliefs, particular 'positions' for the types of social subject that participate in that practice (e.g., doctors, patients,

interviewees, newspaper readers), and particular relationships between categories of participants (e.g., between doctors and patients). In so far as conventions become naturalized and commonsensical, so too do these ideological presuppositions (p.94).

Institutional genres and other conventions are successful patterns in local discursive forms and functions. Over time, they have proven effective at producing the meanings desired by or required of the community. Moreover, they are durable and capable of being adapted to meet and influence changing conditions. In other words, they work; but for whom and for what ends? As Fairclough implies above, the ideological effects of discourse are often obscured by habitual practice. Jay Lemke (1995) makes a similar point when he argues that 'Discourse functions ideologically in society to support and legitimate the exercise of power, and to naturalize unjust social relations, making them seem the inevitable consequence of common sense necessity' (p.20). Lemke also argues that discourses 'function to get us thinking along particular lines, the lines of common sense, which are not as likely to lead to subversive conclusions as using other discourses might' (p.13).

Along what lines does the discourse of social work get people to think? How do the texts and textual practices of social work align workers and clients, or workers and other professionals? How and where do they locate writers and readers in the webs of power created by discourse? How do social work discourse conventions function to make common sense? In the next section, in an effort to answer some of those questions, I offer reflections from my research into social work writing and consider samples of social workers speaking about recording.

The Discourse of Recording

For almost 20 years I have had a fascination with social work recording. I have examined texts and interviewed workers in agencies, hospitals, treatment centers, and group homes. I have spoken to educators and students in schools of social work, and followed students into their field placements and first jobs. I have interviewed supervisors and tape-recorded their interactions with students. In an effort to capture something of their composing process, I have given tape recorders to workers and asked them to write their records out loud.

Initially, I was merely curious about how workplace texts were created, and whether university writing instruction was adequate preparation for that task. As a teacher of writing and literacy researcher, I wanted to know how then-current theories of the writing process matched the realities of workplace writing; the choice of social work as the field of study was largely a matter of convenience.

What I discovered about professional writing in social work has given me a career full of speculation and investigation (see, for example, Paré, 1993 and 2000; Paré and Szewello, 1995). In brief, I discovered a profession in which writing played a central and powerful role, but was rarely and almost never critically discussed. Workers complained about writing, of course, often and vociferously, but at the time (mid-1980s) there was little in the professional or scholarly literature about the role and effect of writing in social work. There were articles and books on how to record more effectively, efficiently, objectively, or scientifically – that is, on how to 'improve' recording – but almost nothing on how recording might shape practice, produce tensions between workers and clients, create and obscure inequities, or otherwise have a decisive influence on the nature and dynamics of social work.[7]

Even the term 'recording' seemed naïve, at best. After all, texts do not capture individuals and events with anything like the detachment of a video or tape recorder. As Hanks (1987) notes, 'Even would-be realist description is at best selective, a refraction of what it claims to portray' (p.671). Clearly, when producing professional documents, social workers do more than record: they select, arrange, interpret, imply, hypothesize, infer, categorize, simplify, and on and on. They do not merely relay information, they *create* re-presentations.

Moreover, for someone trained to ask questions about writing, as I was, the social work profession appeared to have no shortage of contradictions, conflicts, and paradoxes related to writing. Documents were *about* clients, but not *for* them. Many documents were archived immediately and never consulted. In some settings – hospitals, for instance – social work texts were ignored or under-valued by other professionals. Custom, law, and codes of ethics required workers to be dispassionate, objective, and unbiased, but workers reported that the most useful records were often filled with intuition, hunch, speculation, and interpretation.

One phenomenon I noted (an example of which is described in Paré, 1993) vividly illustrated the effect of regular documentary practices on the creation of a communal common sense. That phenomenon might be called 'the self-fulfilling text.' For example, the first section of many social work documents asks for 'presenting problem.' The effect of this is described by Margolin (1997):

> Every case example begins with a pressing problem or series of problems and maladjustments that justifies social work's involvement at the very moment that it diminishes and stigmatizes the client. In fact, it is by describing clients in terms of their problems that the social work invitation is accomplished in the first place (p.73).

Before the client even walks into the worker's office, the record and its opening section exist as discourse spaces to be filled. The worker, used to writing the record and anticipating its requirements, *sees* the client immediately in terms of problems. In the future, other workers, reading the completed text in advance of meeting the client – again, a regular documentary practice – experience the client first as a problem. As Dorothy Smith (1974) explains, 'Socially organized practices of reporting and recording work upon what actually happens or has happened to create a reality in documentary form, and though they are decisive to its character, their traces are not visible in it' (p.257). So, for example, because frequently-required official records demand particular information, circulate to predictable readers, and lead to a finite, predetermined list of outcomes (e.g., admission, transfer, incarceration, referral), workers are predisposed to ask certain questions of clients, to look for particular behaviours and attitudes, to expect typification; in other words, patterns in recording lead workers to experience and create patterns in the people and events about which they write.

In addition, each repeated document places the worker-writers in particular relationships to readers, to clients, and to the ideas and attitudes being expressed. According to de Montigny (1995), 'The text is a mask concealing the embodied speaker who utters this or that claim. Through the text, social workers can promote their claims as though these were the universal wisdom of the profession in general' (p.64). Early in my research, I became troubled by this effect of recording on students and new practitioners. In the following interview except, a student (St) attempts to describe this professional persona:

> St: ...the tone of your writing and the way in which you say something... can reflect your emotions and your feelings about a certain person. And you have to be very careful to be unbiased and unjudgemental.
> R: Why?
> St: Why? It's professional, and I think it's about learning to separate yourself and that's been a very hard lesson to learn. It's that you cannot let yourself get emotionally attached or involved with your clients; and there has to be a point where you remove yourself... from becoming involved in their problems and sympathizing with them. You can sympathize with them, but no, wait. You can empathize with them, but you cannot sympathize with them. You have to harden yourself to some degree.

As Davies and Collings (this volume) might ask, where is there room for the worker's and client's emotions in this model of professional practice? Will this student be able to explore her own feelings 'as a source of creative insight,' as Davies and Collings encourage? Her belief that separating herself and remaining emotionally unattached suggests otherwise. 'The professional self is a fractured self,' de Montigny says, 'a piece of the self exchanged for a salary, and once exchanged it finds 'itself' a participant in production guided and directed by commands, forms of order, relevancies, and discourses that transcend the spheres of immediate experience' (p.14). This process of fracturing the self is dramatically illustrated in the following excerpt from a conversation about recording between a supervisor (Su) and her student (St):

> Su: Now, when we write as social workers in a dossier, we kind of depersonalize it as opposed to taking 'I'; and we use 'the worker' or 'the social worker.'...
> St: It has to be impersonalized as in 'the worker,' even if it's you, you have to say 'the worker'?
> Su: That's right. So you wrote here, 'I contacted.' You want to see it's coming from the worker, not you as Michael, but you as the worker. So when I'm sometimes in 'intake' and [working] as the screener, I write in my Intake Notes 'the screener inquired about'... So it becomes less personal. You begin to put yourself into the role of the worker, not 'I, Michael'... [I]t's a headset; it's a beginning. And even in your evaluations, when we use the global evaluations, the bio-psycho-social, the same thing: as opposed to 'I,' it's 'worker,' and when we do a CTMSP for

placement for long-term care, 'the worker.' So it positions us, I think. It's not me, it's my role; and I'm in the role of a professional doing this job...
St: So in the notes all the 'I's – 'I did this, I did that' – should be eliminated; and just 'worker' and it has to be like impersonal.
Su: Impersonal yet you're identifying yourself professionally. It's not 'I,' a regular person going into somebody's dossier, but it's in the capacity of a professional...

Here the professional newcomer is introduced to regular textual practice and the 'headset' it promotes. At one level, the moment is trivial: from the English lexicon of words that could be used to symbolize the 'self,' the student is instructed to select 'worker' over 'I.' The implications, however, are profound, as the student exchanges himself for a professional role (see Davies and Collings, this volume, for further discussion of this phenomenon). In another setting, a veteran worker told me that 'the 'I' in the record is not the same 'I' that sits at home on the couch, eating a hamburger, and watching T.V.'

The professional role raises the worker above the contradictions, inconsistencies, and weaknesses of a given individual into the pure realm of professional rationality. Gerald de Montigny (1995) again: 'For a professional's claims to be heard as warranted, simultaneously requires a skilful self-negation and constitution of an abstract organizational standpoint' (p.150). In narrative terms, the writer becomes omniscient: not an actor or character, but an observer outside and above the action. Hydén (1997) calls this 'the view from nowhere... a story told by an implicit narrator who is all-embracing and all-knowing. In this way, a specific effect is produced, namely, the impression of objectivity and impersonal professionalism' (p.259).

More than a disembodied voice is required, however, to pull off this epistemological sleight of hand – a trick in which knowledge floats free from an individual and becomes common sense. 'Objectivity' is also necessary, that untainted view of the world that relies on facts, not bias or personal opinion. But beyond such measurable or observable data as age, weight, hair color, and telephone number – and even some of those might not be what they seem – what human behaviors or qualities might be objectively described? In the next excerpt, a supervisor encourages a student to avoid subjective judgments:

Su: ...I have a hard time when I read assessments and I read something about 'Mrs. T. is a 56 year old extremely attractive woman.' Now to the worker she might be attractive, to another worker the person might not be attractive. That's very subjective... They could say 'She's well-groomed.' Which indicates she maintains herself well, but I do not care if she's attractive or not. That's not objective.

Common sense allows us to see attractiveness as a relative quality, in the eye of the beholder, as it were, while we hold grooming to be universal – a quality that can be safely judged without the influence of our age, or class, or race, or ethnicity. This hunger for an uninfluenced perspective is understandable, of course, especially in a world where the discourses of science hold such sway, and where social workers are held accountable at every turn. Evidence-based practice would not be possible, after all, if evidence could be rejected on the grounds that it was merely opinion or personal bias. As a result, faced with the need to reduce ambiguity and increase certainty and control – the demand of contemporary social work, as described by Nigel Parton (this volume) – the practitioner seeks to 'find' hard evidence.

But what evidence does a worker select for reporting, and for what ends? Of all that *could* be said about an individual or about a situation, what facts or features will the worker choose to report? And how will readers make sense of that report? In Bakhtin's lovely phrase, 'The word in language is half someone else's' (1981, p.293); so, what will readers bring to their half of the meaning that results from a text?

Resisting Dominant Discourses

At the start of this chapter, I quoted some new workers responding to questions about how they had learned to write the social work documents required in their workplaces. As I have discovered over many years, the content and method of the lessons are remarkably similar from place to place and worker to worker (see Paré and Szewello, 1995). New workers are coached by more veteran workers. The teaching-learning process follows a predictable pattern: new workers are encouraged to read the records of other, more experienced colleagues; they draft required documents, and sit with their supervising colleague to get feedback; they often receive multiple, detailed explanations about what to say and what not to say, but rarely an accompanying explanation for why it should be that way, or how it came to be; their first texts either work – that is, do what they were supposed to do – or they get further feedback in the form of a judge's rebuke, the loss of a client's trust, a manager's criticism, and so on. Failure to follow the community's standards can be serious, and so adherence is the norm.

Elsewhere (Paré, 2000; 2002), I have considered the implications of that slide into professional literacy, and I have argued that educators and critical community old-timers must help students and new practitioners resist the transformation that unthinking participation in a discourse can cause. It is not reasonable or realistic, perhaps, to coach new social workers to reject or radically revise an institution's documentary practices and products, since that might lead to serious consequences for the individual worker, but raising critical consciousness is possible.

To help newcomers develop a questioning eye and ear where language is concerned, teachers and veteran workers can draw their attention to the nature and purpose of particular texts, to their uses and consequences, to their history and readership.[8] Certain key questions focus that process – questions that bring us back to the start of this chapter and the call for a critical literacy. For example: What kind of language does a text employ? Is it a specialized language for a closed community of fellow specialists – that is, a language full of jargon and technical terminology – or is it plain language that is easily understood by the client or layperson? Is the writer present in the text as 'I,' or does the writer disappear into a faceless professional voice? Social work documentation began as narrative – as the detailed telling of people's stories – a style and approach that takes time and raises issues of 'subjectivity' and relevance. Currently, a different type of language is favored, one closer to scientific discourse, supposedly more objective, and focused on details, 'evidence,' and signs of dysfunction.

What is the physical make-up of the text? All regularized institutional documents call for particular content in a more or less standard sequence. What information is demanded and in what order? Why? Since most texts are read from front to back, it is worth considering the initial, sequential, and cumulative effects of the text's component pieces. What information do readers first receive, and what attitudes or responses might it engender? How does the subsequent division and delivery of information influence readers?

Who will read the text, how, and why? It is worth noting here that reading is hard work, and is not the mere absorption of information; rather, it is an active process of making meaning from the text, and the reader's purpose in reading – as well as her/his professional role, attitudes, and so on – will determine the 'meaning' drawn from the text. A lawyer will read a social worker's court report very differently from a judge, a parent, a nurse, or a psychologist. In addition, since most social work documents have multiple readers, questions about inter-reader relations arise: how will a particular text affect a client's relationship to his mother, a worker's status *vis à vis* the judge, the doctor's treatment of a child?

Why is the document produced? As social workers are subjected to greater and greater accountability and surveillance, it is worth considering the reasons for any given text. Is there a legal requirement? Is it archived, and, if so, why? (Into what situation might a filed text re-appear?) As I note above, the mere repetition of standardized texts produces a sense of normalcy or common sense, but often the original or evolved purpose of a text is unexamined. Increasingly, although they ostensibly respond to the immediate concerns of clients and workers, textual practices actually serve institutional purposes: they anticipate an unpleasant future, and protect the institution and/or worker from legal, political, or public relations problems.

What actions result from a particular document? How will clients' and workers' lives and relations be influenced and changed? Again, the immediate and institutional goals of the text – the need, for example, to record a specific decision – may mask the longer-term effects of the text on the client's life.

Many other questions might be posed: what is the history of the document? Can it be altered? How much, and by whom? How do veteran workers feel about it? And so on. Once language and the texts fashioned from it are seen to be human inventions, it is possible to begin a critical interrogation of documentary practices; once started, it is difficult to stop.

Workers must often practice resistance against the oppressive effects of language alone, since texts are usually single-authored, but there are ways to generate a more public attention to the issues raised in this chapter. First, during professional schooling, the role of language in the creation of professional roles and relationships can be discussed, as can the deeper link between language and 'reality.' Some years ago, when I read through the university calendar descriptions of all Canadian B.S.W programs, I did not find a single course devoted to writing or to the significant place of language in social work practice. Second, workplace consideration of professional literacy might be sparked by the formation of recording committees – groups of workers who critically address the role and influence of workplace documents, and consider as well the discursive relations with allied professionals (do doctors read social work records? how might workers deal with rules governing admissibility of evidence in court reports?, etc.).

As Jan Fook notes in her chapter in this volume, critical reflection 'can provide a means of reconstructing, and thus changing, the ways in which individuals perceive and relate to their social worlds.' A critical reflection on language holds the possibility of enormous and fundamental change.

Notes

[1] 'The ownership and appropriation of the means of production are central to Marx's analysis of industrial conditions. What he could not have foreseen is that under the conditions of fast capitalism the means of production and modes of information have become the nexus of social relations and power' (Luke and Freebody, 1997, 11). It is not enough to control the tools; one must also control the signs.

[2] For some people, thinking of language as a technology diminishes it by reducing it to a mechanism. But, if we are to consider the relationship between language and agency, we must acknowledge the human invention of language. I think of it as an organic technology, a soft machine that grows and adapts and forms to fit the infinite variety of human purpose.

[3] Of course, the reverse is also true, as demonstrated by Chomsky's famous sentence: 'Colorless green ideas sleep furiously.' We know it is grammatically and syntactically 'correct,' even though it makes no sense; that is, inappropriate lexical items have been placed in the appropriate relationships and sequence.

[4] You may recall that some words are onomatopoeic – that is, they supposedly sound like what they represent (*splash*, *bang*, and *thud* are onomatopoeic). But, as anyone who has read comic books in another language · knows, even this apparently more direct relationship between sign and referent is local: things that *click* in English may *clac* in French.

[5] For the curious, an interesting discussion of this can be found in Hartwell (1985). Consider, for example, this string of words: five, Spanish, women, the, old. For those words to make any sense, in what order would they have to be placed? Would other speakers of English agree with you? What rule are you following? How do you know the rule?

[6] Foucault (1972) says that 'in every society the production of discourse is at once controlled, selected, organized and redistributed according to a certain number of procedures, whose role is to avert its powers and its dangers, to cope with chance events, to evade its ponderous, awesome materiality' (216).

[7] This near-silence on the role of recording has ended, fortunately, and there are now quite a number of critical perspectives on recording (e.g., Parton, 1991; de Montigny, 1995; Margolin, 1997).

8   New workers often bring to the workplace a critical perspective gained in their professional education, and can sometimes raise the issues discussed here. But they are frequently too vulnerable as newcomers to pose difficult or sensitive questions, and require the support of more experienced workers.

References

Bakhtin, M.M. (1981), *The dialogic imagination* (M. Holquist, ed., and C. Emerson and M. Holquist, trans.), University of Texas Press, Austin.

Berlin, J. (1996), *Rhetorics, Poetics, and Culture: Refiguring College English Studies*, National Council of Teachers of English, Urbana.

Britton, J. (1980), 'Shaping at the point of utterance', in A. Freedman and I. Pringle (eds.), *Reinventing the Rhetorical Tradition*, Canadian Council of Teachers of English, Ottawa, pp. 61-65.

Coe, R., Lingard, L., and Teslenko, T. (eds.) (2002), *The Rhetoric and Ideology of Genre*, Hampton Press, Creskill.

de Montigny, G. (1995), *Social Working: An Ethnography of Front Line Practice*, University of Toronto Press, Toronto.

Dias, P., Freedman, A., Medway, P., and Paré, A. (1999), *Worlds Apart: Writing and Acting in Academic and Workplace Contexts*, Erlbaum, Mahwah.

Faigley, L. (1992), *Fragments of Rationality: Postmodernism and the Subject of Composition*, University of Pittsburgh Press, Pittsburgh.

Fairclough, N. (1992), *Discourse and Social Change*, Polity Press, Cambridge.

Fairclough, N. (1995), *Critical Discourse Analysis: The Critical Study of Language*, Longman, London.

Foucault, M. (1972), *The Archaeology of Knowledge and the Discourse on Language*. (A.M. Sheridan Smith, trans.), Pantheon Books, New York.

Freedman, A. and Medway, P. (eds.) (1994), *Genre and the New Rhetoric*, Taylor and Francis, London.

Gee, J.P. (1996), *Social Linguistics and Literacies: Ideology in discourses*, (second edition), Falmer Press, London.

Gee, J.P. (2001), 'Quality, science, and the lifeworld: The alignment of business and education', in P. Freebody, S. Muspratt and B. Dwyer (eds.), *Difference, Silence, and Textual Practice*, Hampton Press, Cresskill, pp. 359-382.

Hanks, W.F. (1987), 'Discourse genres in a theory of practice', *American Ethnologist*, Vol. 14.4, pp. 668-692.

Hartwell, P. (1985), 'Grammar, grammars, and the teaching of grammar', *College English*, Vol. 47.2, pp. 105-127.

Hydén, L.C. (1997), 'The institutional narrative as drama', in B.L. Gunnarsson, P. Linnell, and B. Nordberg (eds.), *The Construction of Professional Discourse*, Longman, New York, pp. 245-264.

Lemke, J. (1995), *Textual Politics: Discourse and Social Dynamics*, Taylor and Francis, London.

Luke, A. and Freebody, P. (1997), 'Critical literacy and the question of normativity: An introduction', in S. Muspratt, A. Luke and P. Freebody (eds.), *Constructing Critical Literacies*, Hampton Press, Cresskill, pp. 1-18.

Margolin, L. (1997), *Under the Cover of Kindness: The Invention of Social Work*, University Press of Virginia, Charlottesville.

Miller, C. (1984), 'Genre as social action', *Quarterly Journal of Speech*, Vol. 70, pp. 151-167.

Paré, A. (1993), 'Discourse regulations and the production of knowledge', in R. Spilka (ed.), *Writing in the Workplace: New Research Perspectives*, Southern Illinois University Press, Carbondale, pp. 111-123.

Paré, A. (2000), 'Writing as a way into social work: Genre sets, genre systems, and distributed cognition', in P. Dias and A. Paré (eds.), *Transitions: Writing in Academic and Workplace Settings*, Hampton Press, Cresskill, pp. 145-166.

Paré, A. (2002), 'Genre and identity: Individuals, institutions, and identity', in R. Coe, L. Lingard, and T. Teslenko (eds.), *The Rhetoric and Ideology of Genre*, Hampton Press, Cresskill, pp. 57-71.

Paré, A. and Szewello, H. (1995), 'Social work writing: Learning by doing', in G. Rogers (ed.), *Social work Field Education: Views and Visions*, Kendell/Hunt Publishing, Dubuque, pp. 164-173.

Parton, N. (1991), *Governing the Family: Child Care, Child Protection and the State*, Macmillan/Palgrave, Basingstoke.

Pinker, S. (1994), *The Language Instinct*, William Morrow and Company, New York.

Smith, D. (1974), 'The social construction of documentary reality', *Sociological Inquiry*, Vol. 44, pp. 257-268.

Williams, R. (1976), *Keywords: A Vocabulary of Culture and Society*, Oxford University Press, New York.

Chapter 7

The Reprofessionalization of Social Work: Collaborative Approaches for Achieving Professional Recognition[*]

Karen Healy and Gabrielle Meagher

Introduction

Contemporary practice theories from critical reflexive to evidence-based practice approaches assume that social workers have certain capacities, including the capacity to critically reflect, to analyze, to use and build practice relevant knowledge, to negotiate and to use their context critically and creatively (see Cheetham et al., 1996; Fook, 1996; Healy, K. 2000; Parton and O'Byrne, 2000; Lymbery, 2001; Meagher, 2002a and 2002b). These practice projects also assume that these capacities are, or at least should be, recognized and supported in human services organizations through, for example, supervision focused on the development of practice knowledge and skills, ongoing professional learning opportunities and scope for professional discretion especially for advanced and experienced practitioners. Unfortunately, in many contexts of human services work, such support and recognition are being withdrawn.

We contend that the de-professionalization of social services industries poses a major threat to high quality social work practice. Research on improving the quality of social work practice, whether from reflective or evidence based traditions, has focused primarily on service delivery policy and practice processes; we suggest that the hitherto relatively neglected broader institutional context of social work practice, including its industrial and cultural dimensions, are also of profound importance to the quality of social services. We aim to shift analytical focus here away from the practice interface to the institutional context of social service work, and to highlight social service providers as a constituency whose interests are deserving of attention.

Our specific purpose in this paper is to suggest pathways for social workers to collectively achieve recognition of social work as a professional practice. We will

[*] Acknowledgment: The authors thank Oxford University Press for permission to reproduce this article, which has previously appeared in the British Journal of Social Work, 2004, volume 34(2).

begin by defining what we mean by de-professionalization and examine how this process is reshaping social services work in western English speaking countries. Secondly, we will critically analyze factors from outside and within the profession contributing to de-professionalization. Thirdly, we will compare how professional associations and unions are responding to the emerging demands for industrial and cultural recognition of social services work as professional practice. Finally, we will consider future directions for collaborative re-professionalization of social work practice.

What Do We Mean by 'De-professionalization'?

We contend that, despite the rhetoric of quality service now pervading public policy, social services work is being de-professionalized around the English-speaking world,[1] and that, unless halted, de-professionalization will continue to affect adversely the capacity of human service organizations to deliver effective services. We use the term de-professionalization to refer, firstly, to the fragmentation and routinization of social work and the concomitant loss of opportunities for the exercise of creativity, reflexivity and discretion in direct practice. Evidence from the US suggests that work routinization, particularly the loss of discretionary decision-making power, is both cause and effect of the large scale retreat of professional workers from public welfare agencies (Gibelman and Schervish, 1996). Secondly, we use the term to refer to the relative decline in professional categories of social service employment. Dominelli and Hoogvelt link these two processes thus:

> The delivery of services which have previously been of a complex processual character have become fragmented and reduced to discretely identified part of empirically stated competencies and quantifiable indicators... [this] permits complex social work tasks to be undertaken by less highly qualified practitioners at lower rates of pay (1996, p.52).

A third form of de-professionalization is the underemployment of professional social workers that find employment in para-professional positions for which their qualifications are neither required nor fully utilized.

We discern at least two paths towards de-professionalization. In Australia, Britain and Canada there is evidence of the de-professionalization of social services work as a 'universal' trend, i.e., as a shift affecting the majority of social service workers. Research in these countries indicates an erosion of opportunities for professional discretion at the practice front and the loss of workplace conditions that enable professional development and recognition (Harris, 1998; Healy, 1998; McDonald, 1999; Harris and McDonald, 2000; Jones, 2001; Orme, 2001; Stephenson, 2001). In Britain, Harris observes that, as a result of public sector reforms, 'social work as an occupation will remain a more heavily constrained part of the state's welfare apparatus than it was in the 1970s and early

1980s' (1998, p.859; Ayre, 2001, pp.892-897; Jones, 2001). Research on the Canadian social services sector suggests that: 'Employment opportunities are good but employment conditions are increasingly taxing and professional recognition is less robust than it has been' (Stephenson, 2001, p.3).

The Australian social services labor force provides startling evidence of the trend towards a relative decline in the presence of professional social workers in the human services field. Table 1 shows the disproportionate growth of para-professional employment compared to professional employment in social service occupations.

Table 1 Growth in four social service occupations, Australia 1996-2001

Occupation	1996	2001	Percentage increase
Social workers	7,193	9,125	27
Community workers	15,804	17,113	8
Welfare workers	6,220	8,992	45
Welfare associate professionals	13,231	18,237	38

Source: Australian Bureau of Statistics, Census of Population and Housing, 1996, 2001.

Table 1 shows that the categories of welfare worker and welfare associate professional grew at substantially greater rates than either social worker or community worker categories. According the hierarchical Australian Standard Classification of Occupations used to code the Census data, welfare workers and welfare associate professionals have technical or life experience qualifications rather than the university level qualifications required by social workers and community workers. Faster growth of employment in para-professional categories employment results in de-professionalization: in 1996 there 118 professional workers for every 100 paraprofessional workers; in 2001 there were 96 professionals for every 100 para-professionals. Cutting across this trend is evidence that professionally qualified human services workers are employed in para-professional categories. For example, qualitative research on the employment destinations of new social work graduates in Victoria (Australia) showed that many are employed in positions not requiring professional qualifications (with generic titles such as youth worker or support worker) because of a lack of professional employment opportunities (Hawkins et al., 2000).

By contrast, in the United States, where professional associations have achieved some recognition of social work as a professional activity, de-professionalization has selectively affected the social services labor force. Gibelman and Schervish (1996, p.121) report that over the past 30 years there has been a 'gradual but steady defection of social workers from the public sector'. Declassification of professional social work positions in public welfare agencies has opened these positions to a broad range of workers and has led to the evacuation of professional workers from state social work practice. Public welfare agencies in the US employ a low proportion of professional workers, and the work is highly routinized, limiting opportunities for professional development. Substantial salary increases for workers in the public welfare agencies have failed to attract professional workers, suggesting that factors in addition to remuneration are important to them (Gibelman and Schervish, 1996, p.118). Instead, professional social workers have tended to congregate in non-government agencies and private practice, particularly in mental health, at least partly because these contexts offer greater professional recognition and autonomy (Gibelman and Schervish, 1996).

Why Has De-professionalization Occurred?

Public policy changes are contributing to the reframing of social services work, especially public welfare work, as a non-professional activity. The most significant policy changes include the trend towards privatization of public services. Privatization refers to the shift of responsibility for service delivery from government to non-government agencies, even though, in the United Kingdom and Australia, governments retain a significant role as a funder of public services (Dominelli and Hoogvelt, 1996, p.49; Healy, 1998; Harris and McDonald, 2000). The process of privatization is itself contentious in the human services. It has been suggested that new public management techniques accompanying privatization have led to increased accountability of social services through linking funding to service outputs and outcomes (Knapp, Wistow, Forder and Hardy, 1994). However, as many commentators point out, the process of privatization, particularly the separation of purchaser and provider roles, involves a distancing of government from its citizens and, in the case of human services, affects the most disadvantaged citizens (Dow, 1999; Healy, 1998).

A second factor in the de-professionalization of human services is the de-regulation of human services positions; manifest as declining employment opportunities for specific professional workers, such as 'social workers' and 'psychologists,' and an increase in 'generic' human service positions, such as 'mental health worker' and 'child protection worker' (see also Franklin and Eu, 1996; Stephenson, 2001). Competition for professional positions is increasingly based on demonstrated competency in a specific field of practice, rather than possession of a specific professional background (Franklin and Eu, 1996). Although competency based approaches have the advantage of focusing on workers' field-based knowledge and experience, they are not necessarily consistent with the enactment of social work as a thoughtful, analytic and creative activity. Competency based approaches do not promote the professional development of the worker independent of their specific workplace, and importantly, do not enhance workers' capacities to critically evaluate accepted workplace practices (Dominelli and Hoogvelt, 1996).

Privatization has facilitated the deregulation of human services work, as, often, private sector providers face less stringent employment and service delivery regulation than public sector agencies. Private organizations have greater scope than public sector agencies to blur boundaries between professional and non-professional work as well as paid and unpaid work. For example, Dominelli and Hoogvelt have observed that in residential homes: 'private sector employers have not been prevented from employing new non-social work staff to do social work tasks at lower rates of pay, thereby driving down general wage levels' (1996, p.52). More concerning still is the potential in a deregulated environment for non-government agencies to circumvent hard won industrial and legal protections for service workers and service users. For example, in Australia, public protest has emerged in response to the allocation of services funding to some charities even though their exemption from parts of anti-discrimination legislation allows them to discriminate against both potential employees and service users whose religious or sexual orientation do not conform with agency policy.

De-professionalization of human services work has been accompanied by the fragmentation of management and service delivery processes. New public management reforms have fostered the rise of 'content free' management, so that, increasingly, managers with little knowledge of service delivery issues make key decisions about the management and delivery of social services. Evidence from the US and Australia suggests that social service professionals are losing management positions in social service organizations to 'traditional' professionals from accountancy, law, and business management (Healy, K. 2002; Healy, J. 1998; Martin and Healy, 1993; Patti, 2000). The increased monitoring of social work practice has occurred concomitantly with changed understandings of the purpose of social work. Parton (1996, p.6) contends that social work practice has shifted from a focus on needs to the 'assessment and management of risk'.

Service workers are also ambivalent about the erosion of the professional status of human services work; viewing status and economic rewards as unrelated to, if not opposed to, quality of service. In research with social services workers in the Australian non-profit sector, Onyx and McLean found that:

> The classic notion of career as consistent with progress upward toward greater prestige, power, and financial reward is simply inapplicable to the majority of respondents. Prestige, salary, and secure tenure were very low priorities when it came to applying for a particular position... there was a very strong commitment to making the world a better place, either by helping other disadvantaged people or by working toward social change at a broader level (1996, p.304).

Our own research shows that workers apparently accept lack of professional recognition and poor economic reward as an inevitable feature of social services work (Healy and Meagher, 2001), allowing funding bodies and employing organizations to take advantage of sexist cultural assumptions that care work is naturally 'women's work', and that female workers do not need an independent living wage.

In addition, the nature of social services work can mitigate workers' willingness to improve their workplace conditions. Social service workers have regular contact with profoundly disadvantaged and often distressed people. This contact can lead social service workers to underrate their own workplace disadvantages, and thus give too little attention to the benefits for both workers and service users arising from improvements in the labor force and workplace conditions.

Another reason for the lack of unified commitment to improving the cultural and industrial recognition of human services work as professional activity is the pervasive misrecognition within the profession about the nature and lived experience of social services work. For example, critical academic discourse represents social workers as powerful middle class professionals, akin in status to the traditional professions of medicine, law and engineering (Healy, K. 2000, p.5). In particular, critical social workers' commitment to this caricature of professional social workers, limits our capacity to grapple with the changing conditions of human service practice and to contribute to the collective revitalization of professional social work. As Jones states:

> I am coming to the conclusion that the silence of the commentators, especially in the academy, says much about the ways in which state social work has changed in the past 30 years. It comes over to me at least as a traumatized, even defeated occupation which has lost any sense of itself (2001, p.550).

Third, there is a small but vocal group within the profession who actively oppose attempts to improve the industrial and cultural recognition of social services work. This group, which we refer to as 'abolitionists', actively opposes the quest for professional recognition for social services work. Abolitionists view the pursuit of economic reward and professional recognition for social services work as elitist and antithetical to the genuine needs of those service users (Bamford, 1990; Illich, 1977; Phillips, 1999). For example, in Canada, the Social Work Reform Group formed in the late 1980s to resist the professional registration of social workers in Ontario (Phillips, 1999). Similarly, in Australia, a founding member of the Australian Social Welfare Union (now amalgamated with the Australian Services Union) observed that 'Most community workers saw the maintenance of their (often radically orientated) organizations, rather than the maintenance of their own salaries and conditions as their major priority and many saw the two as mutually exclusive concerns' (Hayes, 1992, p.183).

We contend that in a context of mass de-professionalization of social services work, abolitionist perspectives are deeply problematic and untenable as a platform to improve the conditions of professional social work practice in this era. Our major objection to this position is its apparent lack of concern with the pervasive gender inequality in the social services sector. Direct social service practice is an overwhelmingly female domain and de-professionalization is increasing the proportion of women from working class and minority backgrounds in the social services labor force. Calls to abandon the project of professionalization ignore the extent to which these workers' knowledge claims are already marginalized through gender, class, and race based discrimination.

Second, despite their radical intent, abolitionist perspectives are consistent with neo-liberal imperatives suggesting that professional knowledge and skill is unnecessary, perhaps even inconsistent with good social services practice. Abolitionists' rejection of professional knowledge is predicated on an excessively narrow approach to expertise, which fails to recognize the unique combination of formal and informal knowledge that advanced social service practitioners demonstrate (see Fook, Ryan and Hawkins, 2000). This approach also fails to acknowledge possibilities for the emancipatory use of expertise, where practitioners exercise formal knowledge in the interests of service users (Leonard, 1996).

The abolitionist position fails to recognize the connection between social workers and social services interests in a highly professionalized and well organized social services labor force. We contend that a poorly trained and inadequately supported human services labor force is not well placed to enact social work as a thoughtful, analytic and creative activity. Moreover, a de-professionalized and de-skilled workforce is not in a good position to defend the interest of service users, especially when these interests deviate from prevailing organizational and policy dictates.

Achieving Recognition: Options for Collective Action

We believe that social workers must organize collectively to re-professionalize social work practice, particularly in public welfare agencies. Collective responses are important for two reasons. First, strong opposition is likely: government funders and service delivery agencies benefit substantially from social service workers' lack of organized resistance to their poor conditions. Only concerted collective action can address these vested interests. Second, individual responses such as individual skill enhancement or promotion to positions of power do little to remedy the extensive 'structural' de-professionalization of social services of recent decades.

In this section, we discuss the transitions in two collaborative strategies for re-professionalizing social services work. The strategies of classical professionalization and the other of classical unionism union organizations are well established in the social services field. These strategies lie at opposite ends of a spectrum, with one side promoting an exclusive approach to achieving re-professionalization and other seeking to align social service workers struggles with those of semi- and non-professional service workers. In recent years, these modes of organizing have moved closer together, as new forms of professionalism and unionism have evolved from 'classical' forms. This shift is represented diagrammatically in the continuum in Figure 1.

Figure 1 A continuum of collective options for reprofessionalization

$\rightarrow$ $\leftarrow$

●--●

| Classical | New | | New Political | Classical |
| Professionalism | Professionalism | Unionism | Unionism | |

We contend that classical pathways to professionalization have emphasized recognition of the distinctive expertise of social service workers, while by contrast, classical unionism approaches have tended to focus on experiential knowledge, such as knowledge gained in specific workplaces or through lived experience. In the remainder of the paper we outline classical professionalization and classical union strategies and then consider how new developments in these strategies are leading to convergences between them.

'Classical' Professionalization

'Classical' professionalization strategies are aimed at achieving occupational closure by asserting that the expertise of a specific professional group is both exclusive to that group and essential to the performance of specific occupational duties. This strategy's institutional expression is the professional association, which is the vehicle used by the elite professions to achieve and sustain occupational closure. These associations pursue what they see as the proper remuneration and status recognition of their members' distinctive knowledge and skills.

Professional associations for social workers are active in most countries where social workers practice. However, these associations have had variable success in achieving occupational closure for social workers. In Australia, for example, social work remains an unregistered profession, while in Britain, there have been recent moves towards accreditation of the profession (Orme, 2001). In both countries, the title 'social worker' is not limited to those holding professional social work qualifications, and few social service positions are reserved exclusively for professional social workers.

In addition, the relational character of much direct social work practice and the diverse organizational contexts in which such practices occur makes it difficult to define a unique area of expertise shared across the profession. The relational, practical and moral character of social service work is incompatible with the technical and rational ideals of conventional models of professional expertise (Davies, 1995; Stone, 2000). The diverse character of social work practices and their interface with a range of other specialties in counseling and public administration for instance, makes it difficult to assert distinctive knowledge claims. Moreover, professional associations also have limited capacity to assert claims for professional recognition and reward for members in the large bureaucratic service organizations that employ many social service workers. The declassification of social work positions discussed earlier further reduces this capacity.

Paradoxically, the pursuit of occupational closure by specific professional groups may itself create barriers to the re-professionalization of the social work field. Exclusionary strategies that elevate the interests of professional workers over those of the para-professionals and non-professionals who increasingly occupy social service roles breed resentment and are 'inconsistent with social work commitments to equality and democracy' (Bella, 1995, p.120).

Classical Unionism

Classical unionism lies at the other end of the spectrum to classic professionalization as a collective strategy for achieving occupational recognition. Classical unionism emphasizes the 'worker' identity of union members, and focuses on the pursuit of their interests. Unlike professional associations, for which professional development and growth are goals, unions exist for the purpose of bargaining with an employer (Raelin, 1989, p.103). Unions typically organize those in working class occupations, as well as administrative and professional workers – like nurses and social workers – employed mainly in bureaucratic organizations. In social services, as elsewhere, unions enable workers to bargain collectively for industrial protection, including coverage of individual rights and wage justice.

Although unions have been important in supporting the industrial rights of social service workers, there are practical, institutional, and strategic limits to the capacity of classical unionism to support the re-professionalization we advocate. One obstacle to the deployment of union based strategies lies in the diversity of practice contexts. Social service practitioners in English-speaking countries work in a broad range of government and non-government agencies and are covered by several unions. The fragmentation of workers across a range of workplaces and unions is a practical obstacle to unions defining and representing common worker interests.

The second obstacle is that conventional industrial relations institutions rely on skill recognition and wages bargaining strategies that overlook the less visible dimensions of care work such as relationship building and use of self (see Macdonald and Merrill, 2002). Social service workers pursuing their interests through trade unionism and the industrial relations system must employ a language that does not readily recognize much of the work they do (see Meagher, 1994). For example, in pursuing claims through industrial relations processes, many of the components of social services work must be described in concrete behavioral terms rather than emphasizing their relationship sustaining aspects.

Third, classical unionism's poor record in enhancing the economic and social status of women (Pocock, 1997, p.10) is also a strategic problem to be reckoned with, given the gender composition of the social services labor force. Research shows that women face a myriad of obstacles in having a voice at all in union organizations, let alone having the distinctive experiences and interests of women workers taken up (Higgins, 1996, p.175).

A fourth obstacle is the reluctance of many social service workers to participate in the oppositional tactics of classical unionism, such as strikes and pickets. In part, this is because professional workers 'are not necessarily convinced they must assume an adversarial role in advancing their cause' (Raelin 1989, p.104). But, also, the service orientation of many social service workers contributes to their reluctance to withdraw their labor, because they see this strategy as hurting service users more than employing organizations (Raelin, 1989; Schumacher, 1997).

A fifth obstacle lies in social workers' continuing commitment to the pursuit of professional status. Historically, social workers concerned with increasing the professional recognition of their practice have tended to distance themselves from trade union activity (Scanlon, 1999, p.591). More recently, Gibelman and Schervish argue that 'the emphasis of unions representing state, county, and municipal employees to promote on the basis of agency experience rather than professional education' (1996, p.121) has contributed significantly to the de-professionalization of human services. Some professional workers have expressed concern that while unions have had some success in bargaining for improved wages and material conditions of work, their activities have done little to halt the loss of professional autonomy and increased standardization of social services work (Raelin, 1989). Classical unionism is not well able to take account of the interests of different subgroups of social service workers, and so tends to reinforce rather than overcome problems of non-recognition of professional activity in this field.

A final obstacle is that, in much of the English-speaking world, classical unionism is itself apparently a movement in eclipse as rates of union membership decline. In the United Kingdom, the United States, and Australia, rates of union membership have fallen sharply in recent years; although in Canada they have remained relatively stable (ILO 1997, p. 6-8). In Britain and the United States, de-unionization is particularly significant because collective bargaining is restricted to union members in both countries (ILO 1997, p. 11). Changes in the institutions of industrial relations, particularly decentralization of wage bargaining arrangements are also inhibiting unions' capacity to represent workers' interests around the world (ILO 1997, p. 107).

Towards Collaborative Re-professionalization? The Convergence of the New Unionism and the New Professionalism

Classical approaches to professionalization and unionization of the social services labor force have focused on the promotion of sectional interests of specific occupational groups, such as 'social worker' and 'welfare para-professional'. In recent years, professional associations and union organized labor have moved closer together in their approaches to enhancing the cultural and industrial recognition of social services labor. The convergences point to some new directions for the collaborative re-professionalization of the social services workforce.

Within the professional social work literature, a new professionalism is being articulated, built on recognition of the potential for professional knowledge to be used in the interests of service users, while at the same time maintaining wariness towards elitist professional claims (Leonard, 1996; Healy, 2000; Lymberry, 2001). The new professionalism finds expression in forms of professional organization that recognizes distinctive expertise of professionals, whilst also providing opportunities for collaboration with other groups of service providers and service users. This can include opening membership of professional associations to those with relevant work experience through to professionals working as partners with service users in grassroots community support and advocacy bodies.

Similarly, in some English speaking countries and Scandinavian countries a new form of unionism is emerging that addresses some of the shortcomings of traditional unionism for enhancing the cultural recognition of social service practice. In recent years, unions representing social service workers have sought to achieve collaboration across semi-professional and professional groups and to enhance workers access to formal qualifications, including professional degrees. The 'new political unionism' (Higgins, 1996) or 'social movement unionism' (Bonacich, 1998) is exemplified in unions such as UNISON in the United Kingdom and the Swedish Municipal Workers Union, or Kommunal, both of which represent public service providers. The new unionism shifts beyond a primary concern with wage justice to the incorporation of pathways for increasing service providers' access to formal qualifications. Through its links to tertiary institutions, UNISON, for example, is able to offer members access to formal qualifications at discounted or no cost. Moreover, UNISON links its objective of ensuring service providers access to training opportunities with maintaining a high quality workforce (UNISON, 2001). Elsewhere, unions maintain strong links with professional organizations, rather than competing with them. The Norwegian Union of Social Educators and Social Workers, for example, is both a Trade Union Federation and a Professional Association, representing the economic interests as well as promoting the professional profile of Norwegian welfare workers.

Secondly, the new unionism does not oppose workers' and service users' interests, but rather highlights their shared interests in high quality service provision. Kommunal, the major union representing blue collar welfare workers in Sweden, maintains alliances not only with professional associations, such as the International Federation of Social Workers and with other public service and trade unions, but also with service users (The Swedish Municipal Workers Union, 2001). Indeed, Kommunal cites as one of its core objectives that 'everyone who requires welfare services shall receive them' (The Swedish Municipal Workers' Union, 2001). The new political unionism recognizes the separate interests of workers and service users while also seeking to redress injustices faced by both groups. Redressing both gender based inequities facing service users in the welfare arena and also recognizing the masculine bias of traditional trade unions, the new political unions align themselves to gender justice campaigns (Higgins, 1996; The Swedish Municipal Workers Union, 2001; UNISON, 2001).

Collaborative alliances can contribute to the professionalization of community services work by providing pathways for non-professional workers to increase their status and skills. In addition to links to tertiary education institutes, collaborative links across service provider groups, training bodies, and service provider peak organizations can be mobilized to develop and promote training programs that increase non-professional workers' formally recognized skills and to recognize better their informal skills. This may involve enhancing the links and exchanges between university and vocation training systems, to provide smooth and flexible routes into professional higher education for employed non-professional social service workers.

At the same time, collaborating parties can mobilize their collective strength to seek to influence government policy makers and funders to recognize the connection between the quality of the social services labor force and the quality of social services in program design, planning, and funding. This requires that the training opportunities, career paths, and remuneration of all social service workers all receive attention. This same collective strength can also be exercised in industrial relations institutions, to attempt as UNISON and Kommunal have done, to address the undervaluation of social services work.

Continuing Challenges in the Formation of Alliances

The shared interest of professional associations and new political unions in the industrial and cultural recognition of service provision as professional activity combined with the promotion of social justice for service users suggests grounds for the formal alliance between these associations to achieve the re-professionalization of social services work. However, to actualize these synergies, it is important to recognize any continuing tensions between stakeholders, especially professional and non-professional workers. The historical separation of trade unions and professional associations in English-speaking countries, and the consequent divergence in some key aspirations of the groups creates barriers to collaborative action in the present. Indeed, the history and culture of unionism in the English-speaking world may itself be a fetter on effective collaboration. The International Labor Organization contrasts the nature of unionism in the English-speaking countries and in continental Europe, particularly the Nordic countries:

> All workers' organizations try through collective bargaining, political pressure and sometimes participation in public or private bodies to defend and improve living conditions. Beyond this goal, their objectives may differ greatly. Traditionally enterprise-oriented, United States unions – and to a varying extent those of other English-speaking countries – have until quite recently sought above all to defend the immediate interests of their members. …in Europe, however, the unions have always sought to represent the workers as a whole, to go beyond labor relations issues and have an influence on the actual vision of society (1997, pp. 23-24).

The employment of social service workers in a broad range of government and non-government organizations and the representation of these workers among a myriad of unions and professional associations is a further obstacle to united action in English-speaking countries. Yet efforts at improving collaboration are both necessary and more time consuming than in more integrated industries, such as the Scandinavian examples.

There are other practical obstacles to collaborations involving a range of actors and organizations. Time, money, and effort are needed to secure working consensus on shared goals and strategies, detracting from resources available to do other work. Increased formalized competition within the sector under the new public management also challenges actors to manage their relationships in new ways, and they may find themselves partners in some contexts and competitors in others. Funding agencies and workers may also resist the loss of autonomy required in collaborative ventures. Many social service workers are motivated by their commitment to serve clients and by opportunities for interesting and varied work. Although collaborative strategies do not necessarily interfere with local responsiveness, they do require some loyalty by workers to shared visions or goals. These strategies can extend the scope of worker action, but they add another layer to the often complex arrangements between service organizations, service workers and service users.

Increased labor market competition and de-professionalization of the social services workforce have themselves exacerbated tensions among subgroups of social service workers. Rather than ignore or suppress these differences, we contend that their recognition, in particular, recognition of the value of different knowledge, could be used to unify the field, perhaps providing a range of pathways for increasing competency and professionalism in the social services labor force.

If, as we advocate, different groups are to work together to improve conditions, there is also a significant risk that the voice of formally qualified professionals, who, our re-professionalization thesis suggests, have reached the 'height' of formal professional qualification, will be privileged. The challenge will be to maintain the 'audibility' of the voices of all sections of the workforce; recognizing and rewarding experiential knowledge is critical to the success of collaborative re-professionalization. Here the character of exchanges between universities and the field are critical. Practice requirements for university appointment, and 'practical sabbaticals' for university educators are likely to be necessary to provide the knowledge and skills educators will need to genuinely contribute to – and learn from – the kinds of collaboration we endorse. The meaning of professionalism itself will change in the process.

For the sake of comprehensiveness, it is important to note that another model of collaboration has emerged recently in the form of 'partnerships' for service provision; indeed Miller and Ahmad report that 'Collaboration and partnerships between agencies, professions, and across sectors in the delivery of public services is now a major policy goal across both the developed and developing world' (2001, p. 1). The concepts of partnership and competition are the odd bedfellows at the center of the new public management (Meerabeau, 2001), and collaboration in this model is often required by legislation (Miller and Ahmad, 2001, p.1), rather than emerging out of the productive interactions of service providers and services users. Given that these partnership models are likely to be decreed, as it were, from the top down, and that they are intimately linked with the new public management techniques that are a key driver of de-professionalization, we are not confident that this model can further re-professionalization on its own. However, to the extent that participating in even these administered collaborations increases contact between relevant worker and user groups, these collaborations might be a 'seed bed' for the kinds of collaborations we propose.

Conclusion

Social service workers are subject to conflicting pressures that impact on their capacity to achieve wage justice and recognition of their work as a professional activity, and to maintain and improve service quality for service users. On one hand, over the past two decades there have been more opportunities for employment in this industry as caring work moves increasingly into the public sphere of the market and the state. On the other hand, social service workers must deal with increasing fiscal constraint and rapidly changing modes of public administration in the sector, and with the entrenched cultural devaluation of caring work. In this paper, we have examined how two models of professional associations and trade unions have moved from classical into new modes of collective action. We have argued for broad-based coalitions that bring together diverse groups within social services, that integrate strategies for industrial protection and professional recognition and that link service workers' and services users' interests in high quality service provision, while also recognizing workers as distinct stakeholders in the community services field.

Note

[1] With apologies to the Quebeçois, we use the term 'English-speaking world' to connote the United Kingdom, the United States, Australia, and Canada. As demonstrated by the frequent use of this term in comparative social policy research, these countries share significant aspects of their histories and cultures and so form a natural and distinctive (albeit loose) group for our purposes.

References

Australian Bureau of Statistics (1998), *Community Services 1995-96*, Cat: 8696.0, Commonwealth of Australia, Canberra.

Australian Bureau of Statistics (2001), *Community Services 1999-2000*, Cat: 8696.0, Commonwealth of Australia, Canberra.

Australian Institute of Health and Welfare (2001), *Health and Community Services Labour Force 1996*, AIHW Cat. No. HWL 19, AIHW (National Health Labour Force Series no. 19), Canberra.

Ayre, P. (2001), 'Child Protection and the Media: Lessons from the Last Three Decades', *British Journal of Social Work*, Vol. 31, pp. 887-901.

Bamford, T. (1990), *The Future of Social Work*, MacMillan, Basingstoke.

Bella, L. (1995), 'Gender and occupational closure in social work', in P. Taylor and C. Daly, *Gender Dilemmas in Social Work: Issues Affecting Women in the Profession*, Canadian Scholars' Press Inc., Toronto.

Bonacich, Edna (1998), 'Reflections on Union Activism', *Contemporary Sociology*, Vol. 27(2), pp. 129-132.

Cheetham, J., Fuller, R., McIvor, G., and Petch, A. (1996), *Evaluating Social Work Effectiveness*, Open University Press, Milton Keynes.

Davies, C. (1995), 'Competence versus Care? Gender and Caring Work Revisited', *Acta Sociologica*, Vol. 38, pp. 17-31.

Dominelli, L. and Hoogvelt, A. (1996), 'Globalization and the technocratization of social work', *Critical Social Policy*, Vol. 16(2), pp. 45-62.

Dow, G. (1999), 'Economic rationalism vs. the community: reflections on social democracy and state capacity', *Australian Journal of Social Issues*, Vol. 34(3), pp. 209-229.

Fook, J. (ed.) (1996), *The Reflective Researcher: Social Workers' Theories of Practice Research*, Allen and Unwin, Sydney.

Fook, J., Ryan, M. and Hawkins, L. (2000), *Professional Expertise: Practice, Theory and Education for Working with Uncertainty*, Whiting and Birch, London.

Franklin, J. and Eu, K. (1996), 'Comparative employment opportunities for social workers', *Australian Social Work*, Vol. 49(1), pp. 11-18.

Gibelman, M. and Schervish, P. (1996), 'Social Work and Public Social Services Practice: A Status Report', *Families in Society*, Vol. 77(2), pp. 117-124.

Harris, J. (1998), 'Scientific management, bureau-professionalism, new managerialism: The labour process of state social work', *British Journal of Social Work*, Vol. 28, pp. 839-862.

Harris, J. and McDonald, C. (2000), 'Post-Fordism, the welfare state and the personal social services: A comparison of Australia and Britain', *British Journal of Social Work*, Vol. 30, pp. 51-70.

Hawkins, L., Ryan, M., Murray, H., Grace, M., Hawkins, G., Hess, L., Mendes, P. and Chatley, B. (2000), 'Supply and Demand: A study of labor market trends and the employment of new social work graduates in Victoria', *Australian Social Work*, Vol. 53(1), pp. 35-42.

Hayes, F. (1992), 'Unionism and community workers: the role of the Australian Social Welfare Union', in R. Thorpe and J. Petruchenia (eds.), *Community Work or Social Change?: An Australian Perspective*, Hale and Iremonger, Sydney.

Healy, J. (1998), *Welfare Options: Delivering Social Services*, Allen and Unwin, Sydney.

Healy, K. (2000), *Social Work Practices: Contemporary Perspectives on Change*, Sage, London.

Healy, K. (2002), 'Managing human services in a market environment: What role for social workers?', *British Journal of Social Work*, Vol. 32, pp. 527-540.

Healy, K. and Meagher, G. (2001), 'Practitioners' perspectives on performance assessment', *Children Australia*, Vol. 26(4), pp. 22-28.

Higgins, W. (1996), 'The Swedish Municipal Workers' Union – A study in the new political unionism', *Economic and Industrial Democracy*, Vol. 17(2), pp. 167-197.

Illich, I. (1977), *Disabling Professions*, N.H. Salem, London.

ILO (1997), *World Labour Report: Industrial Relations, Democracy and Social Stability*, International Labour Office, Geneva.

Jones, C. (2001), 'Voices from the front-line: State social workers and New Labour', *British Journal of Social Work*, Vol. 31(4), pp. 547-562.

Knapp, M., Wistow, G., Forder, J. and Hardy, B. (1994), 'Markets for social care: Opportunities, barriers and implications', in W. Bartlett, C. Propper, D. Wilson and J. LeGrand, *Quasi-markets in the Welfare State*, Saus Publication, London.

Leonard, P. (1996), 'Three discourse of practice: a postmodern re-appraisal', *Journal of Sociology and Social Welfare*, Vol. 23(2), pp. 7-26.

Lymbery, M. (2001), 'Social work at the crossroads', *British Journal of Social Work*, Vol. 31(3), pp. 369-384.

Macdonald, C. and Merrill, D.A. (2002), '"It shouldn't have to be a trade": Recognition and redistribution in care work advocacy', *Hypatia,* Vol. 17(2), pp. 67-83.

Martin, E. and Healy, J. (1993), 'Social work as women's work: Census data 1976-1986', *Australian Social Work*, Vol. 46(4), pp. 13-18.

McDonald, C. (1999), 'Human service professionals in the community services industry', *Australian Social Work*, Vol. 52(1), pp. 17-25.

Meagher, G. (1994), 'Evaluating women's work: New South Wales nurses and professional rates', *Journal of Australian Political Economy*, Vol. 34, pp. 77-102.

Meagher, G. (2002a),'The Politics of Knowledge in Social Service Evaluation', *UnitingCare Burnside Discussion Paper No. 1,* UnitingCare Burnside, North Parramatta.

Meagher, G. (2002b), 'Making Care Visible: Performance Measurement in Welfare Services', *UnitingCare Burnside Discussion Paper No. 2*, UnitingCare Burnside, North Parramatta.

Meerabeau, E. (2001), 'Can a purchaser be a partner? Nursing education in English Universities', *International Journal of Health Planning and Management*, Vol. 16, pp. 89-105.

Miller, C. and Ahmad, Y. (2001), 'Collaboration and Partnership: An Effective Response to Complexity and Fragmentation or Solution Built on Sand?', *International Journal of Sociology and Social Policy*, Vol. 20(5/6), pp. 1-38.

Onyx, J. and Maclean, M. (1996), Careers in the Third Sector, *Nonprofit Management and Leadership*, Vol. 6(4), pp. 331-345.

Orme, J. (2001), 'Regulation or fragmentation? Directions for social work under New Labour, *British Journal of Social Work*, Vol. 31(4), pp. 611-624.

Parton, N. and O'Byrne, P. (2000), *Constructive Social Work*, Macmillan, London.

Patti, R. (2000), 'The landscape of social welfare management', in R. Patti (ed.), *The Handbook of Social Welfare Management*, Sage, Thousand Oaks.

Phillips, C. (1999), 'A new provincial voice for social workers! History as the present', *The Networker: Newsletter of the Social Work Reform Group*, Spring, 1999.

Pocock, B. (1997), *Strife: Sex and Politics in Labour Unions*, Allen and Unwin, Sydney.

Raelin, J. (1989), 'Unionization and professionalization: which comes first?', *Journal of Organizational Behavior*, Vol. 10, pp. 101-115.

Scanlon, E. (1999), 'Labor and the intellectuals: Where is social work?', *Social Work*, Vol. 44(6), pp. 590-593.

Schumacher, E. (1997), 'Relative wages and behavior amongst registered nurses', *Journal of Labor Research*, Vol. 18(4), pp 581-592.

Stephenson, M. (2001), *In Critical Demand: Social Work in Canada*, http://www.socialworkincanada.org.

Stone, D. (2000), 'Caring by the Book', in M. H. Meyer, (ed.), *Care Work: Gender, Class and the Welfare State*, Routledge, New York, pp. 89-111.

The Swedish Municipal Workers' Union (2001), *The Swedish Municipal Workers Union and the Future*, http://www.kommunal.se/english. Accessed: 5/9/01.

UNISON (2001), http://www.unison.org.uk Accessed: 7/9/01.

PART III
NARRATIVE, CRITICAL
CONSCIOUSNESS, EMANCIPATION

Chapter 8

Older Women Negotiating Uncertainty in Everyday Life: Contesting Risk Management Systems

Amanda Grenier

Introduction

Older women are not often encouraged to talk about their experiences of 'frailty', decline and death. Ironically, this is especially the case in health and social care services, where interviews and assessments are reduced to managerial processes and response to 'frailty' as 'risk'. This chapter draws on narrative interviews conducted with twelve 'frail' and 'non-frail'[1] older women of diverse social backgrounds[2] in Montreal, Canada. The aim was to understand how older women negotiate their experiences of disability and decline and address the powerful messages within risk management systems. Listening to these stories provide valuable insights for social work practice within the current managerial context. Older women's stories about 'frailty' reveal disjunctures between fixed professional and organizational conceptions and older women's more fluid conceptualisations of their lives and experiences. Older women's accounts lead us to reflect on the importance of questioning narrow constructions of 'frailty', to recognize the tensions between these accounts, and to create the time and space for older women's accounts. Their stories also illustrate how they relinquish the need for that certainty and control that are commonplace within corporate social work practices.

Managerial and Organizational Practices

'Frailty': A Socially Constructed Concept and Imposed Identity

There are two interconnected ways in which 'frailty' is understood in relation to the health and social care context for older persons. First, 'frailty' is understood as an 'actual' condition or situation of physical impairment or disability, which occurs with age (Hammerman, 1999). For example, 'frailty' is marked by three or more of the following characteristics: unintentional weight loss, self-reported exhaustion, weakness (e.g., grip strength), slow walking speed, and low physical activity (Fried et al., 2001). According to professionals (e.g., medicine) there are certain realities that result in an older person being considered 'frail'. Second, 'frailty' is understood as a socially constructed service discourse connected with eligibility for public services (Kaufman, 1994). Although the division between these two ways of understanding are evident within the published literature – which tends to focus on either the definition of 'frailty' or the lives, meanings and social experiences of 'frailty' – in practice they become intertwined and take on particular meanings for older persons interacting with health and social care services.

In health and social care services, 'frailty' is used as a guide to measure and assess risk. Ideas about what constitutes 'frailty' (i.e., the definitions) are standardized into assessment forms and organizational practices to discriminate between cases, sort eligibility and allocate public services. The managerial and/or corporate context within which this occurs, however, influences the construction of 'frailty' and subsequent response to older persons receiving care. Being classified within health and social care services as 'frail' combines medical and professional judgements about the body and managerial priorities intended to apply standard procedures across cases and control cost. In the current competitive context – where only the worst-case situations will qualify for services – eligibility is reduced to minimal conceptions of bodily risk. In this case, eligibility concepts must not only be identified, but also stressed (Tanner, 1998). Consider, for example, the way that professionals emphasize the 'frail' or 'very frail' status of the older person in case records and service allocation meetings in order to compete for their 'clients' eligibility and/or access to service. In stressing the struggles, difficulties and/or weaknesses, however, they must downplay the strengths, abilities and/or coping strategies of the older person at hand.

'Frailty' also takes on specific meaning in relation to age and Western social values, social stigma and negative assumptions that accompany old age. Old age is a socially constructed concept including various assumptions such as 'burden' and 'dependence' (Phillipson and Walker, 1987). 'Frailty' is an example of a concept constructed in reference to old age – older persons are constructed as 'frail' because they are old. Although they may share characteristics of 'risk' with other population groups (e.g., poverty, isolation, etc), only older persons are considered 'frail'. Like burden and dependence, 'frailty' is a complicated construction. On one side, 'frailty' is emphasized to make demands for access and services.[3] Yet, on the other side, their 'risk' when combined with old age, is accompanied by a lack of 'future potential'. Whereas risk in relation to children implies the risk of a poor, difficult or troubled life, 'risk' in relation to older people seems to hold less social importance. Older people are, as Gadow (1996) suggests in her critical metaphor of 'aging as death rehearsal', expected to experience functional problems, and decline into death. This sentiment, however, is not merely abstract – notions that interventions are wasted in old age operate explicitly throughout public discourses (e.g., media discussions of older hospitalized persons as bed blockers) and practices of health and social care. For example, in my interview with Margaret, she says, 'I ...need... two new knee caps, but they, won't even entertain doing them for me because I'm too old...he (the doctor) said, "You'll be 92," '. Being old and 'at-risk' (i.e., 'frail') within the current context of cost effectiveness and lack of social value means that the concept of 'frailty' imposes its own devaluation on the lives of older persons eligible for care.

Limiting Cost, Time and Space: Controlling Anxieties and Uncertainties

Organizational practices of risk management focus on cost containment, expediency, and applying standard processes across a range of situations. Rooted in the pursuit of objectivity and aiming for uniformity, these standard processes are intended to produce rapid assessments and limit the costs and scheduled times of interventions between the health care professional and older persons. In doing so, however, these processes limit the space given to older women and their experiences. For example, in standard assessments such as those in Quebec home care services, workers have a specific amount of time to ask older women standard questions about activities of daily living which are listed on the assessment form. Decisions regarding eligibility are often based on standards allotted to particular recognized illnesses or interventions. Any discussions or experiences not required for the standard form are considered surplus and may or may not appear, depending on the discretion of the worker. The idea that this information is surplus does not necessarily reflect the views or training of the worker, but larger managerial priorities. However, in the constrained context of practice, discussions outside those listed on the form may rarely take place between the assessor and the person in need of care, nor in the decisions about the allocation of services (Grenier, 2002; Hughes, 1995; Ray 2000).

In this sense, the managerial processes of risk management, which direct the interactions between professionals and older women, seem to also control anxieties and/or uncertainties associated with the needs of older persons. That is, in positioning knowledge, science and objectivity as the only acceptable truths, the subjective, emotional and human experiences that accompany bodily changes are excluded. From a managerial perspective, these issues would be costly, and require both the time and space of the home care workers. Yet, the tension here is that risk management is practised within a context where older persons are not only experiencing disability or decline, but also the social and emotional processes which accompany these changes. This situation creates a contradiction between the managerial and organizational practices and the experiences of older women receiving care. Turning to older women's accounts, we may begin to understand how they interpret these issues in light of their experiences.

Stories from the Everyday Life Experiences of Older Women

Forget 'Frailty': Let's Talk about My Experiences

The older women I interviewed rejected the concept of 'frailty' to describe themselves and their experiences (Grenier, 2002). Clara says, 'I don't consider myself, I don't want to consider myself frail', while Elizabeth says, 'I don't think of myself as frail. I think of myself as being, I suppose, handicapped to an extent'. In general, older women responded to my inquiries about 'frailty' by saying something like Ella's statement: 'that wouldn't be me'. Examples about someone else who was frail then followed these statements. For instance, Annie and Margaret focus on physical descriptions of 'frailty':

> Annie: Frailty is frailty physically, I think frailty is someone whose bones may crack...Someone who is slightly bent over and they when they walk, its as though they're not sure their feet are going to find that solid ground there and um, pallid complexion, withdrawn...

> Margaret: You've got to be small and skinny.... If you want to see frailty, you will see them down there...on their tippy toes...

Martha depicts the struggle with an environment not conducive to persons with disabilities:

> Martha: I just saw a frail man the other day, he was on the bus...and was so hard for him to come up, get up the steps to get into the bus and he sat down so, just so difficult for him, then when he had to get off, it was a big procedure for him, it was a big job...but, like, when he sat down at first he says, omigod thank god I'm sitting, you know, that's frail.

Elizabeth connects 'frailty' with the deaths of her family members:

> Well, as I say my parents and my aunt, they're the ones that I, in recent memory, saw, uh, when they were dying and this period of sickness before they died. You know they all ended up in the hospital and were essentially at the end, helpless.... As I say, we all get there in the end... You get frail and then you die.

Even when older women's stories about themselves and others corresponded with health care professionals' descriptions of risk (i.e., focused on illness, strength, mobility), the older women did not see themselves as 'frail'. For example, Margaret spoke about her perceptions of using adaptive equipment, and the way she would integrate this into her views of herself as active:

She said that she thinks that I will have to have …a walker, eventually have a walker. But I'm not going to have a walker unless I have to have it.…A walker is a walker, you know.…I use a walking stick… I wouldn't like to go down and use a walker… I'm not that bad, you know what I mean?…I walk very quick when I walk…I don't know.…I'm going to fight the walker until I have to have one. But when I do get one, in fact I might get one, just to have it in case, because when the nice weather comes, if I can walk and sit, I can walker further. Do you understand what I mean? …I can walk, sit, and walk again and sit. That way I can do a little bit more exercise you see. Strengthen my legs as much as I can.…Yeah, so I'll have to get a walker.

Martha spoke of her distaste for the rocking chair:

I used a rocking chair when I had a baby. But I wouldn't want a rocking chair now…Well, because rocking chairs are associated with old people, or young mothers who are nursing, or, or, feeding their child…Once you're out of that stage of feeding the baby, then old, then the rocking chair is for people to fall asleep, to rock yourself asleep…When you're not well and you can't do anything, well, that's, that's what happens…

Yet, all the women I interviewed refused to see themselves as 'frail'. Only Elizabeth, who explicitly used her 'frail old lady card' to negotiate the health and social care system, used the concept of 'frailty' openly:

It's a way of talking about getting help. I mean I think I get the help anyway, I don't, I don't say I am a frail old lady carry my computer. [laughing] But I, if somebody's offering to carry my computer, I might refer to this as playing the frail old lady card…Well some of this is just getting, you talk about ideas, it makes the ideas more acceptable. I mean, um, it, it's sort of reverse denial, you kind of talk yourself into situations…Whatever denial is – this is the opposite of it, it's kind of, uh, anticipatory acceptance of a change in one's living conditions.

Yet even she is ambivalent about the use of this term when she says, 'Perhaps I should not use this term anymore, it is hitting too close to the bone'. Despite similarities between professional classifications, women's experiences, and the practical use of 'frailty' as a negotiation tactic (Grenier and Hanley, 2002), the older women rejected the concept of 'frailty' as a descriptor of themselves.

Although these older women did not label themselves as 'frail', when approached from a narrative method,[4] they spoke fairly openly about their experiences related to disability, decline, and death. These 'frailties' or 'risks' however, were different from the fixed concept of 'frailty' used within services. Older women's stories were fluid and shifted between context, time, and situations. For example, they spoke of the connections between their experiences and the social and environmental context (Grenier, 2003). Margaret talks about her experience on the bus:

I'm frightened on the bus, dear...You see, when you get on the bus, you just put your money in, or you put your ticket in, and that's alright, but then he starts the bus. And then you... unless you've got something to hang you're really wavering. And one sharp movement can throw you right down.

Despite differences in stories, the connections between social contexts and experiences, and the way frailties may shift through time, suggest a difference between the dominant assumptions present within the fixed concept used in health and social care services and the lived realities. Older women's stories suggest a general resistance to the concept of 'frailty' and social constructions of aging – of which 'frailty', disability and decline are a part. As such, they raise questions about rigid professional classifications and organizational practices.

'I'm Not Sure': Older Women Living with Disability and Decline

Older women's discussions were often framed or located in the uncertainty of their everyday lives. For example, Carrie makes the statement: 'You never know what your world will bring'. In each case – despite exact references (e.g., difficult times, illness or disability) – the older women's stories shared a common point of uncertainty. That is, they prompted a sense of 'never knowing' and the strategies used to adapt or accommodate to this uncertainty. Janet talks about the uncertainty of her current facial paralysis:

I'm not sure how long this will last...I don't know when it will go away and I don't know what I will be left with when it does...It'll either go away or I'll have it for the rest of my life I guess, huh, better have to get used to it.

Alice talks about the uncertainty of her health and the impact this has on making future plans:

I don't know what will happen again, another time. You never know. Things change so fast sometimes you know, you think you're going to do the same thing all the time and then all of a sudden, bingo, the circumstances change, eh....So this is it, you just can't make your long-term plans, you know. You live for day by day...you make goals...You don't have any plans...You adapt everyday to your circumstances. You can't, because you don't know.

Uncertainty also played a daily role in times of crisis or illness, disability or decline. Older women wondered what would happen to them and how this would affect their body and/or their sense of continuity – that is, their identities and the strategies they have used throughout life. Will I get over this illness or grief? What is going to happen to me in the future? Where will I be in a few years? What will happen to me between now and then? Will I be able to live my life in the way I expect and want to? How will this change the way I have always been, who I am and who I expect to become? These uncertainties are not only located in individual changes (e.g., illness, condition, or potential for coping) – as services may have us believe – but, also from outside influences, including changes in eligibility for service or changing caring relationships (Ray, 2000).

Death: Something to be Certain About

Older women's discussions of uncertainty reveal the presence that death has in older women's lives. Across all of the interviews, discussions of their lives and experiences (i.e., the experiences that made them feel frail) were contextualized within life review and/or connected to their various perceptions of death. In fact, it seems death was discussed in contrast to uncertainty – it was one of the only things the older women were sure about. For example, speaking generally as an older woman, Carrie shares her perspective on life: I do feel that our days are numbered for us. While this may seem to strengthen the socially constructed notions that age and death are connected, more importantly, it reveals how older women grapple with and confront their own mortality. These discussions reveal the stance of acceptance that women may have adopted in relation to their own mortality and challenge the certainty, distance and avoidance maintained in health and social care services:

Carrie: I imagine this will be my last time (to visit her birthplace) because I'm sure after that the angels will come and get me – this will be the last time I go home.

Martha: I know I haven't got that many years ahead of me.

Clara: Yeah, yeah, it brings you to this point. And it's a good place, I'm in a good place now, ready to go up, to the good Lord, ready to go up, oh yeah, for sure, I'm ready to go up. I know I'm sure of that.

Although there was a certain avoidance of naming death within some of the discussions (e.g., references to 'luck', their mothers and 'the angels') the certainty of death was ever-present. Older women expressed a sureness or certainty about their mortality – the uncertainty was related to the process by which this will come about. In this sense, it is likely that each new change or onset of illness causes a question in an older woman's mind about whether this is 'it'. Is this the decline that will lead to the end of my life? Or is it another change for which I will have to modify or adapt? In this sense, older women's accounts reveal how they live with an uncertainty deeply connected with mortality that conflicts with the bureaucratic certainty expressed in managerial processes and organizational practices.

Contesting Risk and Negotiating Uncertainty

Reacting to Risk, Management and the Search for Objectivity

Older women's stories may be understood as a response to being constructed and labelled as 'frail' or 'at-risk' by managerial and organizational practices. In rejecting 'frailty', women may actually be reacting to the way aging is socially constructed as 'devalued', as well as the seemingly rigid expectations that accompany the classification of 'being frail'. These many include, for example, expectations of weakness, passivity and compliance. Consider Margaret's statement, 'I'm not that bad' or the repeated use of the rocking chair as metaphor – a symbol which is associated with passivity and dependence. Older women's stories suggest that they reject the label of 'frailty' because their experiences are somehow 'different' from organizational notions of 'frailty' and risk management. Rejection of 'frailty' or risk may be particularly strong where they interfere with a life-long identity or particular life strategies that are usually unrecognized by risk management systems. For example, Clara's identity as a 'strong black woman' and Alice's life strategy of 'living for day-by-day' are not recognized within the social constructions of age and disability that operate in general and throughout health and social care.

Older women's stories may be understood as reactions to managerial processes such as risk management and the anxiety which surrounds discussions of 'frailty' and death. Their stories about risk and 'frailty' illustrate how organizational practices of assessment and managerial priorities may result in a reductionist approach to assessment (Hughes, 1995). Despite the apparent surface level congruence between professional classifications and women's real experiences (i.e., certain realities of disability and decline) the current conceptions of 'frailty' and risk have been reduced to functional abilities of the body. As older women's stories show, however, their experiences are not only about the body, but also their lives and cumulative life experience. As such, their accounts expose the problematic nature of efforts that attempt to squeeze the complexities and variations within and between older women's stories into tick-boxes based on medical-functional criteria. Part of the problem here is that assessments do not allow the time to hear how older people are managing or coping with their challenges – stories which would challenge or contest 'frailty' and risk (Ray, 2000). Older women's stories challenge risk management systems and organizational practices of health and social care in which the interconnections between the social, emotional and death are rarely heard. The differences in the way that older women perceive and negotiate 'frailty' and risk, and the tension these concepts represent between care and control, provide insight into their resistance.

The fixed concept of 'frailty' in health and social care leaves out the potential for older women to move between times of 'frailty' and 'stability' – that is, the times when they are able to 'manage'. Despite the varying reasons provided by my referral sources, Clara, Alice, Margaret, Ella, Carrie, and Doris were referred to me by home care services, and therefore fixed as 'frail'. Their stories, in combination with the stories of Elizabeth, Maizie, Martha, Kumiko, Annie and Katherine – whom were not considered 'frail' – show that the organizational concept or label of 'frailty' does not reach far enough into the older women's experiences. A segment from Alice's narrative illustrates this clearly: 'It's tough, I just can't do it today'. In saying this, Alice implies that there are many times when she can and does do things. The temporary times of 'frailty' become very clear when considered within her entire narrative strategy of 'managing'. Her statement challenges the professional label, which does not permit space for the time and circumstances when she does not feel 'frail'. Similarly, Katherine's understanding of the 'frailties of life' reflects a general preference to see difficult moments as temporary and passing as opposed to fixed and enduring. These statements challenge the standard, objective and fixed classifications within the professional context of health and social care, where once defined as 'frail', there is no other available identity. As Ray (2000) indicates, the professional terms commonly used to determine eligibility become 'total'.

At another level, older women's stories may be understood as a response to the illusion of certainty and truth embedded within managerial organizational practices. Risk management embraces standardisation, objectivity and professional distance as ideals. This means that particular practices of risk management are grounded in certainties of 'how things are expected to be'. For example, 'frailty' is expected to be caused by age and/or physical mobility (Bortz, 2002; Fried et al, 2001; Rockwood et al, 1994; Strawbridge et al., 1998) and place the person at risk for hospitalisation and greater service use (Hammerman, 1999) and therefore, the use of more public funds. Older women's difficult times in life, existential questions and struggles within the social and environmental context, fall outside of these standardized contingencies. This creates a situation whereby risk management practices impose a false certainty on the experiences of older women receiving care, but where there is no space for unrecognized needs, such as the struggles on the bus or doing activities that may require taking risks. Consider Alice's example of the need to take chances to increase her quality of life:

> Well, they suggested, practically forbid me…instilled upon me – not to go down to the basement because it's very dangerous if I fell. Of course I know that…But I still like to take the chance at this point in time. Maybe I'll get better, maybe I won't. Time will tell. So I can go on the outdoor steps stay out there- that I can do that- they don't say anything about that.

As such, risk management approaches may easily be interpreted as striving for and/or grasping certainty or control in an uncertain environment. In embracing the certainty and truth of what 'frailty' 'should' look like (i.e., body injury or risk), managerial and organizational practices overlook the complexity of experience and the varying interconnected practical uncertainties. They overlook, for example, the qualities of life that may come from going outside and/or continuing to live in a certain way. They also overlook the way that 'thin' assessments of risk which do not address the complexities of older people's experiences, may actually be dangerous or pose further risks to other service users (Tanner, 1998). Older women's reactions may, therefore, represent resistance against organizational priorities and services which make certain or 'truthful' claims about how their experiences related to disability and decline are to be understood.

At another level, older women's stories illustrate the lack of space given to particular emotional experiences such as thoughts about mortality, which women seem to perceive as intricately connected with their experiences of disability and decline. Women's stories about the certainty of death reveal the tension that exists between risk management's avoidance of death and women's understandings and need to discuss their mortality. Standard risk management practices provide little or no room for women to talk about these experiences. I experienced this lack of space when my research related discussions about death were silenced by health care professionals and colleagues as being 'too difficult' or even 'morbid'. My experience can only be partially reflective of what older women experience daily. Yet, where given the space (e.g., in the narrative interviews), women elaborate on the connections between their experiences of disability and decline and thoughts about their own lives and mortality. In this sense, older women's narratives provide a privileged location within which they could discuss death, despite even their own reluctance to name death. Though managerial approaches strive for control, prediction and certainty, the most obvious certainty within older women's everyday lives – death – is avoided.

In the discrepancies between professional classification and women's experiences, the focus on certainty seems an intentional way to avoid difficult and time-consuming issues and instead focus on managerial priorities of cost containment, efficacy and standardisation. Distance from sensitive issues of disability and philosophical issues of death are maintained at various levels within service. While standardized services create distance in a more general sense, assessment focused on risk maintains distance at an immediate level between the older person and the worker. During her narrative, Martha comments on the emotional nature of working with older people and the difficulties that older people have in caring for another older person. It can only be expected that some younger professionals experience this as well:

> ...It's hard for an older person to look after another person...it's emotional and physical too...But most of it is emotional I think... but I cannot, uh, uh, and I haven't got the guts like to go and help somebody, like feeding somebody, uh, friend of ours'...there's another reason, because you put yourself in that, it could be me. And you don't wanna face that, it could be me....So you don't know what you have facing you and you don't wanna face that 'cause that could be your, your future.

It is no surprise, then, that priority is given to objective answers, which are quantifiable and may be compared across persons. Yet, these priorities and practices prevent workers from taking the time and space to explore the subjective feelings associated with loss and death. Herein lies a major contradiction, that older women in public services have been constructed as 'frail' because they are old and constructed as 'waiting to die', yet services will not address the emotional issues that are related to difficult issues of loss and death. Maintaining the focus on risk management and managerial priorities also excludes the material conditions and organizational practices that may create and sustain constructions such as 'frailty' in the first place. It is no doubt that women see through these contradictions and have little faith in a perspective that refuses to recognize and address its own limitations.

Living In and With Uncertainty

Older women's stories voice everyday experiences of uncertainty within and between the certainty of risk management systems. Their stories address subjective issues such as loss and the existential questions that accompany age, disability and decline and how they negotiate and live with bodily change. Their narratives also describe the tension between the impending certainty of death and the uncertainty about the manner in which death comes (i.e., the how and the when). While there is a strong societal death taboo that keeps death as the avoided or unspoken subject, older women's accounts are filled with their thoughts about death. Ella says, 'I'm grateful for the life I've lived and I'm ready for the angels to take me away....I wouldn't change anything'. Interestingly enough, however, it was not only women who would be classified as 'frail' who lived with the imminence of death. All of the women expressed heightened awareness of death and had accompanying life strategies to negotiate their experiences such as resistance or acceptance. The uncertainties that older women experience hold a potential both for women to create ways of living and negotiate their experience, as well as provide an alternative model for living with situations that are uncertain, unpredictable or beyond control.

Changes in both the body, such as illness, disability, decline and/or older women's circumstances are often beyond their control. Consider Doris' statement, 'I don't know whether this will go away' and Elizabeth's, 'You get frail then you die'. Despite different viewpoints and experiences, the common message between accounts is that control as it was previously understood is no longer a reality. According to the older women, they must negotiate, resist, adapt and/or find a way to cope. Here, the older women's statements echo with an important message for the organizational practices which intend to create illusions of certainty. Instead of overlooking or trying to control the uncertainties within their lives, older women create accounts and ways of being that, in a sense, normalize and allow them to adjust to the extent of uncertainty in their everyday lives. Older women's stories expose the gap between professional understandings focused on certainty and older women's experiences of living in and with uncertainty – forming a direct contrast to the uniform, standard and certain expectations and approaches of risk management systems and organizational practices. Where risk management systems would likely attempt to control or predict circumstances while ignoring death, women's responses are more along the lines of relinquishing control and accepting both their bodies and their mortality.

Uncertainty was present at several levels and had origins in a range of challenges and/or turning points in older women's lives. Where in general, the older women's life situations would have seemed to portray general patterns or portraits of risk, older women's responses were much more varied. In the face of change, older women either accept, reject or negotiate the new circumstances. Each older woman seemed to have her own unique strategy or path, which seemed less determined by the objective criteria or cause of their difficulty (e.g., hip fracture), and more based on their ongoing life strategies, identities and expectations (e.g., negotiating services or racism). Older women's stories reveal the importance of selecting strategies used throughout their lives. While Kumiko's strategy is to 'make the best of things', Annie 'chooses not to forget the death of her daughter', and Martha has decided: 'I don't run for buses anymore'. Clara, on the other hand, completely resists and/or denies the changes using her strategy of 'mind over matter'. Here, the uncertainties in the older women's lives seemed to be matched with various acceptable ways of living as opposed to standard responses. Older women's strategies highlight the absence of a single predictable acceptable response and show that uncertainty is a negotiated rather than controlled reality.

Older women's strategies to address uncertainty often become the stories the older women decide to live 'with and by' (Holstein and Gubrium, 2000). These stories are not fixed accounts of the experiences related to disability and/or decline in 'old age', but are based on life strategies. As Biggs (1999) indicates, the 'mature identity' is located not in age alone, but in cumulative life experience. Older women's stories are contextualized throughout their life course and contain several references to the strategies they have used throughout their lives to address challenges or turning points. Women's stories are not fixed in time, but evolve and change with their experiences. As such, the telling of the story not only gives a voice to uncertainty, but provides space to work with or negotiate the story and the way it may 'fit' with the self. Stories may give women the space and time to put changes into perspective, and integrate them into their identities and life experiences. As such, these stories reveal the extent to which these complex lived uncertainties extend beyond a mere reductionist categorisation as 'frail'.

Insights for Critical Social Work

Older women's stories provide a glimpse into the specific location of 'frailty', revealing practice tensions, critical questions for social work and care, and guidance for good practice. Both older women receiving care and social workers providing care are located within and affected by the corporate practices of risk management (e.g., limited recognition of need, stringent eligibility criteria and expectations of compliance). Both strive for some sort of certainty or understanding while also encountering uncertainty in daily life or practices. Older women's stories about risk and uncertainty reveal the tensions between silence and space, certainty and uncertainty, and assumed and lived experiences. The current disjunctures between health and social care services and the experiences of clients reveal the need to develop a critical practice to bring these two perspectives closer (Brechin, 2000). This is especially the case in social work, where Ray and Phillips (2002, p.108) call for debate about 'what should properly and appropriately constitute social work with older people'. At the same time, however, the disjunctures and complexities within accounts also reveal the challenge faced by the critical practitioner.

Contesting Constructions and Negotiating Uncertainty

Older women's stories encourage critical social work to question the meanings and implications of professional language or constructions and organizational practices. Older women's rejection of the concept of 'frailty' raises questions about the priorities and processes that construct service users in particular ways. 'Frailty' is only one example of such a construction. The example of 'frailty' reveals how managerial priorities, processes and case management systems may have particular implications for the client group – in this case older women. If 'frailty' is understood and applied as a fixed and measurable concept, older women may be assigned an identity that is problematic, denied their own views and perspectives, and given little space for strengths or movement. In such an application, once an older woman is classified as frail, she has little possibility of negotiating an alternative identity; the frail label sticks with her and accompanies her throughout her dealings with health and social services as well as in her larger everyday interactions. Yet, when organizational processes of risk assessment and management are questioned, spaces to discuss accounts and negotiate experiences become available. Consider Maizie's quote on negotiating your needs:

> The thing is there's a ...view...you don't need services anyway if you don't push the issue, and make sure that they understand that you're entitled to the services... they want to tell you they can only give you an hour, well then you've got to show them... what your needs are... you have to insist on telling them you are entitled to...Because they, that anything they do for you, are what they can better their programs and their agenda, is good for you, but no, you have to tell them. You have to explain to them....You know, and they're going to always say 'oh you can still do this, you can still do that' you have to tell them, 'I know what I can do, I'll tell you what I can do'. And, you know what I need to have.

Older women's experiences related to illness, disability and decline and involvement with health and social care systems highlight that the realities of particular experiences such as disability and decline are negotiated in various ways (e.g., rejection, resistance, adaptation). Despite similar circumstances which could, and often are, classified as 'frailty' or 'risk', women's stories reveal how these categorisations must be constantly negotiated and/or contested when they do not 'fit' with women's lives, experiences and identities. That is, they highlight the importance of rejecting concepts or practices when they either do not represent experience (e.g. the emotional and the social) and or correspond with the person's view of themselves (e.g. strong and independent). Their stories highlight how current experiences and/or difficulties in age are not separate from, but connected with their lives and past experiences. Professional classifications must begin to recognize this continuity that exists within the lives of service users. Further, what is clear from women's accounts is that experiences related to crisis, illness, disability and/or decline are not standard, but uncertain and varied, and that these experiences require a negotiation of uncertainty that has previously remained unrecognized.

Recognizing Strains and Creating Time and Space

Older women's stories highlight the importance of integrating 'care' (Armstrong, 2000) back into health and social care practices. As professionals, we must work with differing shapes – regardless of whether they 'fit' neatly into our professional moulds. We must recognize that our classifications and practices intended to 'help', may at times completely contradict their experiences or the way they wish to receive 'care' and that our re-shaping may serve only our professional interests. Recognizing the instances where practices and experiences do not 'match,' such as in the case of older women's understandings of 'frailty', may assist in developing practices which are more in line with actual experiences and expectations. Yet, these critical practices must be supported by the both resources and a general willingness to work in a different way.

Older women's stories about risk and uncertainty stress the need to move outside of current conceptions in order to recognize existing strains and understand various forms of resistance, which operate within practice. For example, critical social work practitioners could pick up some of the messages within statements such as 'I don't run for buses anymore' in order to develop better understandings and more appropriate responses. The disjuncture between professional accounts and older women's stories reveal the role that location and perspective may play in the interpretation of needs. Professional understandings of 'frailty' and risk are seen through a particular lens. Yet, resistance may look different than previously understood. Recognition of the experiences of strain and the lives of those whom experience these strains may reveal the subtle forms of resistance and continuity that occur daily. By expanding or even differentiating the location of social work from risk-based assessment to the experiences that exist within and behind risk, social workers may both see and encourage new forms of meaning and living within experiences.

The importance of time and space cannot be overlooked. Currently, women do not have the opportunity to speak about how they see themselves or their views on impending death. The lessons from older women reveal the way that practice maintains distance from issues such as loss and death. When, for example, do we close the space for women to talk about the meaning of their 'frailty' or their fears of death? In a sense, we must look for what is not asked – the experiences which fall between our assessments and the differences in ways of seeing things that result in resistance and misunderstanding. For example, the difference between the realities associated with 'frailty' and the way it is interpreted as negative because of the socially constructed assumptions and connections it conjures up for older women. We must recognize and open these spaces to listen to women and their experiences.

Listening to older women would mean selecting a 'fluid' and flexible approach as opposed to a rigid one. It would also mean establishing a comfort level within the discourses on death. Part of this task of creating space may be achieved through open formats of research and practice such as narrative, which allow the person to author their experience by allowing for open-ended stories. It was only through the in-depth accounts of older women that various meanings, experiences and the connections between medical-functional concepts of risk and the social-emotional could be understood. This was particularly the case in relation to issues related to mortality and uncertainty. Yet, under current constraints, this raises critical questions. How can workers negotiate both agency requirements and accommodate women's needs to discuss their interconnected experiences from a self-defined perspective? Admittedly, it is difficult to find a place to start; however, women's accounts reveal the importance of doing so. For in not doing so, we may address only universally recognized needs and overlook the culturally specific and individual needs (Leonard, 1997) – putting services into place that are unsuitable and therefore, result in complete rejection.

Relinquishing Certainty and Truth

Finally, older women's accounts highlight the need to relinquish quests for certainty and 'truth' in everyday practices and learn to recognize and live with flexible, shifting and uncertain experiences. Older women's narratives may be considered narratives of uncertainty that both push against certainty and question the very roots of our need for certainty. Their life stories and accounts about age, disability and risk, beg the question: Do we really need to be so certain? They stand as direct challenges to corporate and managerial social work practices of objectivity and certainty. That is, they reveal the partiality of 'truths', expectations and the hidden experiences – such as the emotional – that exist within and behind professional understandings and current practices. As such, these older women are in a position to teach and provide examples of how to negotiate uncertainty in everyday life. They give us examples of various ways to relinquish the need for certainty as previously known, and show how, in doing so, they have created meaningful experiences through negotiation. Older women's stories emphasize Brechin's (2000) call to relinquish truth through an open and 'now-knowing' approach. By questioning our 'truths' – our understandings of the way things are in relation to risk and practice – older women's accounts expose the situation that if we are willing to listen and change our practices, there is space to relinquish some of the need for control and certainty.

Relinquishing the need for certainty, however, does not mean floating in a sea of endless uncertainty – instead, it means taking a more flexible and varied approach to the uncertainties of everyday life and practices of health and social care. Depending on the situation and experience, this may range from a strong position from which to contest or reject unsuitable practices to moving with the changing tides of uncertainty. For example, this may be as simple as recognizing the disjuncture between a woman's identity-based needs to remain strong and the expectations of receiving services (e.g., being identified as 'frail'). It may also mean rethinking not only what is classified as risk, but providing spaces for older persons to engage in activities which we may consider 'risky'. Overall, relinquishing certainty would mean taking a more fluid approach to the experiences associated with disability and decline. Similar to older women, critical social work may recognize strains and adopt strategies to live within uncertainty that instil a sense of meaning and empowerment. Instead of grasping for certainty within the current context, we may instead relinquish control in order to open the spaces for lived experiences and stories. In doing so, we may continue to learn from the way older women contest risk management systems, and relinquish certainty and 'truth' in order to adapt strategies they can live within.

Notes

[1] 'Frail' older women were referred by multi-disciplinary professionals. Older women's status as 'frail' was determined by clinical judgement and the eligibility criteria for home care services within Quebec. Snowball sampling identified older women who were not considered 'frail'. These older women were not service recipients.

[2] The social backgrounds of the older women varied according to ability, age, culture, ethnicity, 'race', and socio-economic status.

[3] This is especially the case when the low social value of older persons may mean that they remain invisible within society.

[4] Note that I changed my method to an open-ended narrative early in the process in response to the older women's candidacy about their experiences of disability and decline. When approached in a more structured and direct manner, the women seemed to resist and restructure their stories accordingly. When a narrative approach was used, they elaborated on the issues for which they would be seen as 'frail'.

References

Armstrong, P. (2000), *Heal Thyself: Managing Health Care Reform*, Garamond Press, Aurora.

Biggs, S. (1999), *The Mature Imagination: Dynamics of Identity in Midlife and Beyond*, Open University Press, Buckingham.

Bortz, W.M. (2002), 'A Conceptual Framework of Frailty: A Review', *Journals of Gerontology: Medical Sciences*, Vol. 57A, No. 5., pp. M283-M288.

Brechin, A. (2000), 'Introducing Critical Practice', in A. Brechin, H. Brown and M. Eby (eds.), *Critical Practice in Health and Social Care*, Open University/Sage, London.

Fried, L., Tangen, C., Walston, J., Newman, A., Hirsch, C., Gottdiener, J., Seeman, T., Tracy, R., Kop, W., Burke, G., McBurnie, M. (2001), 'Frailty in older adults: Evidence for a phenotype', *The Journals of Gerontology*, March 2001, Vol. 56A, Iss.3, Washington, pp. M146-M157.

Gadow, S. (1996), 'Aging as death rehearsal: The oppressiveness of reason', *The Journal of Clinical Ethics*, Vol. 7, No. 1. pp.35-40.

Grenier, A. (2002), 'Diverse Older Women: Narratives Negotiating Frailty', Unpublished Doctoral Dissertation, McGill University, Montreal.

Grenier, A. (2003), 'Diverse older women's accounts on "frailty": Contextual and social locations of experience', paper presented at the British Society of Gerontology Annual Conference, Newcastle upon Tyne, September 4-6, 2003.

Grenier, A. and Hanley, J. (2002), 'Resisting "frailty" and using "frailty" to resist, paper presented at the Canadian Association of Schools of Social Work, Toronto, May 25, 2002.

Hammerman, D. (1999), 'Toward an understanding of frailty', *Annals of Internal Medicine*, Vol. 130, Iss. 11, pp. 945-950.

Holstein, J.A. and Gubrium, J. (2000), *The Self We Live by: Narrative Identity in a Postmodern World*, Oxford University Press, New York.

Hughes, B. (1995), *Older People and Community Care: Critical Theory and Practice*, Open University Press, Buckingham.

Kaufman, S. (1994), 'The Social Construction of Frailty: An Anthropological Perspective', *Journal of Aging Studies*, Vol. 8, No. 1, Spring, pp. 45-58.

Leonard, P. (1997), *Postmodern Welfare: Reconstructing an Emancipatory Project*, Sage, London.

Phillipson, C. and Walker, A. (1986), *Aging and Social Policy: a Critical Assessment*, Gower, Aldershot.

Ray, M. (2000), 'Continuity and Change: Sustaining Long-term Marriage Relationships in the Context of Emerging Chronic Illness and Disability', Unpublished PhD thesis, Keele University.

Ray, M. and Phillips, J. (2002), 'Critical Practice in Social Work: Older People', in R. Adams, L. Dominelli and M. Payne (eds.), *Critical Practice in Social Work*, Palgrave, Basingstoke, pp 99-109.

Rockwood, K., Fox, R.A., Stolee, P., Robertson, D., Beattie, B.L. (1994), 'Frailty in Older People: An Evolving Concept', *Canadian Medical Association Journal*, Vol. 150(4), pp. 489-95.

Strawbridge, W.J., Shema, S.J., Balfour, J.L., Highby, H.R., Kaplan, G.A. (1998), 'Antecedents of frailty over three decades in an older cohort', *The Journals of Gerontology*, Series B, Psychological Sciences and Social Sciences, Vol. 53B, S9-S16.

Tanner, D. (1998), *Jeopardy of Assessing Risk*, Practice 10, Vol. 1, pp. 15-28.

Townsend, P. (1986), 'Ageism and Social Policy', in C. Phillipson and A. Walker, *Ageing and Social Policy: A Critical Assessment*, Gower, Aldershot.

Chapter 9

Disrupting the Narrative of White Tutelage: Reflections on Post-colonial Social Work Education

Laura Mastronardi

Introduction

Aboriginal people in Canada, like those in Australia and elsewhere around the globe, struggle to overcome the legacy of white colonialism. Education has emerged as a key ingredient in their visions for a future as self-determined peoples. As a vehicle for individual and collective empowerment, aboriginal education typically pursues the dual objectives of fostering skills relevant to participation in a global economy and reinforcing cultural identity (Canada Ministry of Supply and Services, 1996). In 1972, the failure of federal, provincial, and territorial governments to implement policies to achieve aboriginal objectives led to their demands for native control of native education. Since then, Canadian federal policy has been directed toward restoring control of aboriginal education to aboriginal communities, but progress has been slow and the overall results have been disappointing (Canada Ministry of Supply and Services, 1996).

The ongoing struggle for educational jurisdiction as a core element of aboriginal self-government has given rise to an intensified and increasingly sophisticated critique of education at the cultural level in which public education has been analyzed as an instrument of internal colonialism (Perley, 1993), cognitive imperialism (Battiste, 1998), and cultural colonialism (Smith, 2000). Against this backdrop, postsecondary education programs designed specifically for the training of Canadian aboriginal social workers offer a unique site in which to investigate how contemporary discourses of empowerment in education constitute practice and enable or limit possibilities for progressive change toward aboriginal self-determination. Such programs are strategic sites within which to prepare students to participate more fully, and with greater influence, in the process of taking control (Freisen and Orr, 1998). To appreciate the experience and potential of these programs, we must contextualize them within the emerging anti-hegemonic and anti-Eurocentric discourse of aboriginal education (Hesch, 1996, 284). These discourses provide a counter-narrative of western education in which themes of power and identity, and concepts of oppression and resistance grounded in an understanding of the history of racist schooling in Canada, are central. These analytic constructs permit an alternative reading of our pedagogy, and its supporting curriculum, and alert us, as critical educators, to the potentially oppressive consequences of our emancipatory practice ideals.

This chapter deals with a community outreach program of social work education offered by the McGill University School of Social Work for Inuit Students in Nunavik, which is the vast arctic region of the province of Quebec. My own experience of the program, in a variety of roles over fifteen years, is that it functions as a contradictory site where teachers, students, and others participants interact to produce a cultural form that both enables and limits opportunities for an Inuit approach to social work to evolve, including the construction of new forms of worker identity and practice. The program has both liberating and oppressive tendencies in that, while it mediates, it does not fully challenge dominant society conceptions of social work practice and education. The primary contradiction in our practice emerges from simultaneously preparing students to participate in institutions of the majority, non-Inuit society, while attempting to reinforce their cultural identity (Haig-Brown, 1995, p.266). The tensions and dilemmas that arise from efforts to realize this conflicting duality in educational objectives lie submerged but at the heart of our pedagogic practice. By deliberately foregrounding and focusing our gaze on these elements in our work, we can begin to see more clearly how local social relations and practices of oppression are sustained and how they might be resisted and transformed (Healy, 2000).

In this chapter, I will argue that if our intention is to deepen prospects for an Inuit narrative of social work practice to emerge, we must confront the problematic mission of our program, specifically its complicity in cultural colonialism, by deconstructing our pedagogy within the context of decolonisation and Inuit self-determination. In keeping with a view of knowledge as contingent, I begin this chapter by acknowledging the self-reflective character of this text with a brief account of how I came to my present work and of the contextual factors that shape my experience and questions, thus permitting readers to judge the strengths and limitations of my analysis. Having situated myself as author, I then locate the Nunavik social work education within its socio-historical context to illustrate how this position shapes and constrains activities directed toward progressive change. Next, I describe the northern practice setting and the distinctive needs of Inuit students and their communities to highlight some of particular challenges that confront us as mainstream educators. I then reflect critically on some of the difficulties I experience in attempting to bring an emancipatory orientation to bear in my own work. To conclude, I suggest, from my analysis, some possible future directions to enhance educational program responsiveness to Inuit and aboriginal considerations.

Critical Pedagogue as Subject: Through the Glass Darkly

My purpose in studying the Nunavik social work education program is to learn how to think more critically and to act strategically on the nature of my own practice and the institutional contexts in which I work (Liston and Zeichner, 1991). Thus, when I talk and write about my program experience, I am speaking from my location as a subject embedded within the object of my study, actively engaged in the micro-politics of everyday practice. In essence, this text is part of my own ongoing struggle to learn how to teach and write from my own story (Zapf, 1997). Bannerji advises us that 'since political agency, experience, and knowledge are transformatively connected, where but in ourselves can we begin our exploratory and analytic activities' (1991, p.99). At the heart of this endeavour lies the personal contradiction I experience as a white, middle-class, university-educated professional advocating for Inuit control of social services and education. Given the historic relation between Inuit and qallunaat (whites), this contradiction compels me to recognize my own pedagogic and research practice as problematic (Haig-Brown, 1995; Hesch, 1995). However, I did not enter social work practice with the same insight that enables to me make such an observation now.

I began to practice social work in rural northern Ontario in the mid 1970s with no formal training for the job. I suspect that I was hired on the strength of my academic credentials from a respected university in the related discipline of psychology, a common enough practice in northern districts where it remains difficult to attract and retain 'qualified professionals'. My formative practice ideologies as a social worker were constituted in part within the child welfare agency where I was employed. As I joined the social work practice community, what I came to regard as good practice, and consequently 'the being that I aspired to be', was consistently challenged by my interactions with aboriginal communities who were mobilizing politically at that time to contest child placement and adoption practices that devalued aboriginal people and threatened cultural genocide. The opportunity to work collaboratively with aboriginal communities as they struggled to secure jurisdiction over their own child welfare services initiated a process of learning that radically challenged the authority of much that I had come to know. My own politicization and commitment to work alongside aboriginal people in their quest for equity and social justice evolved as I struggled to make sense of the 'shadow side of my work' (Colorado, 1995, p.74) and to come to terms with my own complicity and investment in institutionally-based processes that continued to subordinate and to oppress the people who I meant to serve. Offsetting the painful moments of self-recrimination, questioning, and doubt, as I grappled with the spectre of my own white privilege and power, were the invitations I received to learn and teach with aboriginal groups and traditional Elders in the cultural classroom of their communities, a message from them that I was 'on my right path' and that I was not alone.

There are two contexts for my present work, the first being my administrative responsibilities as coordinator of the Nunavik program and the other, my activities as a doctoral candidate in educational studies. My professional and academic roles do not sit easily together; the former requires that I act as an agent of constraint, and the latter, as advocate of change. There are times when I am decidedly uncomfortable with the curriculum that I represent, just are there are moments when I am uneasy with my socialization into an academic career. Attempting to clarify and to articulate my unease with the status quo seems to me an important first step toward engaging in a more thoughtful dialogue about the program with its various participants.

The process of critical reflection in which I am presently engaged involves a re-reading of my practice experience through the lens of contemporary discourses of empowerment in education, including feminist, critical, and anti-racist approaches to education, as well as aboriginal resistance struggles. As I continue 'coming into theory' (Lather, 1991), I have appropriated elements of these discourses to illuminate and make meaning of my own teaching and learning experiences. I draw upon and remain committed to the critical tradition embedded in modernity at the level of both theory and practice in social work and education. At the same time, I want to develop a reflective critique of the tradition itself by interrogating the potential of contemporary discourses of critical pedagogy to create and sustain a vision for transformative social work education.

As Fook discusses elsewhere in this volume, taking a critical reflective approach holds the potential for emancipatory practices in that it questions and disrupts dominant structures and relations and thereby lays the groundwork for change. Using my own experience as a touchstone to develop a theory and practice link, I have been attempting to explore and to better understand how the current operation of the Nunavik program perpetuates inequities in Inuit-white relations. Deconstructing my practice has involved developing a 'Foucauldian awareness of the oppressive side of potentially liberating forms of discourse' (Lather, 1991, p.10) that guide my work as a critical educator-in-training. Of necessity, this process entails a continuous effort to understand my own formation, and that of Inuit teachers and students, as educational subjects within the institutionally-based structures and processes of social regulation in which our pedagogy is grounded. Doing deconstructive academic work has allowed me to begin to more clearly perceive my own participation in discourse and discursive practices that inscribe Inuit into non-liberatory frameworks and to understand how we are differently caught up in complex webs of structural inequality, the threads of which are beyond our control (Ellsworth, 1989).

Contextualizing Inuit Social Work Education

If we are to the understand the curriculum presently offered for Inuit students, we must examine it in relation to the social and historical contexts in which it is embedded (Goodson, 1994). From a social constructionist viewpoint, the meaning of the curriculum needs to be understood in relation to the complicated configurations of dominance and subordination that are external to it (Apple, 1998). In this respect, the study of postsecondary education in arctic Canada provides an opportunity to reflect upon the shifting nature of power relations between Inuit and Euro-Canadians in the contemporary movement for Inuit self-government (McLean, 1997).

Any attempt to portray life in present day Nunavik must begin with an explicit acknowledgement that it continues to be dominated by the colonial encounter between Inuit and whites. Brody (1975) notes that in their material, ideological, and economic structures, Inuit communities are largely a creation of white, southern intrusion that has been directed from the outset toward the incorporation of Inuit into the mainstream of Canadian society. Early missionaries and fur traders in the pre-war era desired the moral and economic incorporation of Inuit, while newer state institutions seek incorporation that is broadly ideological, national, and political through education, law and medicine, and local government respectively. These objectives were initially facilitated by the dependency relationship that quickly arose between Inuit and whites during the pre-war period when, largely as a result of situational factors such as disease and famine, Inuit came to depend for their survival, or were convinced that they depended, on things that only whites could provide. Ongoing government intervention in the contemporary north perpetuates the colonial aspects of pre-war contacts between Inuit and Euro-Canadians although, as Paine (1977) correctly identifies, the form that the current relationship takes obscures the fact that Inuit continue to be devalued by the institutional arrangements between themselves and the dominant society.

As McLean observes, critical scholarship about the nature of internal colonialism in the arctic has focused historically on the economic exploitation, cultural domination, and political control of Inuit, and makes the following three claims:

> Inuit economic self-sufficiency has been destroyed through a spiral of dependency which began in the eras of whaling and fur trading, and continues in the current era of wage labour and welfare assistance; since the 1950s, Inuit cultural integrity has been undermined thorough explicitly assimilationist state programs and the immigration of large numbers of Euro-Canadian mangers, trades people, and professionals; and Inuit political autonomy has been compromised through the constitutional and legal structures imposed by Euro-Canadian governments (1997, p.22).

Attempts to assimilate Inuit into the mainstream of Canadian society have been largely unsuccessful as evidenced today by kinship and family breakdown, and high rates of violent death, child abuse, alcoholism, and suicide, particularly among Inuit youth. While the negative consequences of neo-colonialism are all too familiar to aboriginal people, to focus only on aboriginal subordination is to undervalue their collective strength and resilience, which have given rise to the alternative perspectives they have developed as most suitable to their reality. While we cannot ignore the organized state and systemic oppression that continues to impose severe limitations on the lives of Inuit, we must also recognize their historical strengths as agents of change in their own world. That Inuit make decisions for themselves still comes as a surprise to many whites.

Perhaps the most definitive feature of life in 'postcolonial' Nunavik is the shifting relations of power between Inuit and whites, which reveal themselves in the following ways:

> While economic dependency remains acute, neither unequal exchange nor the extraction of surplus value characterize many Inuit communities; while a cultural division of labour still pervades wage employment in most communities, explicit assimilationism is no longer official policy and Inuit are assuming many supervisory and managerial roles; and while sovereignty remains with the federal state, Inuit have attained a degree of self-government through provincial politics, national Inuit organizations, and the Nunavut agreement (McLean, 1997, p.23).

In light of these changes, it becomes apparent that if we are to maintain a critical analysis of Inuit-white relations in the postcolonial era, a narrow focus on overt colonial processes will not suffice. In addition, we need to examine the more subtle forms of governance operating within contemporary arrangements between Inuit and dominant society institutions, including social services and education:

> The sociological insight that governance may be less of an explicit project of political rule than a subtle and diffuse structure of experiences through which people take on the capacity and desire to govern themselves needs to be expressed in contemporary discourses concerning aboriginal self-determination and self-government (McLean, 1997, p.22).

The potential for progressive change in Nunavik is constrained by the legacy of dependence and divisiveness brought about by fifty years of rapid change under white tutelage and its sub-structure, patronage. Brody (1975) describes how Euro-Canadian pluralism in the north ultimately gave rise to two polarized value systems at the local level, a development that renders leadership, consensus, and collective action problematic. Conservative, traditional values, he tells us, lead to an uncompromising cultural stance that precludes client-patron relationships with whites, while transitionalist values, more pragmatic and conciliatory in nature, accept the presence of white institutions while, at the same time, seeking to alter the distribution of power and privilege between Inuit and whites. Although transitionalist ideology is the more politically persuasive one for most Inuit because it addresses the bicultural aspects of today's northern communities, traditional values continue to play a crucial role. As Inuit seek to reconstruct their cultural identity within the emerging narrative of self-government and self-determination, they are reconnecting with the beliefs and moral values (e.g., mutuality, interdependence, reciprocity) that gave coherence and meaning to their lives before white intrusion, enabling them to survive their harsh environment for many generations. While some might perceive traditional beliefs and values to be anachronistic within contemporary social structures, local initiatives that bring elders and youth together in a project of shared learning aimed at giving contemporary expression to traditional Inuit values attest to their ongoing importance.

The potential for change in Nunavik is also constrained by the extreme intrusiveness of white tutelage, an everyday lived experience that conditions both Inuit and whites. It is difficult for Inuit to maintain a perception of themselves that is independent of whites, their culture, and especially their help, which is made to seem all the more necessary by the application of white norms of public administration (Paine, 1977). Relegated to the margins of their own communities, at the center of which stand white institutions, many Inuit today experience a deep sense of loss and uncertainty. However, it is not only Inuit who experience uncertainty in the current situation. Whites are increasingly unsure and ambivalent about their ongoing presence and function in Nunavik: 'An increasing number of them have difficulty in accepting unequivocally that they are only givers; they may also see themselves as takers (of natural resources for instance), and as deprivers, depriving a people of their prerogative to make decisions, and even as destroyers' (Paine, 1977, p.14). The ambiguity that characterizes Inuit-white relations in present day Nunavik, brought about in part by the slippage in historically specific constructions of self and Other that constitute the structure of white tutelage, opens up possibilities to envision alternative ways of knowing and being. Using ambivalence as a constructive resource for change entails making use of the 'difficult knowledge' that comes when we begin to confront the contradictions in our pedagogic practice.

I turn now to the question of what kind of educational experience is required to enable students to construct new forms of social worker identity and practice within the context of decolonization and Inuit self-determination. How can we assist students to co-author an Inuit narrative of social work practice with their communities? In his analysis of aboriginal teacher training programs, Hesch notes that 'the problematic posed by the processes through which students develop their formative practice ideologies centers on the extent to which they will or will not be engaged in the reproduction of hegemony in their cultural and ideological practices within their communities' (1996, p.281). Applying his insight to my own work, I am prompted to ask whether we are successfully resisting the temptation to create Inuit social workers in our own likeness or simply grooming them to replace us.

Inuit Students and Their Practice Context

By contrast with their mainstream counterparts who typically come with all of the prerequisites for postsecondary study and attend a full-time program on campus, Inuit students enrolled in the Nunavik program are adult learners with family responsibilities, varied academic backgrounds and preparation, and jobs in social service agencies for which they are concurrently being trained. They practice social work in remote settlements where they must contend with a high incidence of social problems including family violence, substance abuse, child sexual abuse, and suicide, all symptomatic of the psychic consequences of various forms of oppression. Many of the students have experienced personal and family trauma with the same issues they must address in their work.

The small size and isolation of arctic communities are significant features of the students' practice context where overlapping and intertwined relationships between workers and family members, colleagues, and leisure companions belie western conceptions of professional social work, including worker and client identities and relationships. State-organized social services in the north replicate the bureaucratic structures and divisions of labor characteristic of southern, mainstream practice, along with its attendant shortcomings. Perhaps most troubling for workers and their communities is the fragmentation of services into specialized practice and the creation of vested interests in discrete service sectors, both of which function to undermine collective action for change. Moreover, the fragmentation of services has been thoroughly institutionalized by funding agreements with external agencies (e.g. health, education, justice) that reinforce dependent links to both federal and provincial jurisdictions (Brant-Castellano, Stalwick, and Wiens, 1986).

The Inuit workers' location within the service bureaucracy parallels that of aboriginal people in the broader social, economic, and political contexts of Canadian society where, as members of a minority group, they are discriminated against in their efforts to participate fully in dominant society institutions (Bolaria and Li, 1990). Although the increased presence of Inuit in the social service sector may imply a shift away from the paternalism that characterizes historic relations between Inuit and whites, the current administration's insistence upon the correctness of its own institutional rules leaves the structure of white tutelage intact (Paine, 1977). Accountable to both agency and community for their interventions, Inuit workers find themselves in a subordinate and oppositional stance *vis-à-vis* the service bureaucracy. Their need for validation from both the community and their employers constitutes an intractable practice dilemma in that the more they succeed in meeting agency expectations of their work, the more likely they are to be judged unfavourably by members of the community, many of who remain sceptical and suspicious of 'the white man's law' (Mastronardi, 1990).

The social service centers in Nunavik exist in a dynamic state of tension wherein administrators uphold the need for conventional agency models to ensure practice standards while communities press for innovation and local control. The objective for the Inuit is not simply to gain administrative control but to transform social services into more authentic expressions of Inuit culture. The contrast between agency and community priorities gives rise to competing expectations of workers' practice and preparation: whereas administrators emphasize the need to ensure workers' technical competencies (i.e. to meet bureaucratic requirements of their jobs), students themselves acknowledge the importance of technical skills but stress their need to develop knowledge and capacities as healers and agents of change.

Zapf (1995) notes that aboriginal students are frequently less interested in joining the social work profession than they are in acquiring the knowledge and skills to help their communities. The social change agenda implicit in the students' community-based practice suggests that their reasons for pursuing higher education likely extend well beyond self-interest. From this vantage point, students might view higher education 'as a means of reducing inequality and sharing in the opportunities of the larger society; overcoming dependency and neo-colonialism; engaging in research to advance aboriginal knowledge; providing the knowledge and expertise required by their communities; demystifying mainstream culture; and learning the politics and history of racial discrimination' (Kirkness and Barnhardt, 1991, p.5). These learning objectives reveal that:

> a symbiotic relationship exists between meeting the education needs of students and contributing to the social, economic, and spiritual needs of their communities. From an aboriginal perspective, the two are integrally connected in the sense that the individual is dependent on a healthy community for social, emotional, and spiritual sustenance while the community relies on healthy individuals for its well-being (Barnhardt, 1991, p.214).

To balance individual and collective interests in our pedagogy requires that we challenge the tendency in western society and education to promote individual options for achievement at the expense of the social connections that make achievement meaningful (Hampton, 1993). Thus, to ensure a culturally congruent learning experience for students, we need to emphasize cooperative and collaborative strategies that extend the learning project beyond the classroom walls. Providing teachers who share the same cultural background as their students is an important step, but will not be enough if organizational structures compel them to behave in ways no different from dominant society practitioners (Corson and Lemay, 1996).

It becomes readily apparent in the foregoing discussion that in order to work effectively in the social, economic, and political contexts of contemporary Nunavik, Inuit social work students require an educational experience that is significantly different from that provided in conventional, mainstream programs. In other words, it is necessary that we do more than train social workers who just happen to be Inuit; it is crucial that our pedagogy and its supporting curriculum reflect the distinctive needs of students and their communities. While there is general agreement that the conventional curriculum cannot simply be transported into the north (Brant-Castellano et al., 1986; Pace and Smith, 1990; Brown, 1992; Morrisette, McKenzie, and Morrisette, 1993; Zapf, 1995), there are no clear guidelines on how to proceed. What the university has to offer Inuit students will be useful only to the extent that it has instrumental value and connects with their own aspirations and cultural predispositions (Martin, 1993, p.3).

The challenges posed for critical social work educators in the postcolonial context of Inuit social work practice and education are formidable. In the discussion that follows, I describe and reflect critically on some of the difficulties I encounter in attempting to bring a critical orientation to bear in my own practice.

Walking on Thin Ice

The question of what counts as valid knowledge, and who decides, is central to the process of curriculum adaptation to meet Inuit requirements. I use the analogy of walking on thin ice to convey something of the difficulty I experience in attempting to respond sensitively to the broad spectrum of needs and interests that converge in the daily operation of the Nunavik social work education program: the needs of students for a relevant and meaningful learning experience; the requirements of the social service centers that employ the students and expect them to function with relative autonomy in their communities; the requirements of the university; the expectations of program funders, in this instance, the provincial Ministry of Education; and the expectations that I have of my own practice. To balance this complex configuration of interests is a daunting challenge, rendered all the more problematic by skepticism within mainstream institutions, which is predictable when differences in an education program encompass course content, delivery format, student characteristics, and specially recruited staff. The conservatism of universities that tends to equate different with inferior is mirrored by aboriginal communities who voice similar concerns that the designation of 'special native program' might imply lower standards (Brant-Castellano et al., 1986, p.173). They insist, therefore, that while program content and delivery must be adapted to their requirements, the quality of education must not be compromised.

In order to gain access to resources and to maintain program status, the School of Social Work must emphasize disciplinary knowledge in the curriculum. At the same time, to respond adequately to student and community needs, program objectives must be directed toward something that is practical, immediate, and relevant. The cultural appropriateness of mainstream theory has to be balanced with the need to avoid creating a seemingly inferior program by straying too far from acceptable standards of social work practice as articulated by the Canadian Association of Schools of Social Work in its professional code of ethics (Brown, 1992, p.50). Difficulties arise, however, in both social work practice and teaching venues because the professional code fails to take into account the realities of northern practice and the dilemmas faced by Inuit practitioners, including issues that stem from limited supervision and collegial feedback; from having to practice beyond one's competence; from access to too much information; and from dual relationships between workers and clients (Delaney and Brownlee, 1996), which are so common that one of our Inuit teachers coined the phrase 'intervening relatively' to capture this aspect of her work.

In a similar vein, the program must comply with university regulations concerning both curriculum structure and process (e.g., emphasis on literate knowledge, hierarchical organization and fragmentation of knowledge, criteria for admissions and student evaluation). As defined by mainstream institutions, rigorous standards are derived from principles of efficiency, cost effectiveness, accountability, behavioral objectives, standardized testing, and the rhetoric of individualism (Apple, 1998, p.189). Grounded as they are in educational ideologies and values of the dominant society, mainstream standards are not appropriate for evaluating the success of educational programs intended for aboriginal communities. Hampton (1993) notes, for example, how the continued focus on individual versus group achievement in western education constitutes an ongoing assault on aboriginal peoples' collectivist ethic. The competitive success of the individual is an implicit value in western society and education and, as such, is in direct conflict with the value that Inuit place on group success through individual achievement. Alternative sets of standards by which to assess educational program responsiveness to aboriginal considerations have emerged from the experience of tribal colleges and aboriginal training institutes. Kirkness and Barnhardt (1991), for instance, propose that programs should be evaluated on the basis of their demonstrated ability to respect students for who they are, to be relevant to their worldview, to offer reciprocity in their relationships with others, and to help students exercise responsibility over their own lives.

The tension between academic standards and local needs represents an ethical challenge for mainstream educators because it raises the question of whose values are protected in the curriculum (Brown, 1992, p.51). The history of aboriginal education in Canada clearly demonstrates that programs designed to meet aboriginal requirements cannot be a positive force for social change if the goals and content reflect only dominant society culture and values (Taylor, Crago, and McAlpine, 1993). If the Nunavik program is to function as a resource for progressive change, program standards must respect Inuit cultural integrity by reflecting their values and beliefs concerning knowledge, the transmission of knowledge, and the evaluation of learning. My experience with the program suggests that curriculum adaptation fails to meet this challenge insofar as it continues to privilege dominant ideologies of social work practice while leaving the core assumptions, values, and logic of the curriculum itself unchanged. For instance, 'the western notion of a professional helper with recognized knowledge and a skill set that enables her to practice effectively in any location does not fit well with the crucial sense of place that is a foundation of traditional aboriginal knowledge' (Zapf, 1999, p.146).

Although curriculum adaptation might be safer because it is not likely to attract unwanted attention, it cannot honor Inuit values and beliefs in the requisite ways. In order to do so, we must resist interpretations of innovative programming as a question of watering down standards. The fundamental question is whether Inuit can represent their values in the design and implementation of education programs. Their right to articulate and to apply their own standards of excellence is at stake in this debate. Self-determination in education should give Inuit clear authority to create curriculum and to set standards to achieve their educational goals. In order to facilitate the realization of Inuit educational objectives, we must be prepared to negotiate agreements that convey mutual recognition of one another's curriculum decisions and standards.

Disturbing the Balance of Power

Conventional structures within universities provide Inuit with very limited means to ensure the relevance and appropriateness of educational programs that are offered in their communities. The claims to autonomy of powerful interest groups within the university and the privileges of tenure significantly reduce their capacity to exert a direct influence upon the university. Moreover, as Barnhardt suggests (1991, p.222), programs intended to respond to uniquely aboriginal concerns are typically treated as anomalous and outside the purview of the university's customary mission, thereby contributing to a stance of scholarly detachment and aloofness from the communities it is meant to serve.

Within the confines of distinctive aboriginal programs such as ours, located on the margins of university social work education, Inuit are in a position to exert some influence upon curriculum policy. From the outset, the program has been loosely structured as a partnership between the School and the communities of Nunavik designed to afford some measure of community control. In pursuit of this objective, the program has endeavored to develop strong ties with the community it serves through its field-based delivery format, use of local resources, and links with the agencies where students are employed. Although the existing program model offers some possibilities for Inuit control, the program's administrative location within the university constrains the nature and extent of their participation. The connection between the program and the university is a hierarchical not a lateral one and as a result, the decision-making authority is concentrated in the highest echelons. University administrators continue to make policy decisions, for example, concerning admission criteria and student evaluation, on behalf of instead of with Inuit.

Having to implement policies such as these, formulated without the full participation of Inuit, is a particularly troubling aspect of my work as program coordinator. These situations evoke for me disturbing images of white tutors deciding the best interests of their Inuit protégés. The maintenance of institutional structures and processes that exclude Inuit as full partners serves only to reinforce white privilege and to sustain the unequal relations of power that emancipatory pedagogy seeks to challenge. The contradiction that I experience, the disconnect, between the values that guide my work and the actual practices in which I participate, albeit sometimes very reluctantly, is difficult to reconcile within the institutional setting of the university.

A different picture emerges at the level of site-specific curriculum development (i.e., individual courses), for it is here that Inuit are actively engaged in policy decision-making and where I experience a much greater degree of congruence between my own values, beliefs, and practices. The following features of current practice have evolved over time through dialogue and collaboration between Inuit teachers and students, their workplace supervisors, and university staff working in the Nunavik program: decisions regarding course content and process are made collaboratively; Inuit content knowledge and methods are explicitly highlighted; courses are taught in Inuttitut and students complete all written work in their choice of language; students are supported to question the relevance of what they hear (i.e., qallunaat worldview) in relation to what they know from personal and professional experience; and students are supported to conceptualize and to articulate Inuit approaches to helping and to develop new tools and strategies as required, for instance, to manage the authority and exercise of discretion that are particularly difficult aspects of their daily practice (Mastronardi, 1990).

While the existing possibilities for Inuit participation in decision-making helps to ensure a more culturally appropriate and relevant learning experience for students, and supports the conceptual and practical development of an Inuit approach to social work, these will remain temporary gains unless Inuit also acquire the power to determine what is useful and valid knowledge for social work practice in their communities. As we have seen, even with all of the ambiguity that it brings, community control is a critical issue for proponents of aboriginal education among whom community participation and ownership are crucial as vehicles to empowerment and as a means to ensure educational program relevance (Martin, 1993, p.2). Local control, therefore, is not just a philosophical or political good but instead it is a defining characteristic of aboriginal education.

Where to From Here?

The issues that emerge for critical social work practice and education in the postcolonial era demand a focus on the deconstruction of white privilege and our ability to listen to and to support aboriginal voices in the reconstruction of their cultural identity and self-determination. If we are committed to 'working on the side of Inuit', we must engage critically with the tension involved in trying to move toward the transformative end of the education continuum while being pushed toward the domesticating end by material and ideological forces with which we contend in our daily practice (Mayo, 1999, p.5).

For aboriginal people the challenge is to translate the well-honed critique of colonial institutions into initiatives that go well beyond the deconstruction of oppressive ideologies and practices to give expression to aboriginal philosophies, worldviews, and social relations. For non-aboriginal people, the challenge is to open up spaces for aboriginal initiatives in schools and colleges, work sites, and organizations so that indigenous ways of knowing can flourish and intercultural sharing can be practised in a spirit of coexistence and mutual respect (Brant-Castellano, 2000, p.23).

In the reflective critique of my own practice, I identified some of the practices of resistance in which staff and students currently engage to create spaces for Inuit social worker identity and practice to evolve, for example, by problematizing mainstream knowledge, by negotiating course content and objectives, and by challenging fixed identity categories of worker and client, as well as teacher and student. While I believe that participants in the Nunavik program have made some important gains in this regard, we need to remain concerned with engaging in educational processes that are not meant to consolidate 'what is' but are driven by a vision of 'what should and can be' (Mayo, 1999, p.5).

Universities have an important role to play in redressing the historical inequities between Inuit and state institutions. Institutional legitimating of indigenous knowledge and skills, or a re-valuation of knowledge not derived from books, is essential if universities are to respect Inuit cultural integrity. An ability to help students articulate and build upon their customary forms of consciousness and representation as they expand their understanding of the world in which they live is also crucial (Kirkness and Barnhardt, 1991, p.8).

As the service provider in this instance, the School of Social Work needs to take the initiative to create and support opportunities for a dialogical process of shared learning to unfold among all program participants. Together, we need to address the question of educational objectives in a forthright manner. If the Nunavik program is to meet Inuit requirements more adequately, our academic goals must complement community development goals in such a way that the process of education becomes intertwined in local development processes. This would entail ongoing struggles and projects in the community becoming an explicit curriculum concern.

Repositioning our pedagogy on the borders or the meeting place between Inuit and white cultures would enable us to appreciate the value of cultural conflicts as a source of learning for developing a more emancipatory pedagogy. The articulation of competing perspectives and expectations of the curriculum would be a productive first step toward a more meaningful dialogue among program partners.

Lastly, in order to develop the requisite cross-cultural insight, it is imperative for us as mainstream educators to resituate ourselves and to be open to learning from our students. We would do well to heed the words of Ojibwe Elder Howard Contin, who teaches that the Creator gave two ears and one mouth so that we could listen twice as much as we speak.

References

Apple, M. (1998), 'Social crisis and curriculum accords', *Educational Theory*, Vol. 38(2), pp. 191-201.

Bannerji, H. (1991), 'But who speaks for us? Experience and agency in conventional feminist paradigms', in H. Bannerji, L. Carty, K. Dehli, S. Heald, and K. McKenna (eds.), *Unsettling Relations: The University as a Site of Feminist Struggles*, Women's Press, Toronto, pp. 67-107.

Barnhardt, R. (1991), 'Higher education in the fourth world: Indigenous people take control', *Canadian Journal of Native Education*, Vol. 18(2), pp. 199-231.

Battiste, M. (1998), 'Enabling the autumn seed: Toward a decolonised approach to aboriginal knowledge, language, and education', *Canadian Journal of Native Education*, Vol. 22(1), pp. 16-27.

Brant-Castellano, M. (2000), 'Updating aboriginal traditions of knowledge', in G. Sefa Dei, B. Hall, and D. Rosenberg (eds.), *Indigenous Knowledges in Global Contexts: Multiple Readings of Our World*, University of Toronto Press, Toronto, pp. 21-36.

Brant-Castellano, M., Stalwick, M.H. and Wiens, F. (1986), 'Native social work education in Canada: Issues and adaptations', *Canadian Social Work Review*, Vol. 4, pp. 166-184.

Brody, H. (1975), *The People's Land: Eskimo and Whites in the Eastern Arctic*, Penguin Press, Aylesbury.

Brown, L. (1992), 'Social work education for aboriginal communities', *Canadian Journal of Higher Education*, Vol. 22(3), pp. 46-54.

Canada Ministry of Supply and Services (1996), *Report of the Royal Commission on Aboriginal Peoples: Gathering Strength*, Author, Ottawa.

Colorado, P. (1995), 'Coherence: A process of social work education with aboriginal students', in K. Feehan and D. Hannis (eds.), *From Strength to Strength: Social Work Education and Aboriginal Peoples*, Grant McEwan Community College, Regina.

Corson, D. and Lemay, S. (1996), *Social justice and Language Policy in Education: The Canadian Research*, Ontario Institute for Studies in Education Press, Toronto.

Delaney, R. and Brownlee, K. (1996), 'Ethical dilemmas in northern social work practice', in R. Delaney, K. Brownlee, and M.K. Zapf (eds.), *Issues in Northern Social Work Practice*, Laurentian University Press, Thunder Bay, pp. 47-69.

Ellsworth, E. (1989), 'Why doesn't this feel empowering: Working through the repressive myths of critical pedagogy', *Harvard Educational Review*, Vol. 59(3), pp. 297-324.

Freisen, D. and Orr, J. (1998), 'New paths, old ways: Exploring the places of influence in role identity', *Canadian Journal of Native Education*, Vol. 22(2), pp. 188-200.

Goodson, I. (1990), 'Studying curriculum: Towards a social constructionist perspective', *Curriculum Studies*, Vol. 22(4), pp. 299-312.

Haig-Brown, C. (1995), *Taking Control: Power and Contradiction in First Nations Adult Education*, University of British Columbia Press, Vancouver.

Hampton, E. (1993), 'Toward a redefinition of American Indian/Alaska Native education', *Canadian Journal of Native Education*, Vol. 20(1), pp. 261-309.

Healy, K. (2000), 'Reinventing critical social work: Challenges from practice, context, and postmodernism', *Critical Social Work*, Vol. 2(1), pp. 1-14.

Hesch, R. (1995), 'Aboriginal teachers as organic intellectuals', in R. Ng, P. Staton, and J. Scane (eds.), *Anti-Racism, Feminism, and Critical Approaches to Education*, Ontario Institute for Studies in Education Press, Toronto, pp. 99-128.

Hesch, R. (1996), 'Antiracist educators *sui generis*? The dialectics of aboriginal teacher education', *Canadian Review of Sociology and Anthropology*, Vol. 33(3), pp. 269-289.

Kirkness, V. and Barnhardt, R. (1991), 'First Nations and higher education: The four R's – respect, relevance, reciprocity, and responsibility', *Journal of American Indian Education*, Vol. 30(3), pp. 1-15.

Lather, P. (1991), *Getting Smart. Feminist Research and Pedagogy Within the Postmodern*, Routledge, N.Y.

Liston, D. and Zeichner, K. (1991), *Teacher Education and the Social Conditions of Schooling*, Routledge, New York.

Martin, P. (1993), 'Considerations for aboriginal adult education programming', *Canadian Journal of Native Education*, Vol. 20(1), pp. 247-254.

Mastronardi, L. (1990), 'The Inuit community workers' experience of youth protection', in L. Davies and E. Shragge (eds.), *Bureaucracy and Community: Essays on the Politics of Social Work*, Black Rose Books, Montreal, pp. 103-135.

Mayo, P. (1999), *Gramsci, Freire, and Adult Education: Possibilities for Transformative Action*, Zed Books, London.

McLean, S. (1997), 'Objectifying and naturalizing individuality: A study of adult education in the Canadian arctic', *Canadian Journal of Sociology*, Vol. 22(1), pp. 1-29.

Morrisette, V., McKenzie, B., and Morrisette, L. (1993), 'Towards an aboriginal model of social work practice', *Canadian Social Work Review, Vol.* 10(1), pp. 91-107.

Pace, J. and Smith, A. (1990), 'Native social work education: Struggling to meet the need', *Canadian Social Work review*, Vol. 7(1), pp. 109-119.

Paine, R. (1977), *The White Arctic: Anthropological Essays on Tutelage and Ethnicity*, Memorial University, St. John's.

Perley, D. (1993), 'Aboriginal education in Canada as internal colonialism', *Canadian Journal of Native Education,* Vol. 20(1), pp. 235-246.

Smith, L. (2001), *Decolonizing Methodologies: Research and Indigenous Peoples*, Zed Books, London.

Taylor, D., Crago, M., and McAlpine, L. (1993), 'Education in aboriginal communities: Dilemmas around empowerment', *Canadian Journal of Native Education*, Vol. 20(1), pp. 176-183.

Zapf, M.K. (1995), 'Teaching social work in aboriginal outreach programs', *Human Services in the Rural Environment*, Vol. 18(4), pp. 182-197.

Zapf, M.K. (1997), 'Voice and social work education: Learning to teach from my own story', *Canadian Social Work Review*, Vol. 14(1), pp. 83-97.

Zapf, M.K. (1999), 'Location and knowledge building: Exploring the fit of western social work and traditional knowledge', *Native Social Work Journal*, Vol. 2, pp. 138-152.

Chapter 10

Social Work Practice and Research as an Emancipatory Process

Kamal Fahmi

Introduction

For a profession like social work, committed to social justice and to the empowerment of oppressed and excluded social groups, participatory action research (PAR) seems, in the eyes of many social workers and researchers, consistent with this commitment (Healy, 2001; Finn, 1994; Reason, 1994; Sohng, 1996). Indeed, PAR is now endorsed as an alternative methodology able to respond to the philosophical and methodological challenges facing contemporary social work and research, especially the need for development of effective strategies for social inclusion (Bradbury and Reason, 2003; Healy, 2001). This promise is consistent with the fact that the PAR methodology, as developed by Freire (1970, 1973) subscribes to the basic tenets of critical theory; it seeks to link theory and practice through an understanding of praxis that occurs across both the personal and the political; and it questions dualistic modes of thinking and adopts a dialectical perspective suggesting that creative change can emerge in the tension between binary oppositions. PAR further asserts that knowledge and action cannot be separated and focuses on the production of knowledge that can help oppressed groups articulate and meet their needs. Lastly, PAR strives to promote the dialogic method whereby researchers, workers, and participants engage in relationships of mutual education within an overall context of reflexivity.

The 'promise' of PAR (Finn, 1994) has understandably generated high expectations (and scepticism) amongst its critics, especially those who adopt a poststructuralist/postmodernist perspective and have thus added to the tension between this perspective and those informed by critical theory. In this chapter, I will demystify some of the PAR promises, not to discredit the methodology, but to highlight the nature and scope of the political, technical and emotional challenges that need to be addressed for a PAR undertaking to be emancipatory. My objective is thus two-fold. I want to both ascertain and confirm the prospect for emancipatory social work practice and research as promised by PAR as a methodology well-suited for interventions that target excluded and oppressed populations. I also want to argue that PAR promises of democratic participation and empowerment are not ipso facto fulfilled by simply adopting a PAR stance;

instead, they should be conceived as challenging ideals to be actively pursued in an open-ended process of collective action to pre-figure a more just society.

To realize my objective for this chapter, I will draw on my experience as PAR practitioner and particularly on a participatory action research undertaking that spanned eight consecutive years of fieldwork with street kids in Cairo, Egypt between 1993 and 2001. Although I will focus only on the preparatory and 'getting-in' phase of this undertaking, I believe that the discussion of the challenges that characterized this phase well represent the essence of my argument.

How It Started and the Context

The PAR undertaking with Cairene street kids that I partly narrate here was initiated by two practitioners/researchers (myself and a colleague) who had previous experience of action research with street populations. We both wanted to *do something* with respect to the social phenomenon of so called *street children* that was becoming then, in late 1993, a priority on the international development agenda[1,2] In analysing the global failure to adequately address this complex and very diverse phenomenon, it seemed to us that it was the result of conceptual confusion with respect to defining who a street child is. The dominant discourse on street children defines them as victims or deviants. This reductionist and objectified definition, combined with a mode of practice emphasizing risk assessment measurement, has justified intervention approaches informed by a rescuing mentality that precludes any positive value to street life. Such approaches to intervention also occlude the capacity of many of these children for human agency and ipso facto exclude them from participation in the construction of solutions to their problems.

My colleague and I wanted to start from a different perspective. We assumed that street children could justifiably be represented as social actors who play a more or less active role in the development of their situation and are capable of participating in making decisions that affect them. This was our starting premise, despite a local context in which state officials trivialized the phenomenon (if not negated it altogether) and where the mainstream viewed street children as immoral perpetrators of serious social violations. Their very presence contradicts the state's official discourse on family values and ideas about public order and safety. Such transgressions justify the periodic 'cleaning up' of children from the streets, arrests, imprisonment, institutionalization, and torture (Human Rights Watch, 2003). Street girls are doubly marginalized in that they are viewed as blatantly violating dominant standards of femininity in the Egyptian context.

My colleague and I started working on a tentative PAR design that would evolve in developmental stages, with the overall objectives of:

- Infiltrating street children's milieus and establishing a meaningful participatory presence, using a street ethnography methodology;
- Understanding the magnitude, underlying factors and conditions, and persistence of the street children phenomenon;
- Developing community-based alternatives to institutionalization with the individuals and groups concerned.

The design needed to remain flexible in order to accommodate the new data expected to emerge in the process and to add progressively more depth to our understanding of the social realities of the individuals and groups that we would be engaged with.

Initiation of the PAR Process by 'Outsiders'

One common claim in the PAR literature is that PAR processes are usually initiated by a group of oppressed individuals who come together with a view to undertaking action to improve their situation and become more empowered. Reason (1994) acknowledges that 'many PAR projects could not occur without the initiative of someone with time, skill, and commitment, someone who will almost inevitably be a member of a privileged and educated group' (p.334). Yet Reason refers to this fact as a 'paradox ... [with which] PAR appears to sit uneasily' (p.334). It would seem appropriate now, after decades of PAR practice and documentation, to acknowledge the fact that the majority of PAR undertakings, like the one presented here, are initiated by outside researchers and/or practitioners who often come from the ranks of intellectuals by virtue of their privileged economic and social status. This recognition can pave the way for divesting PAR discourse of the dogmatic claim that the initiation of the research process itself comes from or should come from members of the oppressed groups. The majority of such groups, including street kids, have neither the abilities nor the resources to initiate a PAR process without help from outsiders.

Getting Started

Before proceeding with fieldwork, we needed to attend to a number of technical and political issues. The awareness that the project was to be implemented in a conservative and repressive climate of state surveillance necessitated the development of an institutional and political framework that was acceptable to state officials, *even if they did not completely approve of it.* Our next hurdle was to work out the intricacies of how to obtain approval for fieldwork from the relevant Egyptian authorities in a context that did not encourage the undertaking of such research.

Simultaneously, I started recruiting individuals to carry out the projected ethnographic investigation of a marginal and highly sceptical population of children and youth. I had difficulties identifying social workers willing to go down the streets and link up with kids in their life settings. It seems that for a great majority of social workers, this kind of activity is not consistent with a professional view of what social work is. I thus relied on informal networks to identify and recruit two lay persons, one male (Samir) and one female (Ranya), with the view to educating, training and equipping them *on the job* with necessary skills and knowledge using a reflective methodology. Through snowball recruiting, Ranya and Samir subsequently introduced and participated in the training of additional workers.

Last, but not least, we needed to overcome our fears and prejudices about the target population, the street kids. This meant also resisting the discouragement of colleagues, friends, and families who warned us that we were embarking on a 'difficult and dangerous' mission.

Observation Work: Identifying Key Street Localities

The main objective of observation work was to identify street localities where substantial numbers of kids were hanging around and to find potential points of entry. The work consisted primarily of roaming around the streets of Cairo at different hours of the day and night. In our search, we followed our own prior observations and knowledge, as well as following the kids in the streets. Friends and colleagues who knew of our undertaking passed on information and told us that they were surprised to observe that there were many more kids on the streets than they had initially thought. Keeping an eye open made us all see better.

Twenty-seven street localities were identified over a period of three months. They included strategic busy street corners, bus stops and terminals, railway stations, public squares, markets, commercial streets, vacant lots, areas around mosques, garbage dumps, spaces under bridges and overpasses. However, in the course of identifying these localities, we also observed a wide variety of individuals and activities. The street localities looked like living social milieus with numerous interactions, transactions and activities, many of which we were initially unable to discern or grasp. In some localities, the kids seemed to be actively engaged in some type of work, such as helping in a street food vending set-up, shoe-shining, or peddling goods such as selling paper tissue boxes to drivers at traffic lights. In other instances, the kids seemed to be just wandering around, or sniffing glue, or participating in some group activity, which was difficult to identify with precision. Some localities were empty by night time, whereas some kids were still to be found in other areas late at night and even slept there. We started to wonder whether some children went back home at intervals. Furthermore, many of the interactions between street kids and their surroundings were incomprehensible to us. Who were these youths and the adults often found in the immediate vicinity of street kids and who seemed to be involved in some kind of relationship with them?

In short, we were unable to tell on many occasions exactly what was going on. We had to contend with the fact that the answers to many of the questions and puzzles confronting us could only be revealed once we managed to infiltrate some of the street milieus.

Managing Emotions

Fear and Prejudice

During early participant observation work, our fear had to be acknowledged – fear of violence, of being ridiculed by the kids, or of looking stupid, and, certainly, the fear of being unable to handle sensitive situations that might suddenly arise on the street. We realized that many of our fears originated in the stereotypical fantasy about the wildness and havoc of street life and the belief that street kids would readily, for the sake of survival, commit violent acts. We had to remind ourselves constantly not to let these prejudices exaggerate our fears and unduly immobilize us.

Later, as the work progressed, many of these prejudices were challenged. Most of the violence takes place in-group and is directed against members of the group, seldom against outsiders. The crimes committed by street kids are of a petty nature; e.g., stealing hanging laundry and goods in marketplaces. Contrary to widespread belief, over the eight-year duration of the program, no evidence emerged tying these kids to the drug industry or to terrorist groups, as is often assumed.

We also needed to come to grips with the repugnant appearance of many of the kids. Barefoot, wearing shabby and dirty clothes, most had black dirt on their faces, arms, feet, and on every exposed part of their bodies, which were often also covered with scars. Their fingernails were quite long and full of dirt. It was difficult not to feel unnerved after shaking hands with them, and as the closeness of the rapport with them increased, so did the physical closeness so characteristic of Middle Eastern societies, which further intensified our feeling of discomfort.

However, this initial apprehension dissipated gradually as the development of a closer rapport with the kids made us less disturbed by their physical appearance. Subsequently, we found out that most of them enjoyed and appreciated personal cleanliness. Access to water and washing facilities were indeed some of their main problems. Interestingly, we also learned that the black dirt on some kids' bodies was self-administered, using mud. They resorted to this practice while they were begging, hoping to elicit enough disgust amongst prospective donors so that they would contribute some change hurriedly in order to get away from these 'filthy young monsters'. Furthermore, we came to appreciate that long fingernails are kept for defending oneself against assault.

Later, when the drop-in center was opened, the street workers felt no hesitation about helping some of the younger children to shower. Periodic hairdressing of all the kids and application of medicated lotion became a regular practice in order to minimize hair lice.

Witnessing Destitution

During early participant observation work, one of the most tormenting issues that we had to handle was our feeling of being incapable of providing much help regarding some situations of utmost destitution and misery facing young children. I still recall one late winter night when we met two girls holding hands and going around parked cars trying to identify a convenient sleeping spot. The older girl, who was seven or eight years old, told us that they had to sleep under a car so that they did not get picked up by the police. Under her arm, she was holding a piece of cardboard to use as a mattress for her and her younger sister, who was crying desperately. 'She is very tired and wants to sleep,' said the older sister, who looked exhausted and pale herself. She nevertheless made the effort to explain to us that they had fled from a police raid on nearby Ataba Square earlier in the evening, where their mother had been arrested. We knew that an urban upgrading plan was about to be implemented in the area of the square. This, as is often the case, was accompanied by the eviction of street people, who had managed to eke out a living and make a habitat around this busy square for many years, surviving by selling tea, soft drinks, and food to travellers waiting for buses at a main terminal located in the vicinity of the square. The dilemma for the older sister was that she did not really trust sleeping under a car. She was worried that she might not notice if the car started moving and that it might run them over. It was getting late and cold when it occurred to us to ask the doorman of an apartment building if he would let the two girls sleep in the building entrance hallway for few hours. To our relief, he agreed.

Later, in my warm bed, I was thinking of the strong desire that I had felt to bring these two girls home, to make them safe and comfortable and to accompany them to look for their mother the following day. Such situations occurred repeatedly afterwards, and we had to learn to acknowledge the limits of our ability to help.

Getting In: Infiltration

Faced with the question as to which street locality to use as an entry point, we decided on a place that was most familiar to the street worker, Samir. It was situated in the neighbourhood where he had been brought up, and where he still had good relations with influential and ordinary people alike.

The chosen street locality was strategically situated at the beginning of a major commercial thoroughfare, at the end of which are the famous Giza pyramids. The area also harbours many hotels, as well as one of Cairo's most active red light districts.

We had noticed that many kids hung around this locality and seemed to have relationships with the storeowners in the area. One of these shops, a small grocery store, belonged to a friend of Samir.

It was planned that Samir would pay more frequent visits to his friend at the store. Hanging around and having informal exchanges with his friend and the neighbouring milieu of shop owners was a convenient means of conducting close, covert observation of the kids in the area.

A few weeks after Samir started intensive observation at this street locality, Ranya, a female street worker, was recruited and prepared to embark on a similar venture, targeting a community of street girls and women whom we had noticed in our preliminary field observation. The street locality where Ranya started working was in the busy vicinity of a major railway station, where kids running away from Upper Egypt disembark from the train. This is a key street locality, which groups of street people had been occupying for many years and still are. This locality had the added advantage of being close to Ranya's work place.

Ranya started by approaching female sidewalk vendors, who make tea and sell flat cakes and cookies that they purchase from nearby bakeries. Buying cookies and exchanging greetings with the girls and women on a daily basis, Ranya gradually became a well-known, friendly figure.

From Observation to Participant Observation: Accompanying the Kids

The main objective of this getting-in phase was infiltration and establishment of relationships of trust with some street kids. Conceived as *a process of learning and acculturation*, participant observation concentrated on observing routine activities, social organizations, behaviour, conversations, and events, and on identifying values, norms, power structures, and patterns, as well as learning the language of the street.

To facilitate the building of relationships of trust, Samir and Ranya were instructed not to be too inquisitive, but to display interest, care and humour, and to create some complicity over trivial matters. In short, the strategy consisted of gaining the kids' friendship and esteem while leaving them eager for more of the street workers' company.

In his observation work at the grocery shop, Samir noticed that there were relationships between the shop owners and the kids. Cleaning the sidewalk in front of the shops, bringing tea from a nearby café or going to change a large bill were some of the petty tasks that the kids occasionally did in return for a little money. In this way, Samir started to establish contact with some of the kids by asking them to buy him tea.

Being a professional athlete, Samir quickly became an idol and a great deal of his early exchanges with the kids revolved around sports. Ranya, being a mother herself, started sharing with the street mothers concerns and problems regarding child rearing and parenting. She noticed that the girls were interested in the way in which she applied make up and so, picking up on it, she started to give them some hints and advice.

As noted by Prus (1996), the move from observation into participant observation adds a new and vital dimension to ethnographic work as researchers come much closer to the lived experiences of the people they are studying. In accompanying the kids through their everyday living in street milieus, Samir and Ranya capitalized on the use of the self as a powerful tool for mutual trust building. The building of non-threatening identities and relations of solidarity was the first task that had to be undertaken in order to develop reciprocal trust and respect.

In establishing a meaningful, participatory and sustained presence in the street milieus frequented by the kids, Samir and Ranya and the street workers who subsequently joined the team were able to develop *accompaniment*[3] relationships that were not exclusively, or necessarily, 'help-oriented'. Instead, the objective was to develop rapport and relationships that were basically ones of acceptance, trust, complicity and solidarity, created by the repeated sharing of the ordinary, warm and tender gestures of everyday life: laughing together, seeing each other in different situations that might even be ridiculous, allowing the other to live and express different emotions, playing and having fun, contemplating, creating, going for walks, joking, and allowing the other the right to live a crisis, to express disappointment, fear, suffering and a desire to die. As such, the primary role of street workers was to offer their 'being' through the use of self in a sustained participatory presence in the everyday life of the kids they came to know.

Thus, after several weeks of rather superficial participation activities, some kids and mothers started to tell their personal stories, interests, concerns, complaints and problems to Samir and Ranya. The street workers became a 'buddy' for some and a 'big brother/sister' for others. Some kids and mothers started to compete for the street workers' attention, to the extent of secretly telling them about the 'bad' behaviour and 'strange' stories of peers. From then on, as dialogical relationships developed, the specifics of street life, the cultures and norms of its inhabitants, and the viewpoints and practices of the kids themselves were progressively revealed.

Infiltration and Ethics

Maurice Punch (1986, 1994) maintains that *infiltration* is a key skill in field research methods, despite the fact that this concept/technique is fraught with negative connotations and associated with police and espionage techniques. At many of the public presentations I have given over the last ten years on our work with street kids, objections have been made to the use of the term *infiltration* to describe the strategy of accessing the street milieus. Disdain has often been expressed at the analogy between a scientific endeavour and an intelligence methodology, one that is viewed as being one of the uglier aspects of repressive state conduct. Upon closer verification, the objection is often based on ethical and moral concerns that argue against deception and for the fully informed consent of the research subjects. The objection is even stronger in PAR, where subjects are supposedly viewed as participants/partners, thus 'to dupe them in any way would be to undermine the very processes one wants to examine' (Punch, 1994, p. 89).

The issue here is whether *covert* research is ethical or not. The debates over the covert-overt issue in the literature are far from conclusive. While some writers totally reject covert participant observation, others argue that without it, many street-style ethnographies would be practically impossible to undertake. In my view, the choice of when and how to resort to covert participant observation has to be consistent with the research objectives and the methodology used, and must always be guided by principles related to the dignity and privacy of individuals, the avoidance of harm, and the confidentiality of the research data. In other words, 'sound ethics and sound methodology go hand in hand' (Sieber in Punch, 1994, p. 95).

I would like to elaborate on this covert-overt dilemma using the example of the PAR presented here. Had Ranya or Samir from the outset revealed to the kids that they were involved in some research that aimed at understanding their situation, it would have been impossible for them to establish relationships of trust with the kids. Although it may sound contradictory to say that the establishment of trust necessitated concealment of the research agenda, this was the case in this particular situation. Continually harassed by security agents and passers-by, regularly picked up and maltreated by police, and always suspected of different crimes, street people are understandably cautious and suspicious of inquisitive intruders. Introducing oneself as a researcher or data collector would have elicited enough mistrust to subvert the establishment of a meaningful and sustained relationship with the kids. Furthermore, most street kids are not spontaneously enthusiastic about telling their *true* stories to outsiders. These stories are sometimes the unique thing over which they may have some control. Understandably, they do not wish to readily relinquish this control to satisfy those questioning them.

Furthermore, in the case of PAR presented here, concealing the street workers' identity, both as practitioners and researchers, was necessary in light of the uncertainty regarding the development of the PAR enterprise. During this initial phase, there was no guarantee that we would be able to identify and obtain the necessary funds that would have enabled us to make the switch from research *on* street kids to action and research *with* them. Indeed, we were eager not to elicit unrealistic expectations on the part of the kids; had we not been able to move further in the work, the promises of PAR presented to the kids would have been the source of major disappointment.

Invisible Others: The Gatekeepers

Prior to infiltration work, we had hypothesized that street kids did not live on the streets as isolated individuals. Rather, we assumed that in order to survive, most kids would join some group or street organization in which the leaders might not welcome outsiders poking their nose into their affairs. As such, we expected that the kids contacted by the street workers were also being observed by peers and leaders who would question them regarding the identity of the workers and their motives. A non-obtrusive form of infiltration was deemed necessary in order to avoid a rapid rejection by the milieu, providing another reason for being covert.

This hypothesis required the street workers to be very careful about how they presented themselves, the impressions they gave and the questions they asked. The leaders had to be neutralized. In addition, the state security agents and informants, who we felt were also bound to be mingling with the kids and their surroundings, had to be taken into account. They, too, had to feel that we were benign for them to let us proceed with our work.

These *invisible others* were thus the *gatekeepers* who had to *authorize* and not hinder our access to street milieus. Being invisible meant that our messages to them regarding who we were and what we were doing had to be conveyed indirectly through the kids and the street individuals with whom we established contact and relationships.

The Kids' Manipulations and the Workers' Acculturation

On a practical level, it was necessary to appreciate the physically and emotionally demanding nature of direct, day-to-day street work. The workers were relating not only to the children, but also to their surroundings and the street community as a whole. These included a wide variety of street adults who, in some capacity or another, influenced the daily existence of street kids: natural leaders, police informants, street food vendors, tea makers, security agents, street employers, grocery and coffee shop owners, shoe-shiners, commercial sex workers, and others, who were part of the children's surroundings in the streets. Although many children were forming attachments with individual workers, the workers began to realize that such gratifying relationships could also be very taxing if they were not adequately managed.

Further complicating the situation was the tendency of the kids to manipulate. Presenting untrue, well-rehearsed stories about experiences, family background, current situation, age and reasons for leaving home is often well integrated into the behaviour patterns of street kids. This misrepresentation seems fundamental to survival and is related to an ability to manipulate the environment. The street worker becomes another facet of the environment that children must successfully manoeuvre in order to survive. There are other reasons why the children manipulate information: it allows them to get back at a society that devalues them. Falsified information also serves to keep society from knowing the details of their lives. Consequently, the street workers had to learn to accept a degree of 'healthy manipulation' from the children, who were seeking to maintain a sense of control. This also facilitated the development of a relationship between the child and the street worker based on the child's terms.

Moreover, there is a delicate balance to be observed by street workers, who not only have to maintain professional integrity and identity, but also to be versatile enough to move comfortably in the street child's domain without trying to become one of the children. There is a danger of 'false acculturation', whereby street workers over-identify by assuming cultural characteristics that are unnatural for them. All of the above required the maintenance of a high level of engaged support and self-investment.

The Progression of the PAR Process

It took over two years to accomplish the getting-in phase outlined above, to acquire an adequate understanding of the phenomenon of street children and to establish a comfortable level of complicity between the kids and the street workers. The acculturation required to achieve this necessitated a long-term self-investment. While ethnographic street work constituted the essence of fieldwork undertaken during this phase of gaining access, the socio-political act of going onto the street, infiltrating street milieus and developing relationships of mutual trust and acceptance with street kids and their surroundings involved bridging a formidable gap between mainstream society and a 'deviant' group. The construction of the necessary bridges for this operation was facilitated by the implementation of a non-obtrusive and carefully designed street work methodology. This allowed us to access marginalized and dissident street kids in the very context of the street organizations and milieus in which they were active actors.

Through observation and participant observation, the street workers were covertly observing behaviours, informally interviewing and collecting various accounts including family background, circumstances that led to the street, nature of street life, relations with peers and street leaders, modes of survival and acculturation and other data. The analysis of the data recorded in field notes was an on-going group activity for participating street workers. The increasing 'intimate familiarity' (Blumer, 1969) developed with groups of street kids often involved unpredictable situations in which uncertainties and ambiguities gave rise to a large number of ethical issues. Pondering on these issues was the major gateway promoting the workers' capacity for critical reflection. From the outset, reflexivity became for us a 'survival mechanism' to feel our way, to manage the ethical dilemmas raised, to acquire and develop conceptual understanding, and to contain our own affective states.

It should be noted that the getting-in phase consisted mostly of research *on* street children. The participation dimension was focused on educating and enabling the street workers to become practitioners-researchers and, consequently, increasing their participation in the design, implementation, and monitoring of the different activities. The explicit participation of the kids was not possible as long as the work was being conducted covertly.

Accordingly, at the beginning of the phase that followed, we revealed our identity as street workers-researchers to the kids with whom we had established trust relationships during the first phase of ethnographic street work. This 'coming out' was needed so we could shift from doing research *on* street kids to doing research *with* them within a PAR framework. Indeed, this shift fitted well with the sense we were making of the realities of the kids and the milieus in which they live. By then, we had amply observed and understood that far from being mere victims or deviants, these kids, in running away from alienating structures and finding relative freedom in the street, often become relatively autonomous and capable of actively defining their situations in their own terms. They are able to challenge the roles assigned to children, make judgements and develop a network of niches in the heart of the metropolis in order to resist exclusion and chronic repression. In short, many street children and youth are already actors actively engaged as agents of change in their own lives. As self-reflecting beings, they can and do direct, monitor, assess and adjust their own behaviour over time.

It was thus clear for us, as we came out to the kids, that the prospect for emancipatory research and action with them was contingent upon recognizing them as 'agents in the transformation of reality, through a constant dialogue which gives priority to their participation in the whole process' (UNICEF, 1987). Our political agenda was clear: we had the intention of siding with the excluded groups of kids to transform personal problems into collective advocacy for inclusion and a greater stake in the public good. The kids signed on and the second phase was launched.

The opening of the drop-in center and the intensification of accompaniment work, along with non-formal educational activities and collective soft advocacy, were the major features of the second phase together with the ethical issues and dilemmas they raised. A detailed account of this phase can be found in Fahmi, 2004 (see references). Here I conclude with some reflections regarding this kind of practice.

The 'In-Between' Position: Concluding Reflections

PAR processes of the kind described in this chapter are understandably very time-consuming, labour intensive, field based, longitudinal, and engaged undertakings that require extensive patience, perseverance and a capacity to handle a great deal of ambiguity. They also require a certain experiential knowledge that allows practitioners to venture into the life-worlds of the other while being careful not to provoke fusion and confusion problems by over-identifying with the other. Moreover, by taking the side of the excluded, PAR practitioners put their own identities on the line and subjugate their viewpoints to those of the many 'moral entrepreneurs'[4] (Becker, 1963) who may have a variety of vested interests regarding either the non-respectability of some people or practices being studied or the ethics of some aspects of the methodology employed. Furthermore, the promotion of values and notions such as empowerment, equity, self-reliance and commitment to the interests of local participants often entail challenging oppressive political and social arrangements, such that the research group is often positioned in opposition to dominant and mainstream forces.

We were quite aware of the fact that in accompanying street kids we were situating ourselves in an in-between position, dissident youngsters on one side and a scornful and hostile mainstream society on the other. While mediation between the kids and family, school, police, social and probation workers, reception centers and other instances was certainly an important aspect of fieldwork, it did not mean that we remained neutral. On the contrary, we sided with the kids as a means of validating their experiences, not so much as victims or deviant but more as active actors who were trying to cope with being excluded. Obviously, this was a politically sensitive position. However, it enabled us to witness their day-to-day reality and to advocate not only for an increased mutual tolerance between mainstream and deviant street societies, but also, and more importantly, to advocate for a genuine, humane representation of a young excluded population living precariously on the fringes of society.

However, despite the fact that we had opted for a soft collective advocacy approach, it did not save the NGO under whose auspices the PAR project was undertaken from being dismantled by Egyptian state officials in April 2001. The NGO went to court to contest the decree and the case is still being reviewed. This raises a question regarding the appropriateness of soft advocacy in light of escalating conservatism in the North and repressive regimes in the South. Behind this question is the issue of *resistance*, an issue which fortunately seems to be making its way again onto the agenda of social activists, albeit slowly and tentatively.

In both the North and the South we are witnessing the rise of a wave of political discourses that heavily invest in the revival of one of the most pernicious, yet stable, dichotomies constructed by human thought, namely, *good versus evil*. This can only add fuel to a mounting fundamentalism, which may have well started in the South but is today equally manifest in the North. Resisting this global and exclusive binary of 'good and evil' as advanced by the fundamentalists is no easy task for today's activists. The intensification of surveillance mechanisms[5] and the blatant exercise of power (under the guise of pre-emptive security measures). Activists in the North are now experiencing some of what has been until recently considered to be the 'fate' of their Southern counterparts, namely, the shrinking of the democratic margin of manoeuvre permitting the existence of nuances and a dialectical sensitivity to go beyond the simplistic/fundamentalist discourses of good versus evil.

In the face of such a regressive state of affairs, many activists understandably feel pessimistic regarding the prospect for any meaningful emancipation in terms of social justice, at least for the immediate and medium terms. However, even if the prospects for emancipation at the structural level seem dim, if not nil, this does not preclude the prospect for pursuing emancipation through social processes at the local level. This becomes even more important when we realize that the present situation is further aggravated by the resonance the fundamentalist discourses have among the masses. This resonance carries the risk of waking the dormant totalitarian in us and we are likely to witness the insurgence of moral entrepreneurs with different vested self-interests ranging from fear and desire to protect oneself, to power trips and even psychic disorder. These moral entrepreneurs are familiar faces in the South and include those who give themselves the right to impose on others what they consider to be the right and good way to live. They are not found solely in the ruling hierarchy, but are also comfortably niched in the social fabric of the day-to-day reality of ordinary people. In the North, some moral entrepreneurs seem to be coming to the surface in the context of such groups as the moral majority as well as in the context of rising patriotism and the war against terrorism.

It would thus seem that today's activists need increasingly action strategies at the local level that aim at resisting the trickle down of oppressive tendencies with a view of saving some of the essential values of the humanist project. Such action strategies can be articulated using the practice of *emancipatory resistance*. Emancipation here gets its (new) meaning in the collective process of resisting fatalism, of elucidating the dynamics and the underpinnings of the global situation and its ramifications at the local level, and of identifying means to resist. While these acts of resistance may not have a significant impact at the macro level, their values reside in the very process through which local communities and groups come together to resist the hegemony of fundamentalist discourses, of individualistic and market values, of capitalist rationality and the often ensuing fatalism.

In April 2001, after the forced closure of the NGO, participants, including myself, felt overwhelmingly discouraged, if not depressed. It took more than a year to recover and to start re-organizing. In December 2002, Ranya and Samir, along with two other street workers and the kids who had started to assume street work tasks just prior to the dismantling of the NGO, decided that they would not wait an extended time period for the court to settle the dispute between the NGO and state officials. Instead, they began to study the feasibility of establishing a new NGO. In November 2003, the new association was officially set up in to resume work with street kids. The revitalization of the emancipatory process is starting up again.

Notes

[1] In Latin America, Africa, Asia and Eastern Europe, children and youth living on the streets are commonly referred to as *street children*. In North America and Western

Europe, the term *homeless youth* is used interchangeably with that of street children/youth to refer to this population.

[2] It is interesting to note that today, a decade later, the number of kids observed in street situations is on the increase world-wide despite numerous intervention programs, and street children are still a priority on the international child protection agenda.

[3] The notion of accompaniment is borrowed from acompanamiemto, which means 'accompanying the process', and is used by 'Latin American development workers to describe a relationship with communities, groups, and individuals that fosters mutual support, trust, a common commitment, and solidarity' (Clinton paraphrased in Bradbury and Reason, 2003, p. 162).

[4] Becker's notion of moral entrepreneurs includes both the roles of 'rule creators' and 'rule enforcers' that individuals and groups may play to regulate morality in a community context.

[5] 'The FBI is currently asking libraries to provide them with lists of the books and Internet sites consulted by their members as a way of building 'intellectual profiles' of individual readers', The *Washington Post*, National Weekly Edition, 21-27 April 2003. Even more frightening is the creation by the Pentagon of a system of 'total surveillance' of all 6 billion individuals that constitute the inhabitants of the planet, as reported in *Le Monde Diplomatique*, August 2003.

References

Becker, H.S. (1963), Outsiders: Studies in the Sociology of Deviance, The Free Press of Glencoe, New York.

Blumer, H. (1969), Symbolic Interactionism: Perspective and Method, Prentice Hall, New Jersey.

Bradbury, H. and Reason, P. (2003), 'Action Research: An Opportunity for Revitalizing Research Purpose and Practices, Qualitative Social Work, Vol. 2, No. 2, pp. 155-175.

Fahmi, K. (2004), 'Participatory Action Research: A View from the Field', unpublished Ph.D. thesis.

Finn, J.L. (1994), 'The Promise of Participatory Research', *Journal of Progressive Human Services*, Vol. 5, No. 2, pp. 25-42.

Freire, P. (1970), Pedagogy of the Oppressed, Herder and Herder, New York.

Freire, P (1973), Education for Critical Consciousness, Seabury Press, New York.

Healy, K. (2001), 'Participatory Action Research and Social Work: A Critical Appraisal', *International Social Work*, Vol. 44, No. 1, pp. 93-105.

Human Rights Watch (2003), 'Charged with Being Children: Egyptian Police Abuse of Children in Need of Protection', *Human Rights Watch*, Vol. 15, No. 1(E).

Prus, R. (1996), Symbolic Interaction and Ethnographic Research, State University of New York Press, New York.

Punch, M. (1986), The Politics and Ethics of Fieldwork, Sage, California.

Punch, M. (1994), 'Politics and Ethics in Qualitative Research', in Norman K. Denzin and Yvonna S. Lincoln (eds.), Handbook of Qualitative Research, Sage, California.

Reason, P. (1994), 'Three Approaches to Participative Inquiry', in Norman K. Denzin and Yvonna S. Lincoln (eds.), Handbook of Qualitative Research, Sage, California.

Sohng, S.S.L. (1996), 'Participatory Research and Community Organizing', Journal of Sociology and Social Welfare, Vol. 23, No. 4, pp. 77-95.

UNICEF (1987), Paulo Freire and Street Educators: A Critical Approach, Project for Alternative Treatment of Street Children, Rio de Janeiro.

A Concluding Reflection

Linda Davies and Peter Leonard

As we described in the Introduction, the McGill Social Theory Group at the School of Social Work existed prior to the production of this book and continues to meet. Participation in this group has become a source of both intellectual exchange and emotional support for its members as educators, students or practitioners. We see the McGill group as an opportunity for resistance in an academic context of increasing managerial and corporate control within Western universities.

Various and long-standing inter-connections amongst and between all the contributors to this book also proved to be important. Although we each came to the table with individual preoccupations, we seized the opportunity to spend time together as a whole group to reflect on some of the key challenges and debates facing social work educators and practitioners today. These face-to-face meetings were also valuable in sustaining the intellectual comraderie and perseverance necessary to realize this book. One of the outcomes of this collective process is that it allowed us a deeper appreciation of each other's perspectives and experience.

Our discussions enabled us to explore the historical antecedents of the problems social work is facing today. We see a growing theoretical and practice literature in social work, which is positioned primarily in one of the two major traditions of the profession. The most influential and powerful one is perhaps that which is heir to the modernist tradition of valuing, above all, prescriptions for practice within a paradigm of science, reason and moral discipline in its pursuit of professional legitimacy. But there are also indications of renewed demands for social reform and for structural transformations as a precondition for human welfare. This emancipatory strand in social work practice and politics tries to maintain its optimism while at the same time facing the paradox of drawing upon a radical but often pessimistic deconstruction of the Western emancipatory tradition itself. This is the wider context within which we see our book situated: a contribution to continuing efforts at reconstructing critical social work as a reflexive and resistant practice. But to face an uncertain future with some optimism demands more than the intellectual capacities needed to engage in the reflections and skeptical questionings that we hope this book raises for the reader as it has done for the authors. What is needed, we would argue, are exercises of the imagination.

We have explored in this book the various tensions and oppositions that are characteristic of social work at this particular historical juncture. This exploration was pursued not only in an attempt to contribute to social work *praxis* – a process of both reflection and action – but also to argue, in the end, for the greater use of our imaginations. We cannot expect to sustain any contribution to the positive side of the modern project of emancipation unless we are able to imagine alternatives to the existing order of things. We need to imagine the relationships, institutions and practices of a society that does not yet exist. Such a projection is difficult in a context in which rapid transformative change is already taking place. It is a change committed to a planet-wide global capitalist system in the interests of 'human progress'. In previous historical periods of revolution and anti-colonial struggle, it was possible to see the future as a positive state of being already on the horizon. The old order was dying and the new was yet to be born, Antonio Gramsci maintained, optimistically.

For us, such optimism may be more difficult to sustain without leaps of the imagination. We need to use our imaginations when we attempt to develop new forms of relationships with others – democratic and dialogical – in our daily practices as social workers and educators. Such practices pre-figure, in our imaginations, a society that does not yet exist. This utopian thinking allows us to see emancipation as a process as well as a goal. Pre-figurative social work and educational practice might be seen as a growing form of resistance to an oppressive, scientistic and cynical world. Imagining alternatives becomes a means by which we can challenge the existing dominant institutions and practices in the name of an, as yet unnamed, more just, more equal and more inclusive society. As a contribution to the building of alternative social institutions and relationships, a revitalized critical social work has its part to play.

Index